CONSUELO

CONSUELO

Portrait of an American Heiress

JAMES BROUGH

Coward, McCann & Geoghegan, Inc.
New York

First American Edition 1979

Library of Congress Cataloging in Publication Data

Brough, James, date.
  Consuelo: portrait of an American heiress.

  Includes index.
  1. Balsan, Consuelo Vanderbilt. I. Title.
CT3150.B34B76   973.8'092'4[B]   78-21244
ISBN 0-698-10782-9

PRINTED IN THE UNITED STATES OF AMERICA

BOOK ONE

I

A Portent of Glory

She had not as a rule been given to brooding, but then she had never before felt a child quickening in her womb, making it impossible to avoid mulling over what the future might bring, a boy or a girl, joy or sorrow. The baby would be born before winter ended. No one could be sure that by then chaos would not have returned and set Americans killing each other again in the name of national destiny.

The fighting before had lasted until she was on the threshold of puberty, almost thirteen years ago. The North's victory and liberation of the family slaves on the Alabama plantation had spelled ruin for her father. It would take a cataclysm, of course, to destroy the family Alva Smith was married into now. The War of Secession, which had driven the Smiths into flight to Paris, had multiplied Vanderbilt money ten times over.

Pretty, petulant and plump as a turtledove, Alva Vanderbilt was restless, cooped up in a nondescript little brownstone house in Manhattan's newly fashionable forties for the final trimester of her pregnancy. Unrest across the land might be surging into flood, but she felt certain that no matter how high it rose she would be capable of staying afloat. Ambition for herself and her child stirred within her. She would soon have to start modeling her life along lines worthy of her talents. That would take money, a lot of money. She would need to be firmer with her husband, Willie, whom his grandfather, the ancient Commodore, liked to keep on a parsimonious financial string along with all his other kin.

7

The old man was beyond caring what happened except to himself and his fortune. The richest living American had not set foot outside his Greek-columned mansion on Washington Place for the past nine months. The patrician neighbors, who ostracized him for his crudities, missed the chance of snubbing the white-whiskered octogenerian with the pink cheeks and glittering blue eyes as he took the air on elegant Washington Square. Bent on softening the value of his shareholdings to make a bear-market killing, some Wall Street brokers hastened now and then to spread the word that he was already dead.

"After I'm gone," he grunted, "there'll be hell to pay."

Not a shred of evidence indicated the existence of affection between Alva and the founder of the Vanderbilt dynasty. If she spent any time at all by his bedside, it was always in the presence of the corps of physicians attending him or with the company of his young second wife, Frank, whom he loved within his limited experience of the unsettling emotion.

Cornelius Vanderbilt, "Corneel" for short, who would be eighty-three next birthday, resented having been ordered to bed. Overweening vanity persuaded him at first that he was well enough to dress up again in one of his tightly cut suits and immaculate white chokers, both out of style in the present generation. Then, he argued, he could make a public appearance in his fur-lined topcoat and plug hat, cane in one hand and cigar in the other, to provide a sight as familiar to New Yorkers as the Croton Reservoir that towered above Fifth Avenue between Fortieth and Forty-second Streets.

He accepted his doctors' advice that he could no longer go around to the stables on Fourth Street behind the house, where he once kept a dozen of the fastest trotting horses he could buy. Handling the ribbons of a lanky pair like Mountain Boy and Mountain Maid, he would climb up into his curricle every afternoon, weather permitting, to race through Central Park and up Harlem Lane as far into the unspoiled countryside as One Hundred and Sixty-eighth Street, passing every other driver on the road except unbeatable Robert Bonner, who published *The Ledger* and owned Dexter, the world champion, clocked covering a mile in two minutes, seventeen and a half seconds. But spindly, high-sprung curricles and the bony steeds that pulled them were as outmoded as the suits in the old man's wardrobe.

New York gentlemen these days went in for more ornate, less dashing carriages and plumper horseflesh.

The first rumor of the Commodore's demise had brought a gaggle of reporters to present their calling cards at the front door of 10 Washington Place. Frank had them admitted into the parlor, where they stood inspecting a marble bust of the old man while he crept from an upstairs couch to eavesdrop on the landing. She went in to deny the tale of fatal illness and protest that her husband was almost entirely recovered from a bout of inflammation of the bowels. A sudden volley of curses from the top of the stairs supported what she was saying.

"I am not dying," old Corneel bellowed. "Even if I were, I could knock out all the truth there is in the wretches who start those reports. That would cause the biggest job for the undertakers that Wall and Broad Streets have afforded for a great number of years."

He would apologize to Frank afterward. He had been doing his best lately to curb his tongue and stop spewing out the waterfront profanity he had picked up as the eighteen-year-old proprietor of three ferryboats carrying passengers and freight across New York harbor. The Reverend Charles Deems, whose Church of the Strangers was a $50,000 gift from Vanderbilt, found his nightshirted benefactor in tears one day.

"Oh, God damn it," the aged reprobate wept, "I've been a-swearing again, and I'm sorry."

Suspicions that he might be as mortal as the next man had been planted by his daily inspection of the newspapers, the only reading he could set his razor-edged mind to. First came news of the death of William Backhouse Astor, whose fortune had once surpassed the Commodore's, in his new house on Murray Hill, a region of Manhattan Island where duck and quail had abounded in his youth. Vanderbilt had little cause for grief; the Astors declined to associate with Vanderbilts outside of business occasions.

Then Alexander T. Stewart, an immigrant boy from Belfast who piled up his millions as the proprietor of New York's grandest department store, had been carried to his grave from the grandiose white marble palace he had built on Fifth Avenue and Thirty-fourth Street, the most pretentious residence in the city. He had lived there for nine years, childless, virtually friendless and spurned by upper-class citizens as a mere tradesman, although, after Astor, he was the largest landowner in New York. Rough, rambunctious Corneel could sympathize with a fellow pariah.

For all the pretense of recovered health, he was failing fast and stricken with disturbing symptoms of guilt. The doctors prescribed champagne to brighten his disposition. "Champagne?" he snorted, mentally totting up what his illness was costing him. "I guess sody water will do. I don't want to go into the presence of my Creator under the influence of liquor." This was another change in his thinking. He had been used to downing straight gin by the tumblerful, sweetened with lumps of sugar.

His moods varied by the hour. One of the team of physicians recommended adding more wool blankets to the bed. Frank's reply that blankets were "very expensive" brought another outburst from the patient. "God damn the expense! Buy a bale of 'em!" He wolfed down so many cookies that Frank thought it provident to ration the supply. One day when she substituted a bowl of soup for the nibbles he craved, he gulped a mouthful, then hurled the dish across the room. "Who in damnation salted that soup?"

Alva's interest in the old curmudgeon centered not so much on his condition as on how he proposed to dispose of his millions. In spite of his tantrums, he was obviously dependent on Frank, who'd been married to him for nearly eight years but never pregnant, and his first wife, Sophia, had borne him eleven other children besides William Henry, known as "Billy," who was the father of Alva's husband, Willie. The precise size of Vanderbilt's fortune could only be guessed at while breath remained in him. If the pie were to be cut into too many thick slices, it could be reduced to crumbs before Willie inherited his share.

Willie, curly-haired, handsome and pliable, was an attentive husband, as youthful in looks as when he was a schoolboy in Switzerland rubbing shoulders with the sons of European aristocrats. At his grandfather's order, he had been working his way up through the management ranks of Vanderbilt railroads since he was nineteen. These days he came home conscientiously and promptly from his office in Grand Central Terminal to relieve Alva's monotony.

The turmoil that the country was in did not concern her. It

mattered little to Alva whether Rutherford Birchard Hayes or Samuel Jones Tilden would be declared the legitimate successor to President Ulysses S. Grant when Congress concluded its survey of last November's contested election. Republican businessmen envisaged revolution unless Hayes were declared the winner; Democrats smelled a conspiracy designed to keep their opponents in power; talk of troops being called out to seize control in Washington was commonplace; but what Alva wanted to talk about was what would happen to Corneel's money when he died.

She and Willie went down the intimidating list of relatives. Her father-in-law, plodding, placid Billy, had always tried to stay on the leeward side of his father. For his pains, he was abused as "blatherskite" and "sucker"—the Commodore called any number of people "suckers." Billy's luxuriantly whiskered jowls would sag in dismay, but he would make no answer. The patriarch foresaw this son amounting to nothing more than a bookkeeper until Billy's health failed after he was married and the Commodore set him up as a farmer on Staten Island, Corneel's birthplace.

The acres of top-grade corn, oats and potatoes Billy raised did not impress the old man half as much as his son's shrewdness in a deal to buy manure from the Fourth Street stables. "It's worth four dollars a load to me," he said. The Commodore jumped at what he took to be a fool's offer; a carload of fertilizer sold elsewhere for two dollars. The following day at the Battery dock, he spied his son beside a scow heaped high with horse dung.

"How many loads have you got there, Billy?"

"One," young Vanderbilt snickered. "One scowload."

Part of the $10,000 a year he earned from the farm went to affording his two sons, Willie and his elder brother Cornelius II, the education that the half-literate Commodore had neglected to provide for Billy. The boys were sent to boarding school on the banks of the Hudson and then away to Switzerland. When Billy wanted to add to his acreage, he had to mortgage the farm because Corneel refused to lend him a nickel. "Billy," he raged, "you don't amount to a row of beans. You won't never be able to do anything but bring disgrace upon yourself, your family and everybody connected with you. I've made up my mind to have nothing to do with you."

For once, Billy spoke up for himself. "I engaged to pay off the

mortgage at a certain date. I shall do so. I cannot see that I have
anything to be ashamed of." And, for once, his father relented.
"Will that man take his money now?" The Commodore drew a
check for $6,000. "There may be something in the boy after all,"
he grunted to his cronies over some later hands of five-point
euchre, which had replaced whist as his evening pastime.

Alva knew he would never have said as much about Billy's
younger brother, Cornelius Jeremiah. He had a record only of
failures—as a law clerk, leather merchant, revenue agent and
farmer. The single ability he demonstrated lay in gambling away
a fraction of his father's wealth over the faro tables at George
Beers' casino on University Place and at Matthew Dancer's
downtown parlor. "I'd give a hundred dollars," the Commodore
groaned, "if he'd never been named Corneel."

He warned his agents in other cities, "There is a crazy fellow
running all over the land calling himself my son. If you come
into contact with him, don't trust him." Cornelius Jeremiah, in
his parent's judgment, "is a very smart fellow, but he has a cog
out."

The missing cog was the result of epilepsy. When he felt early
symptoms of an attack, he would sit tugging at his white neck-
cloth to loosen it around his throat while Corneel watched, unmoved. If the convulsions persisted, his father would have him
put away in places such as the Bloomingdale Lunatic Asylum.
Only once did he show any sign of pity. On his parlor mantelpiece stood a solid gold model of the steamboat *Cornelius Vanderbilt*, in which President James Knox Polk had once sailed into
New York. "I'd give that ship and her b'ilers, too, to cure Corneel of his ailment," the Commodore confessed.

But Alva could dismiss the possibility that Cornelius Jeremiah
might inherit any great share of the fortune. He had sought to
talk with his father when old Vanderbilt was closeted with Billy,
charging him with the duty of carrying out the terms of the will
he had drawn up, which was still his secret. "I don't want to see
Corneel whether I'm dead or alive," snarled the monarch of the
railroads.

If his youngest son had lived, his prospects might well have
been brighter than anybody else's. George Washington Vanderbilt, muscled like an ox, came first in his father's favor. In a family whose males shunned wearing uniform, he was the only one

to serve the Union as a soldier, a West Point graduate commissioned as a lieutenant of infantry. Though he campaigned at Shiloh with General Henry Halleck, it was tuberculosis resulting from exposure in the field that killed him in 1864 at Nice on the Riviera, where the Commodore had sent him in an effort to save his life.

The old man had no fewer than eight surviving daughters to be entered into Alva's calculations, six of them with husbands, two of them widowed. In the twenty-one months of her own marriage, she'd had scant time to know many of them other than by name. The eldest, Phoebe Jane, was Mrs. James Cross and evidently in her father's good graces, since he had taken her and James across the Atlantic with him in his superb steam yacht, *North Star*, of twenty-five hundred tons burthen, with ligneous marble lining the walls of the dining salon under a ceiling painted with medallion portraits of Columbus, George Washington, Benjamin Franklin, Henry Clay, Daniel Webster and John C. Calhoun. Satin and rosewood predominated in the drawing room, with plush-upholstered furniture in the style of Louis XV everywhere. London bankers fawned over him, but the doors of polite society were shut every bit as tightly against the Yankee Croesus as in New York.

The second daughter, Ethelinda, had been aboard, too, with her husband, Daniel Allen. As the Commodore's valued aide in the steamship business, he had his own close ties to Corneel, whose sick bed he haunted nowadays.

Emily Vanderbilt Thorn, third on the list, had also sailed with William Thorn and their daughter Louisa on that vacation, launched with a salute of aerial rockets let off from deck by order of Corneel as *North Star* anchored off Staten Island on her way out to sea. "There was discipline on board that ship, sir," said the Baptist pastor whom Corneel took along as ship's chaplain. "Each man attended to his own business. The Commodore did the swearing, and I did the praying, so we never disagreed."

If great-grandchildren were to be remembered in the old man's testament, Alva had reason for trusting that her baby would be born in time to be included in the patrimony before he departed the earth.

Daughter number four was Eliza, Mrs. George Osgood; George had been one of Corneel's lieutenants when he was fighting to expand his empire by wresting the Erie Railway Company from the greedy control of Jay Gould and his confederates. The son-in-law, however, had not been present to see Corneel's performance in a switch from fox into possum on an evening when Gould, frail and stunted, joined him in the Washington Place parlor at the height of the negotiating.

After some opening minutes of debate, Corneel decided to test the courage and perhaps soften the heart of his adversary. He closed his eyes and slid out of his chair onto the carpet. There, he stretched out limp and still in what appeared to be a dead faint. Gould hurried to the door to call for help, but the Commodore had locked it and pocketed the key. Gould stooped to stir the body on the floor. The only audible sign of life was a choking breath that sounded as if it might be Corneel's last. He kept up the deception for half an hour while Gould's alarm flared into panic. Then at last the possum reverted to fox, Vanderbilt pulled himself to his feet, and the hassling started up once more.

The dramatics achieved him nothing. Gould and his fellow operators, slick Jim Fisk and sly Daniel Drew, held onto the decrepit Erie, and its passengers continued to risk their necks on the worst run railroad in the land. Corneel, losing $7,000,000 on the watered-down stock his competitors had pumped out to entice him, looked for revenge in a rate war, a strategy that had scarred rivals in the past. He announced that his New York Central, a far better run system, would carry cattle from Buffalo to New York for a dollar a carload, in anticipation of stealing every bit of business from the Erie, which plied a similar route. Gould and Fisk responded by secretly buying six thousand steers and shipping every head via the Central. The Commodore decided to call it quits. "From now on, I'll leave them blowers alone."

His daughter Sophia had lost his goodwill in wedlock with Daniel Torrance, whose business abilities his father-in-law despised. Corneel simultaneously confided his opinion of Daniel to one of his doctors and dropped a broad hint about what could be expected when the will was read. "If I had died in 1835 or 1836 or even 1854, the world would not have known that I had lived, but I think that I have been spared to accomplish a great work that will last and remain, for I have taken care that it is to be secured in such a way that the stock cannot be put upon the market after I die. Had I given one daughter $3,000,000 and another daughter $5,000,000, the first move would have been to turn Billy out and put Torrance in, and then they would have got to quarreling among themselves, and in six months the stock would have been down to 40."

Dr. Jared Linsly's long years as the old man's personal physician reinforced normal professional discretion. He did not think of relaying such confidences to anyone. Alva could only go on wondering who the principal beneficiaries would be and how much was due for each of them.

Daughter Catherine, embarked on her second marriage, was now Mrs. Gustave Lafitte, and her father did not disapprove of divorce. That left only the two widows' chances to be assessed by Alva. Marie Louise's late husband, Horace Clark, had carried out some tricky commissions for Corneel, including making a generous contribution to the bail money needed to release Jefferson Davis from Fortress Monroe, Virginia; health waning, he had been kept there in chains, under threat of trial for treason as president of the Confederacy. Alva must have been astounded when she learned of that singular act of compassion.

Corneel thought well enough of Horace to push him onto the Central's board of directors when Vanderbilt was scheming to obtain outright hold of the line, and after he picked up the Lake Shore & Michigan, he promptly installed Horace in the president's chair. He jeered at this son-in-law, just the same, for his pernicketiness at the card table, whereas the Commodore had been known to win as much as $20,000 a day at whist. "I've just seen the funniest thing," he chuckled in public. "Clark and three grown men playing cards for nothing! The *idea* of three grown men!"

Death had removed Horace from the running nearly four years ago. Corneel showed no more affection for the widowed Marie Louise than for his other daughter, Mary Alicia LaBau, who had also lost her husband. He had excelled as a groveler at Corneel's feet, most cloyingly at Corneel and Sophia's golden wedding anniversary, when one hundred and fifty relatives and business acquaintances crowded the house on Washington Place.

A chorus of young grandchildren piped up with, "Dear Grandpa, our thoughts are constant to thee, and true as steel to the star," and so forth, and then LaBau unburdened himself of a

song in his father-in-law's honor: "Staten Island's a nice little island, It's covered with beauty all o'er, It's the prettiest spot in
creation. It's healthy and *wealthy*—that's more."

He went on to lard some of the ladies with his flattery. "You
have three sons and nine daughters, and insensible must be the
man to the influence of beauty who will not admit that the
daughters of Vanderbilt are not only fair, but that they are
among the fairest of America. May the affections of your children cling to and around you . . . May their love be ever
green."

The Commodore, whose comments were usually fanged, restrained himself, though he held no better opinion of his daughters than of most other women. Women were apt to be frail, skittery creatures, serviceable as wives and mothers, but useless in
the business of making money to create a dynasty. Daughters'
offspring were also deficient in the matter of family name. "They
are nice children," he once remarked about Emily Thorn's
young ones, "but they are not Vanderbilts."

The Vanderbilt women, dominated by Corneel, must have
appeared as a collection of milksops to Alva, whose determination equaled his. He had proved susceptible in the past to faces
nowhere near as pretty as hers. If only his health had held up,
she would have grabbed the opportunity to make him aware that
she was no commonplace woman but gifted with brains, beauty
and what would count for most with the Commodore—bravado.

She would not have let his admiration run away with him, as
it had long ago when he set off in amorous pursuit of his children's governess. At that time, Sophia was in the process of
menopause. To clear the way for him to win over the alarmed
schoolma'am, he talked his wife into taking a trip to Canada
with Ethelinda and Daniel Allen.

Sophia was Corneel's cousin, daughter of his father's sister.
Her lack of all desire to make her mark on society perpetually
irked him. She was a homebody who liked to mind her own business, enjoying the company of children and grandchildren in
the comfortable Gothic house and handsome garden the Vanderbilts then had near Tompkinsville on Staten Island. If the Astors chose to lord it over New York, that was their affair.

Sophia's loss of physical attraction for Corneel drove him to
conclude that she must be kept permanently out of the way after
she came back from her enforced vacation. Declaring her to be

mentally disturbed, he had her confined in Dr. McDonald's asylum in Flushing, Long Island.

Rumor accused Alva's father-in-law, Billy, of being the one child who did not protest to Corneel about this brutal treatment of his mother. Billy, who sometimes found it necessary to gloss over unpleasant truths, denied the charge. "I had nothing to do with that. I never in my life interfered in the affairs of my father, and I do not think the others did." It was "always understood," he added, that Sophia "retired willingly to the asylum."

The governess quit, refusing to live under the Vanderbilt roof with Sophia away. It was an altogether different roof. While his wife was interned, he bought the mansion on Washington Place. Rumor continued, alleging that Billy introduced a younger woman into the new household for his father's satisfaction. The arrangement was short-lived. Doctors examining Sophia soon judged her totally sane, and she was released to rejoin her husband.

He used to spend two months every summer taking the cure at Saratoga Springs, first at the United States Hotel, then after that burned down, at the Congress. Sophia's presence was superfluous. He began each day lolling on the piazza, enjoying one of the cigars he carried loose in a sidepocket—if he carried a caseful of them, he would be expected to share his delicious Havanas with the company. "When I take them out of my pocket, they won't know there are any left." In the afternoons, he would have his trotters harnessed up for an airing, and an evening of whist would round off the day. He was at Saratoga when Sophia died of a heart attack at the home of Horace and Marie Louise.

The seventy-five-year-old Corneel waited twelve months before he took as his bride Miss Frank Crawford, aged thirty, who was the great-granddaughter of his mother's brother. Like Alva, she came from Mobile, Alabama, though she had preceeded Mrs. Willie Vanderbilt to New York soon after the war ended. A special train took the honeymooners to the Commodore's summer haunt, the Congress Hall in Saratoga Springs.

At least one other aspirant to a Vanderbilt wedding ring felt she had been cheated. "Didn't you promise to marry *me?*" asked Miss Tennie C. Claflin, known as "Tennessee," a raffish young beauty who manipulated Corneel, body and soul, as a self-proclaimed "magnetic healer."

"Yes," he agreed, "but the family interfered."

He had peculiar ideas about what was good for his constitution. He was careful to keep clippings of his silvery locks out of strangers' hands after he had been barbered, lest black magic be invoked against him by means of a strand of his hair. As superstitious as a savage, he ordered saltcellars set under the legs of his bed to prevent his strength ebbing away through the floorboards. An addict of spiritualism, he relied on mediums to establish contact for him with departed, most particularly his mother, but in an emergency with the shades of rogues like Jim Fisk, murdered on a staircase of the Grand Central Hotel.

Tennessee introduced him to her sister, Victoria, wed at fourteen to Dr. Canning Woodhull, whom she had divorced after bearing him two children. Victoria was adept at raising spirits to order, so Corneel added her as another protégé within the first year of his new marriage.

In an earlier chapter of a checkered existence, the two sisters had gypsied through the Midwest, telling fortunes and peddling quack medicine. With his backing, they opened up as stockbrokers in a suite in the Hoffman House, one office wall bearing a portrait of the Commodore, another a framed motto, "Simply to Thy cross I cling." Before many months had passed, Woodhull, Claflin & Company showed a profit of $500,000.

"I think a woman is just as capable of making a living as a man," said Tennessee, who shared Victoria's taste for wearing curly brown hair cropped outrageously short, mannish jackets, dazzling neckties and skirts that revealed a pair of trim ankles. "I have seen men so vain of their personal appearance and so effeminate that I should be sorry to compare my intellect with theirs. I don't care what society thinks. I have not time to care."

Corneel denied that his lady brokers' success was founded on advance tips about his manipulations on Wall and Broad. To the contrary, he said, he planned his deals on their prophesies of the ups and downs of the market. "Do as I do," he advised one ambitious speculator; "consult the spirits." He recommended another seeker of his counsel to invest everything in New York Central common. "It's bound to go up twenty-two percent. Mrs. Woodhull said so in a trance."

Gratitude impelled him to put up the capital to launch *Woodhull and Claflin's Weekly*, whose masthead proclaimed, "Progress! Free Thought! Untrammeled lives!" Its columns purveyed a brew of spiritualism, free love, abortion and votes for women. It was her personal right, Victoria declared, to have as many lovers as she pleased, as well as run for the Presidency of the United States.

So far as Alva knew from Willie, Victoria and Tennessee had vanished from the scene. A less seductive magnetician, Dr. Frederick Weed, was ministering to the Commodore, who seemed to miss Tennessee's skillful touch. "Why have I been deprived of this so long?" he moaned to Frank. "It is doing me so much good." It was not inconceivable in Alva's view that in his will he would remember the two adventuresses that Wall Street knew as "the bewitching brokers."

Peritonitis had a death hold on him. He had not cared for hymns until now. When Willie and the other grandchildren went to call, he had wanted them to stand around the organ in the parlor, singing comic songs about Scots and Irishmen. If Frank, a devout Christian, tried to add a hymn to the recital, he would snap, "Enough of that. No set-up jobs on me. Give me some more lively music."

On the fourth morning of January, 1877, he focused his thoughts on heaven. "I shall never cease to trust in Jesus," he whispered to Frank. "How could I ever let Him go?" He could feel the world spinning away from him. "Frank, sing me my hymns!" She started up with "Come Ye Sinners, Poor and Needy," while good Dr. Deems of the Church of the Strangers recited the Lord's Prayer. "I am poor, I am needy," Corneel whispered as his life ebbed away a few minutes before eleven o'clock. By noon, the flags over the Union Club and the Manhattan Club hung at half-mast. By the time the market closed, the Commodore's stocks had registered modest gains, and his body lay encased in morticians' ice blocks, ready for autopsy.

In clubs and offices in every major city, men he had made and men he had trampled on gossiped about him with admiration or bitterness, according to his treatment of them. They recalled tales of the hard-fisted lad who had left the family farm two years before George III and a bullheaded Congress blundered into the War of 1812. Corneel's original ambition had run only to earning a living as a boatman with a two-masted sailing barge bought with $100 borrowed from his mother. Before his attention turned from the sea to the golden dividends to be ex-

tracted from railroading, he had acquired twenty-eight steam-
boats and his courtesy title.

Mourners and victims agreed that two American wars had to
be credited for the bulk of his money. With his proceeds from
the first, young Corneel had built two schooners as the start of
his fleet. Transporting armies and supplies to the battlefronts in
the recent war had brought boom years to the railroads, which
Corneel had a passion for buying.

The talk turned to what his detractors had said about him.
"Commodore Vanderbilt owns New York," Jim Fisk once told
reporters. "He owns the Stock Exchange. He owns New York's
streets and railroads." Another critic claimed that "$50,000 of
absolute water" had been poured into every mile of Vanderbilt
track; yet no matter how often they were bilked, investors scrambled for the stock.

Some of his own comments had become as familiar as the axi-
oms in *McGuffey's Readers*. "The law? Why, I have the power
already." . . . "Congress be damned." He believed that "a million or two is as much as anyone ought to have," but there was
no way of disposing of the excess because "what you have got
isn't worth anything unless you have the power, and if you give
away the surplus, you give away the control." And, of course,
everyone remembered his letter to a pair of associates who be-
trayed him: "You have undertaken to cheat me. I won't sue you,
for the law is too slow. I'll ruin you."

On one subject his defenders and his defamers had no quarrel. Vanderbilt would need no monument to his legend; it had
already been built. His original thought had been to make it a
joint memorial to himself and George Washington. In its
finished form, the figure of Corneel stood supported by Neptune
and Liberty in fifty tons of bronze cast at a cost of $500,000 and
anchored to a wall of his downtown St. John's Park freight station.

Falling snow made it advisable for Alva, two months away
from childbirth, to stay away from the burial in the Moravian
Cemetery at New Dorp, Staten Island. The horses had trouble
hauling the hearse up slippery slopes, and the ferries could not
handle all the mourners' carriages that clogged the Manhattan
slips. A handful of his enemies came for a glimpse of the satin-

lined casket to satisfy themselves that Corneel was truly dead at last.

The will was read the following morning. The Commodore had left $105,000,000 to be disbursed in accordance with written instructions left with Billy. The country had never known an individual fortune of this size. The testament contained nothing to cause Alva alarm. As security for the dynasty to which her child would soon be added, it could scarcely have been improved upon.

It contained no mention of Tennessee or Victoria. Frank was to have $500,000 in bonds and the Washington Place house with its furnishings. Alva's potential rivals, Corneel's daughters, were treated stingily. Phoebe Jane, Emily, Marie Louise, Sophia and Mary Alicia would each collect $250,000 in bonds of the Lake Shore Railroad, Ethelinda the income from $400,000, Eliza whatever $500,000 would produce, and Catherine the dividends from $500,000.

Cornelius Jeremiah, unquestionably the neediest, would have to survive on income from $200,000, which would amount to $10,000 a year at 5 percent. The Commodore's grandsons came off much more handsomely. Cornelius, the eldest, was down for $5,500,000 in railroad stock. Willie, like the rest of his brothers, would collect a satisfactory $2,000,000, but that was far short of what he could ultimately receive. Excluding a few more minor bequests, Alva's father-in-law Billy had come into the rest of the inheritance—power, responsibility and $90,000,000. Billy was easy to get along with, and his wife, the former Maria Louisa Kissam, for whom Willie K. was named, was not socially ambitious. Willie and Alva had great expectations of one kind or another, unless the deadlock in Washington remained unbroken and the country exploded into war.

Right now, she had the means and money available to tackle what no Vanderbilt as yet had accomplished, and that was to secure an acknowledged place in polite society. The best people's disdain for old Corneel's crudities extended to his whole tribe: Vanderbilts, in the prevailing judgments, were vulgar barbarians. The injustice of it affronted Alva, who rated herself a trueborn blue blood. Why were the Astors so well thought of when Corneel's contemporary, John Astor, could scarcely speak English and his brother Henry was a butcher? What qualifications did the current queen of Manhattan society, Caroline Schermerhorn Astor, hold apart from the fact that Astor money was now respectably invested in real estate instead of in speculative stocks?

As her child grew in her body, Alva conceived a monumental ambition: somehow she would depose Mrs. Astor and reign as queen in her stead.

Toward the end of February, feuding erupted among the Vanderbilts. Lawyers fired the first shots in surrogate court on behalf of three of Corneel's heirs who felt most bitterly that they had been defrauded. Cornelius Jeremiah, Ethelinda Allen and Mary Alicia LaBau objected to the will that bequeathed all but 3 percent of their father's treasure to Billy and his sons.

On the last day of February, the Forty-fourth Congress went into joint session to tackle the count of the states, a process interrupted by filibuster and continual caucusing as upper and lower houses broke off in turn to vote among themselves. Fresh alarms rang in the capital. General George Brinton McClellan, defeated in his run for the presidency against Lincoln in 1864, was rumored to be raising an army to enforce Tilden's inauguration.

At three-forty in the morning of Friday, March 2, 1877, the last votes were tallied. Wisconsin's ten were added for Hayes, and he was declared President of the United States by 185 to 184. Army regiments were alerted to guard the approaches to the Capitol for Monday morning's Inaugural.

In her bedroom in the Willie Vanderbilts' nondescript dwelling that Friday, Alva bore her child. In the tumult of the day, with strife within the family and fear in the streets over what the weekend would bring, the birth was never officially recorded. Consuelo was the name Alva chose for her daughter.

II

Opening Gambits

The name itself was a kind of talisman, a token of what Alva had in mind for her daughter when she grew up. Friendship with Consuelo Yznaga dated back to Alva's young days as an aspiring belle of Mobile. Don Antonio Yznaga delle Valle, her father, had a Yankee wife and estates south of the Mason-Dixon line as well as in his native Cuba. A son of his, Fernando, was married to one of Alva's sisters.

The war had left the Yznagas' wealth intact, and they were established on the Manhattan scene by the time Alva arrived to live in the city where she was determined to reign as queen bee. Finding William Kissam Vanderbilt as a husband for her had been Consuelo's doing—she introduced them to each other at a party for the Commodore's daughter, Emily, and she had been a bridesmaid at their wedding.

Of greater moment now was the fact that since last May she had been the witty, talented, tantalizing Viscountess Mandeville, one of the first of her generation to cross the Atlantic as the bride of an English nobleman. Another was Jennie Jerome, daughter of a Brooklyn stock promoter, wed in Paris one year earlier to Lord Randolph Churchill, who was a son but not the heir of the Duke of Marlborough. Consuelo's viscount was more advantageously placed in his line of succession. When his father died, he would be the Duke of Manchester and Consuelo his duchess, only one level beneath a princess on the hierarchical pyramid.

Alva cherished high hopes for her baby, whose physical care was delegated to nursemaids. In their style of living, influence and prestige, English aristocrats had no equals. By the simple act of exchanging marriage vows, Consuelo had raised herself close to the summit of international society in a family whose links with its monarchs dated back to the sixteenth century; an ancestor of her husband's committed Sir Walter Raleigh to imprisonment in the grim Tower of London and served as one of the most trusted counselors of Charles I.

Members of the Manchester line had been intimates of kings and queens ever since. Consuelo Mandeville's mother-in-law, Louise, the beautiful, German-born eighth duchess, had a fortune in jewels and a firm place in the affections of the Prince of Wales as well as a succession of lovers from the ranks of British Cabinet ministers. During the years of waiting to follow in her footsteps, Alva's dear, doe-eyed friend could look forward to shining in similar splendor. Meanwhile she was expecting a child who, should it be a boy, was destined to be the ninth duke. She did, in fact, give birth to a son in the course of the year.

Alva had accomplished much in the last few months, but so far as she was concerned, her ascent of the mountainous slopes of social recognition had only just begun. Antebellum society in Alabama had ignored the Smiths of Mobile. Murray Forbes Smith, born in Virginia, was no Southern gentleman but a mere commission merchant. His wife, Phoebe, had better claim to acceptance by the elite. She was a daughter of a Tennessee lawmaker, United States congressman and general of the militia, and an uncle of hers was Governor Joseph Desha of Kentucky. But that was still not enough to save the Smiths and their five children from the stigma of being "in trade." Fellows who had to work for a living could not be considered gentlemen.

Alva had not much to say about her upbringing. She let it be understood that her father had once owned a plantation and that, after his loss of it, she was "educated in private schools in France," which could be interpreted as meaning that the refugee Smiths could not afford governesses for their children. The omission would be made good in the case of baby Consuelo now that her father had $2,000,000 of his grandfather's money to dispose of.

With her mother and two sisters, Alva had moved to New

York in the early 1870s, part of the horde of strangers who invaded the city in that era. Older inhabitants looked down on them as upstarts. One Knickerbocker dowager, Mrs. May King Van Rensselaer, after an arm's length inspection of the newcomers, concluded, "They were outside the pale, but that did not worry them. They aimed for social distinction not by assault upon the established caste but by counter-attraction. They appreciated the value of publicity and employed it." Alva also appreciated the benefits of discretion, particularly in disclosing the circumstances of her earlier days in Manhattan, where Phoebe Smith had conducted a boarding house to support herself and her three daughters.

In the first days of her baby's life, strain within the Vanderbilt family and throughout the nation eased somewhat. The trio of challengers of the Commodore's will withdrew their complaints for the time being, though in November Cornelius Jeremiah would resume rattling the skeletons, insisting that Billy had warped his ailing father's mind, and lawyers would bring a parade of spiritualist mediums to the witness stand to testify that Corneel had been deranged. Victoria Woodhull resurfaced to confide to a journalist, "It would make a splendid, sensational article if we gave the reasons why Commodore Vanderbilt took such an interest in a paper that expressed the most radical of radical views, but our lips are sealed."

In his Inaugural address on March 5, 1877, President Hayes, quaking every time he heard the crackle of fireworks nearby, was out to mollify. His wish was to say nothing to offend anybody. He had appointed a Confederate officer as his postmaster general, and as a priority order of business he proposed to pull federal troops out of every Southern capital. McClellan held his peace. The danger of war was over, but unrest still simmered in the land.

Willie took a lighthearted approach to his new job as second vice-president of the Central, which paid him $300,000 a year. He would rather spend his time playing with his gurgling baby daughter than sit behind an office desk. His father, on the contrary, had too many problems on his hands to spare much thought for his new granddaughter. Every railroad in America was in financial trouble, and slashing ten cents off every dollar of wages was their method of protecting dividends.

During the child's first summer the sun that had shone unfailingly on the Commodore and fellow giants of industry passed its zenith. "Never again, after 1877," one commentator wrote later, "were the moguls to be wholly free, as they had been before, to work their financial wonders without protest from labor, criticism from the public, and harassment by government . . . A new era had set in. The giants and near giants who followed the Commodore, including his own able son, were never to know a moment when they were not under fire."

Violence exploded in July, flaring highest in Pittsburgh, where Pennsylvania Railroad workers rampaged through the city, setting fire to company buildings, the goods depot, coaches and locomotives. In the night, they soaked a freight-car load of coke with petroleum to convert it into an awesome implement of wrath. They shunted it against the wall of a roundhouse in which a thousand Philadelphia militiamen lay sleeping, in sudden hazard of being roasted alive. The soldiers broke out and raced for the arsenal, but the commander refused to admit them, so they turned and ran again through the gauntlet of strikers wielding ax-ahandles, rocks and clubs. Twenty people lay dead when dawn glowed in the smoke-filled sky.

Terror spread to other railroad cities, and damage mounted into the millions. Paint shops blazed like erupting volcanoes. Trains were derailed and tracks torn up to knock out service in an area of devastation reaching from the Canadian frontier to Virginia, from Atlanta to the Mississippi River. Within those borders mail was blocked and food shipments cut off. There had been nothing to compare with this in peacetime since the 1863 draft riots when New York lynch mobs strung up a thousand victims of racist prejudice.

Willie and his father exuded typical Vanderbilt calm, the son by taking a sunny afternoon off from the office to play polo, Billy by vacationing at the United States Hotel in Saratoga, rebuilt with a donation of $50,000 from Corneel in his declining years. Central employees had not yet joined the strike, but they were demanding a 25 percent boost in wages.

Billy said no. "There is a great principle involved in this matter, and we cannot afford to yield, and the country cannot afford to have us yield." The army of strikers was immediately swollen by Central workers, from expert mechanics making $1.20 a day to laborers earning 80 cents.

Billy's reaction was to ask Governor Robinson of New York for twelve hundred militiamen, the bill for whose services he would settle for $250,000. A notice posted in the Central shops read: "The public interest should not suffer from any difference between the road and its employees. Keep at work until the excitement is over, and a fair conference can be had."

When a strike committee called on him at his hotel, he still refused to talk about wages. In the White House, Hayes dithered, unable to decide whether or not to declare martial law, and finished by doing nothing. Two days after the meeting with Billy, the strike on the Central collapsed. Wage cuts, he insisted, would not be rescinded until better times returned, but he set aside $100,000 to be shared in bonuses among his work force.

"Out of the last six months of the year of the Commodore's death," wrote one student of the age of the moguls, "came the first effective labor unions the country had seen. Along with the unions came the first serious efforts of government to make it increasingly difficult for one man to accumulate and leave an estate of $105,000,000 . . . Through the smoke of the tremendous violence of 1877 the capitalist was seen clearly to be an ogre, the natural enemy of man, of the Republic, and of God."

Alva supervised her daughter's upbringing as strictly as a lioness raising a cub, her concentration only briefly interrupted by the arrival of her second child when Consuelo was nineteen months old. After the birth of William Kissam II, his mother called a seven-year halt to further childbearing. She had more challenging matters to attend to, not the least of which was to establish herself as more prestigious than the other four Mrs. Vanderbilts: the Commodore's quiet widow, Frank; Alva's gracious mother-in-law, Maria Louisa; and her two sisters-in-law, Alice, wife of Cornelius II, and Louise, married to Willie's younger brother Frederick. Fortunately none of them represented much competition to a woman of Alva's mettle.

First, she had to secure her position in the family, then take the next step, which was to install herself as the undisputed queen of American society and Consuelo as its princess. At present, the Vanderbilts continued to be treated as parvenus, perhaps deservedly so, as another wedding in the family indicated.

Billy's quaint daughter Florence Adele wore $120 silk stockings and a bridal gown created by the same salon that had served President Grant's Nellie for her White House marriage, but Florence's ceremony had a taint of Donnybrook Fair. Visitors slow in presenting their printed admission cards at the church doors were hustled away by a brace of burly guards. Guests descending from their carriages in feathers, furs and evening clothes were roughed up by a mob of thousands battering their way through police barricades. "One lady in a low-necked dress," *The New York Times* noted, "was thrown under the feet of a pair of carriage horses that had just driven up, and placed in immediate danger of her life." Safe in a pew inside, Alva certainly aimed for something less raucous for Consuelo when the time came.

As far back as memory took her, the girl was miserably conscious of pressure from her mother. Alva dominated her in mind and body. She could recall few words of praise or moments of love from an iron-willed, rosebud-lipped woman who let nothing impede the path toward her goals. Willie was the source of the child's joy, always kind, as she recalled, and full of laughter, but Alva carefully isolated him from his son and daughter most of the time.

Consuelo found it impossible to satisfy her mother. If she misbehaved, she was punished with a lashing about the knees with a riding crop. But worse than the beatings was Alva's scorn for the child. Her mother ridiculed her looks, marred, Alva feared, by an impossible nose with a turned-up tip. Consuelo came to regard her nose as a singular misfortune. The inordinately fancy clothes she was dressed in, fit only for a fairytale princess, were designed to proclaim her superiority over commonplace children. Certain that she was an oddity, she became a precocious introvert, in the habit of searching her infant soul for faults and judging herself inadequate. The sweet temper inherited from her father soured, which meant more applications of the whip to her legs.

She was four years old when she found herself transported into what seemed to be a living nightmare, the new house Alva rated essential as a base for her invasion of society. It also served as notice to the rest of the family that none of them would be allowed to overshadow her.

Billy, in his plodding way, was growing into his role as head of the family. He tried hard to still the scandals that continued to

darken the Vanderbilts' reputation. To ward off further complaints from Cornelius Jeremiah about the Commodore's will,
Billy made over to his enfeebled brother the income from a
$1,000,000 trust fund and presented an extra $500,000 in bonds
to each sister.

One brother-in-law questioned the terms of the settlement.
"William, I've made a quick calculation here, and I find these
bonds don't amount to quite $500,000. They're $150 short at the
price quoted today." Billy gave him a wan smile and a check to
make up the difference.

His gift to Cornelius Jeremiah could not stave off fresh shame.
One Sunday afternoon, his father called for Willie in his stylish
coupé, painted dark maroon, the color the Vanderbilts had
adopted to identify the dynasty. Billy needed a dependable companion on the mission to be performed down at the Glenham
Hotel. In a bedroom there, Cornelius Jeremiah sprawled dying
on a couch. He had shot himself in the head with a .38 Smith &
Wesson revolver.

Meanwhile, Billy had developed a taste for splurging on personal pleasures. With whiskers flying under a plug hat, he
whipped the trotters he had inherited from Corneel at a spank-
ing pace along the same roads his father had driven, and ended
up buying the swiftest team in the world. To build an art collection around the first painting he had bought for $90, he went
shopping in France for pictures that told a story, not the incomprehensible daubs of Renoir, Degas or Monet. He liked canvases with a few farm animals in them. "Well, I don't know as
much about the quality of the picture as I do about the action of
those cattle. I have seen them like that thousands of times." Unlike Corneel, who had feasted his eyes on a shameless "Aurora"
that hung in a sitting room on Washington Place, Billy, who was
a church vestryman, would not look at a nude, but he had such
admiration for the microscopic technique of Jean Meissonier
that he paid $188,000 for seven works by the gray-bearded Pari-
sian and then had him paint his portrait.

Alva could not ignore that kind of challenge. She approached
the same modish Carolus Duran whom Mrs. Astor had patronized and commissioned him to portray Consuelo in red velvet
and Venetian lace, clutching a bouquet of roses in each small
hand and venturing a pixie's smile.

Though his wife Maria Louise was reluctant to move—"I hate

to think of leaving this house where we have lived so comforta-
bly," said this clergyman's daughter—Billy wanted to stay
abreast of the times and live farther north in the most fashionable
section of Manhattan. He and his pictures had outgrown his
home at Fifth Avenue and Fortieth Street. He bought the block
between Fifty-first and Fifty-second streets and proceeded to
have it covered with a monumental, slab-sided dwelling consisting of three houses, the biggest for himself, the others for two of
his daughters, Margaret Louisa, who was Mrs. Elliott Shepard,
and Emily, who was Mrs. William Sloane.

His architects, the sedate Herter Brothers, and contractor
urged him to build in red and black marble in keeping with his
recently attained splendor; other freshly minted millionaires rejected the ugly, unassuming downtown brownstones of older-
established wealth. But Billy was afraid that handling the job in
marble would take so long he might be dead before it was
finished. He settled for brownstone in a structure resembling
nothing so much as a high-class commercial hotel. It cost him
$3,000,000, nevertheless, and once the new gallery was opened
at 640 Fifth Avenue, he proudly sponsored a massive volume,
Mr. Vanderbilt's House and Gallery, for which John Pierpont
Morgan and other business acquaintances dutifully subscribed.

In the matter of residential magnificence, her father-in-law
and his two daughters were getting ahead of Alva. She prevailed
upon Willie to give her a free hand in overtaking them.

Richard Morris Hunt, Paris-trained, had laid the foundations
of his architectural reputation with his work in extending the
Capitol in Washington and then gone on to enhance it as a prac-
titioner of the French Renaissance manner in libraries, chapels
and colleges. What he had lacked so far was a devoted patron
with cultivated taste and money to burn. Alva filled the prescription as snugly as the massive stone blocks were laid, without
mortar, to raise the Pyramid of Gizeh.

Architecture in itself would provide her with a double-edged
weapon for simultaneously putting her relatives back into their
place and for undermining the pretensions of the snobs who
snubbed the Willie Vanderbilts. She knew what she wanted:
nothing less than the most impressive dwelling in New York, sit-
ed directly across the street from Billy's triple construction and
overshadowing it in magnificence. It did not matter that it would

cost Willie as much as his legacy from his grandfather plus
$1,000,000 more.

Hunt had never had a more spectacular commission or a customer so heedless of expense. He turned for ideas to the châteaus he had studied at the École des Beaux Arts, borrowing a
dormer from this one, a tower from that. The principal source
was the manor house of a fifteenth-century French upstart,
Jacques Coeur, who spent a fortune building his Castle of Blois.
Bejeweled New York ladies who regarded Alva as a pushy *ar-
riviste* could not help being intrigued by the house that began to
go up at 660 Fifth Avenue.

As the building took shape, it was recognized that Hunt, under his client's ceaseless scrutiny, had produced a marvel, a fan-
tasy in white limestone. Rival architects came to stand and stare.
Only one of them, Louis Sullivan of Chicago, who insisted that
purpose should prevail over ornamentation, sneered. "Must you
wait until you see a *gentleman* in a silk hat come out of it before
you laugh?" he asked. "Have you no sense of humor, no sense of
pathos? Must I then tell you that while a man may live in the
house physically . . . that he cannot possibly live in it morally,
mentally or spiritually, that he and his home are a paradox, an
absurdity, a characteristically New York absurdity, that he is no
part of the house, and his house no part of him?"

"Pathos" was an odd word, yet it fitted Consuelo's reactions
when she was first led into the intimidating mansion that people
called the "Petit Château de Blois," set back from the sidewalk
behind a low railing, with a flight of steps leading up to its
wrought iron front doors. From the hall, a staircase of Caen
stone curved up for three flights past penumbral landings. The
child imagined that evil spirits waited for her there, fingers out-
stretched first to touch and then to exterminate her. She was old
enough, Alva thought, to be taken from the nursery and put
into a room of her own. In a tower of the château, she was as secluded as Rapunzel. Reaching the door meant braving the stair-
way, which sometimes took more courage than she possessed.
She would slump in a swoon to her knees, praying for strength
to continue to climb. Her father's plight seemed akin to her
own. His dreary little room saddened her. She wanted him to
have the best of everything life could give.

Relatives pitied her. Aunts, uncles and cousins recognized

her to be a frightened pawn in Alva's hands. Aunt Emily, who lived across the street, especially tried to bring a smile to the girl's pale cheeks. Uncle Fred was another jolly soul like her father, and Grandmother Vanderbilt's love seemed a kind of refuge.

None of them, in Alva's estimation, could be considered people of true quality. The nature of Vanderbilts made them money grubbers like the rest of the Northern breed of rich. Only the old, shattered South, of which she was eternally proud, had produced true gentlefolk. In the tales she drummed into her daughter's head, the Smiths were always glorified. Murray Smith became not a merchant but a plantation owner, descended from the Scottish Stirlings with a distant earl among them who, as a courtier of King James I, received vast grants of American land in 1621. Another Lord Stirling, an American inheritor of the title, was a confidant of George Washington and a valiant general of the Revolution who fought at Trenton and Brandywine, Germantown and Monmouth.

Consuelo had to wait until she was old enough to learn for herself that the first Vanderbilts landed in New Amsterdam from Bilt in the Netherlands in the same flow of seventeenth-century immigrants that brought over Claes Van Rosenvelt, forefather of two presidents of the United States.

The reigning queen of New York's elite boasted of similar ancestry. Mrs. William Astor was born Caroline Webster Schermerhorn, a daughter of the Dutch clan that turned up in Albany about 1640 and prospered in New York real estate. By 1800, the Schermerhorns were peers of the Schuylers, the Van Rensselaers and the rest of the solid old Dutch stock that had erected the social ladder and perched on its top. On a rung farther down stood John Jacob Astor, the German butcher's son who sold pianos to New Yorkers, traded for beaver pelts from Indian trappers, and put most of the $30,000,000 he accumulated into real estate.

Caroline's father was worth perhaps $500,000 when she was married to Astor's grandson in 1853. She allowed no one to forget that her position set her higher than her husband, but it was not until after the close of the Civil War that she took it upon herself to impose order on confused post-bellum society, where new rich jostled old, vulgarity threatened to overturn tradition, and hostesses were well advised to provide spittoons for upstart millionaires. "If society was to be preserved," as one historian wrote, "it must not only be made impregnable, but restored to its former high estate."

Caroline began her task as she introduced her four daughters to the social scene. For that, she needed a man at her side, and William Astor, bored with her airs and graces, was an almost permanent absentee, spending summers on his yacht, winters in Florida, and intervals at "Ferncliff," his estate in Dutchess County.

She found the counselor and companion she required in the person of Ward McAllister, a fawning snob from Savannah, Georgia. He dubbed her his "Mystic Rose" and set about organizing the Patriarchs, a standing committee of Astors, Livingstons, a Van Rensselaer, a Rutherfurd, a Schermerhorn and others to create the governing code for a hierarchy more exclusive than British aristocracy in dictating who should be allowed in and who kept out.

At the royal court in London, admission to the presence of the empress was recognition of superiority. In New York, the Mystic Rose presided over similar rites at her annual ball, held every third Monday in January in the art gallery of the red brick and brownstone mansion that her husband had built for her at 350 Fifth Avenue, where the Empire State Building stands today.

Her crown was a diamond tiara, pinned on black-dyed hair, her throne a divan placed on a dais. There she would appear in velvet and satin, with a triple rope of diamonds encircling her white throat, a sunburst of them on her ample bosom, a stomacher of the stones cinching her midriff, strands of them trailing from a corsage, as she accepted the obeisance of her awed subjects. Petulant little Victoria, ruler of the British Empire's twelve million square miles and nearly half a billion people, did not compare with the plump American dowager in height, dignity or gracious ruthlessness. Only patriarchs and their guests qualified to dance under the enormous chandelier William Astor had imported from Italy. Caroline and her preening chamberlain winnowed the list to insure that a summons to 350 Fifth Avenue was a singular honor, and exclusion a mark of shame.

"Why," cooed McAllister, "there are only about four hundred

people in fashionable New York society. If you go outside of that number, you strike people who are either not at ease in a ballroom or else make other people not at ease." He equated "fashionable" with "wealthy," warning would-be eligibles that "a fortune of only a million is respectable poverty." But money alone was no guarantee of acceptance into Mrs. Astor's pantheon. Entry was subject to her personal approval, and she made it as plain as her face that she considered the Petit Château de Blois and its occupants equally pretentious.

With some help from Lady Mandeville, Alva's opening gambit in attacking the imperious dowager was to win over McAllister. Even before the move to their new address, the young Vanderbilts were invited to dance at one of the lesser Patriarchs' Balls, staged in Delmonico's magnificently mirrored restaurant on Madison Square. Willie and Alva trod the same rose-petaled parquet as Mrs. Astor and her youngest daughter, Carrie, in the company of the divinely chosen "nobs" who in McAllister's vocabulary were as superior to self-made "swells" as orchids to radishes. But Mrs. Astor had not so much as a nod for Alva, much less an invitation to tea.

The time had come to press her fight. When Lady Mandeville arrived as a guest in the petit château, Alva announced that she would give a ball in her honor as a housewarming. Consuelo and her brother goggled at the transformation. Monsieur Klunder, the émigré French florist, filled downstairs rooms with red and pink roses in the tens of thousands, $11,000 worth of them. Consuelo sniffed a different fragrance in the supper room, scented by garlands of orchids hung from towering potted palms. Down in the servants' quarters, the gold service was polished and the china and crystal washed for the meal that would be served by the staff of footmen in smart new maroon livery.

Mrs. Vanderbilt, just turned thirty, planned the ball as a fancy dress affair, something fifty-three-year-old Mrs. Astor would never dream of arranging. It must be a frolic on a scale unknown in republican America, an extravaganza worthy of Versailles and the court of Louis XIV, *le Roi Soleil* himself, a ruler who appealed to her. The twelve hundred invitations drove ladies to distraction. How to dress up—as the Four Seasons, Dawn, Sunset, Innocence or more à la mode as Electric Light? As Helen of Troy, Marie Antionette, Rachel, Elizabeth of England or Salome? In banks, brokerage houses and gentlemen's clubs, the question was whether to go disguised as the Count of Monte Cristo, Cardinal Richelieu, Henry VIII, Richard the Lion-Hearted or perhaps Genghis Khan.

Throughout the city, dressmakers and seamstresses labored around the clock in airless workrooms or East Side tenements, sewing costumes for which some of the bills would run to $700 apiece. The *New York World* calculated afterward that the raiment Alva and her guests bore on their backs cost at least $155,730 retail.

No ball was complete without a series of quadrilles, square dances in the French manner practiced weeks in advance and performed by four matched pairs of males, females or mixed doubles. Mrs. Astor spurred her daughter Caroline into drawing in seven other young ladies to rehearse a star quadrille gowned in yellow, white, blue and pale purple, each with battery-powered light bulbs twinkling in their long, unbraided hair.

Alva kept herself informed on the troupe's progress as they drilled in the Astor mansion, biding her time until they had reached the stage of perfection. Then she chilled their bones by letting intimates of Mrs. Astor relay the word that since Mrs. William K. Vanderbilt had never been afforded the pleasure of meeting either the grande dame or her daughter, it would be improper for either of them to be asked to 660 Fifth Avenue on gala night.

With the crumbs of humble pie on her lips, Mrs. Astor summoned her coupé, dark blue in the Astors' distinguishing dynastic hue, to be driven up Fifth Avenue. When she reached the House of Vanderbilt, a blue-liveried footman descended to deliver to the maroon-liveried counterpart who opened the front door a calling card engraved with only two words: *Mrs. Astor.* Alva accepted the surrender. Later in the day, a servant in maroon delivered the last of her invitations to No. 350.

Consuelo may have shared in the jubilation, the cause of which was a mystery to her, by being allowed a look at her mother costumed in glory to pose before a camera when preparations for the night were completed. Alva had turned for inspiration to Alexandre Cabanel, the artist who had directed the École des Beaux Arts under Napoleon III, but not to his "Birth of Venus," hung in the Luxembourg. Garbed instead as a Venetian princess he had painted, she looked, in Consuelo's word, "gorgeous" as she stood unsmiling in an arched, jeweled headdress, low-cut gown of yellow and white brocade revealing soft-skinned shoulders, train of blue satin embroidered in Roman red and gold thread. To record the sight for posterity, she had the photographer include six stuffed white doves, three of them gazing glassy-eyed at her costume, one clasped in each hand, the sixth suspended from a wire as if in flight and about to land on her brown ringlets.

March 26, 1883, probably brought one of the rare evenings when Consuelo was allowed into her mother's capacious bedroom to watch her at her toilette, ready to descend to the two-storied dining hall. At ten o'clock, she would be there to begin receiving her guests, flanked by Lady Mandeville—the Princesse de Croy after the portrait by Van Dyck—and handsome Willie, resplendent in yellow silk tights, striped trunks, yellow doublet and black velvet cloak as the Duc de Guise. One of Consuelo's prayers was that the door of the bedroom safe would not jam, as it did once when Alva was about to leave for another party. On that evening, the child raced to her room to escape her mother's outburst of fury at being deprived of her pearls. Alone, Consuelo pleaded with God, and He answered with what she accepted as a minor miracle: the safe opened on another try. As long as she lived, she retained faith in the power of prayer.

Red carpet covered the sidewalk, and the inevitable throng of gapers and gawkers surged against the customary police cordon. Inside and out, the château shimmered with light as Consuelo crouched behind the balustrade of an upstairs gallery, peeping at the incoming horde. They came dressed in fabrications from fairyland, Mother Goose, Audubon's "Birds of America," heathen myth, the art treasures of Europe, and the *Almanach de Gotha*. With a rapier dangling at his waist, Uncle Cornelius was a Louis XVI courtier, Aunt Alice a dazzling Electric Light, Aunt Eliza a make-believe hornet in yellow satin, Aunt Emily a delicate Bo-Peep, Aunt Margaret a marquise. Grandfather, like General Grant and his wife, contented himself with dressing in nothing fancier than he would wear to any humdrum dinner party.

Miss Caroline Astor and friends executed their star quadrille, but they were outdone by an octet of ladies and gentlemen attired in riding habits and wearing life-size effigies of horses made of genuine hide; fastened around the dancers' waists, they were the essence of the "hobbyhorse quadrille." A military band and Landers' orchestra spelled each other through the night. It would be four the next morning before the last magnum of champagne had been poured in the second-story supper room.

Henry Clews, Wall Street broker, filtered through the rooms, drawing up a mental balance sheet of Alva's coup. "The ball," he judged, "seemed to have the effect of leveling up among the social ranks of upper-ten-dom and placing the Vanderbilts at the top of the heap in what is recognized as good society in New York. So far as cost, richness of costume, and newspaper celebrity were concerned, that ball had, perhaps, no equal in history."

The issue of the *Sun* on sale a few hours later reached a similar conclusion, but in an era of growing unrest at the distant, barely discernible end of the social scale, the newspaper introduced a note of surprise: "Mrs. Vanderbilt's Ball was gorgeously accomplished with no interruption by dynamite."

After Billy had figured the probable expenses of the night, he showed concern for his son's financial situation. Willie was forthwith promoted to president of the Lake Shore at a fat increase in salary. Alva, her status as a rival queen in her own right established by Willie's money and the force of her will, began staking out her territory. Since Mrs. Astor dared not close her doors in Vanderbilt faces again, Alva was content to leave the dowager to bask in her own diminished glory. Mrs. Vanderbilt would dictate not the manners of her followers but their tastes in the arts, architecture and high-style living, with energy to spare for the upbringing of her daughter.

III

'Mid Pleasures and Palaces

Consuelo must be turned into a paragon of the social graces—nothing less would satisfy her mother. Fräulein Wedekind, the living-in governess on whose breath the girl from time to time detected distasteful whiffs of sauerkraut, tutored her in her native German; another governess came in to teach her French. On Saturdays, Alva reviewed her progress by having her recite poetry in both languages and English, too. By the time she was eight, she could read and write in all three.

She was sent out for an hour's exercises in Central Park every day and to music classes, learning French and English songs. At one youthful concert, she grew so mournful singing "Les Adieux de Marie Stuart" that she finished in tears. Fresh pangs of emotion beset her when she was put on display at matinee performances in the brand-new Metropolitan Opera House. Vanderbilts owned five boxes in the "diamond horseshoe," in the first tier.

The blatant yellow structure on Broadway between Thirty-ninth and Fortieth constituted solid evidence of another triumph for Alva. The Vanderbilts led the consortium of new capitalists who built the hall as a showcase for themselves after they were refused boxes by the Schuylers, Bayards and other titans of old Knickerbocker society in the more venerable temple of opera, the Academy of Music on Irving Place, where the parvenu millionaires wanted to put themselves and their diamond-dipped wives on view in the audiences.

Willie's box by the stage was the display case in which Consuelo was exhibited, fingernails manicured, dark hair burnished and tied with an immaculate bow, dressed beyond her years in the Paris silks and satins Alva judged necessary to her status. The child was drilled to sit straight and still as a wax doll, a model of deportment, but it was impossible for her to restrain the emotions that the music engulfed her in. She agonized over Mephistopheles bartering for souls in Gounod's *Faust*. Poor Marguerite! How she suffered! "Folly," Consuelo thought, "became associated with love." She was too absorbed to notice that to the audience around her she was as much of a show as any prima donna across the footlights.

Once a week, adorned in similar finery, she went for lessons in deportment and dancing from an aged instructor who had slid a rung or two down the social ladder since the days of his prime when he taught only the sons and daughters of the old Knickerbocker rich. The classes gave her a rare opportunity to enjoy herself, to allow a bit of the uncowed devilment that lurked in her to reveal itself. In a long white gown and matching slippers, she was pretty enough to incite boys into elbowing each other for the chance to lead her around the floor. She could pick and choose among her partners, and she found that good for her soul. "The competition," she recalled in after years, "gave me a sense of superiority I did not often enjoy at home."

Their eagerness would not have surprised a less introverted girl. She was growing up into timid beauty, dark hair curling on slim shoulders, gentle blue eyes, and a sad mouth to which smiles were strangers. Long skirts hid knees that continued to feel the sting of the riding crop, but she imagined that beatings were every child's lot. Her brother had his share, too, but as his older sister, she expected the first lashing. There was no point in complaining to her father—Alva would take no heed of him.

She insisted that her daughter should know something about running a household. Since she could not be conscripted into service in the petit château, she would be trained on her father's new estate at Oakdale, Long Island. Idle Hour, the villa there, was another commission from Alva for her friend Richard Morris Hunt, together with the teahouse and the stables. Willie ran a little steamboat, *Mosquito*, on the river, stocked his eight hundred acres of woods and farmland with quail, which he hunted, and a herd of blue-ribbon cattle. He also ran into misfortune in his speculations on the stock exchange. "William K. has never asked me for a dollar," Billy claimed. "He has never hinted that he needed help." Nevertheless, one year after Alva's ball, Billy made over to his son a welcome $5,000,000 in treasury bonds.

A bowling alley on the grounds of Idle Hour was converted into a playhouse for Consuelo's apprenticeship. In a state of bliss, she cooked—homemade caramels were a special treat—washed the dishes and cleaned up the place, with little Willie helping her. They waded together in the trickling Great River, probing under the rocks for crabs, learning to fish and handle a sailboat, supervised by servants outfitted in standard maroon.

The stables now were replete with horses, carriages and, best of all, a yellow and scarlet coach, driven four-in-hand by Willie, a "tallyho" in the parlance of ignorant commoners. He had been admitted at last to membership in the Coaching Club, a rarefied group of gentlemen to whom, as one scrutineer remarked, *form* was almost as important as *family*. Decorum called for artificial flowers to be attached to the leathers around each horse's throat.

Coaching was a pastime imported from England, where the Prince of Wales was a devotee, as was the rakish Marquess of Blandford, who one day would become the eighth Duke of Marlborough. Willie, an enthusiastic whip, joined the ranks that included Colonel William Jay, the club's founder; Leonard Jerome, father-in-law of Lord Randolph Churchill, Blandford's brother; and James Roosevelt Roosevelt, of Hyde Park, New York, whose half-brother, Franklin, was then two years old.

Coaching called for a gentleman to put on his club uniform, consisting of bottle-green surcoat with gilded buttons and a boutonnière in the lapel, striped vest and silk topper. Reins in his gloved left hand, whip flourished in the right, he would seat as many pretty ladies and their elegant escorts on rooftop seats as the immaculate vehicle would hold, one comrade at the rear being entrusted with tooting the polished brass horn that was essential to the turnout as the equipage tooled along Fifth Avenue to cheers and jeers from the sidewalks.

Coaching was not for children, however. Consuelo and her brother had ponies to ride—sidesaddle, of course, in her case—and a trap to which they were harnessed. With a stoic's ability to

minimize the cruelties she suffered, she was objective in her assessments of her mother's character. Understanding Alva completely was beyond her power, but she admired many of the
qualities in her, her daring most of all. The girl was out in the
trap one day when the skittery pony took fright and began to bolt
straight toward a water hydrant. Alva, close by, saw her daunted, docile darling in danger of being hurt and possibly scarred if
she were thrown out of the little cart. Running in front of the
animal, she grabbed hold of its bridle to drag it to a halt. Her
mother was brave in what she did as well as in what she thought.
Consuelo hoped she, too, would be one day.

One essential mark of a young lady of quality was the habit of
sitting straight as a poker, refraining from what Alva called
"Vanderbilt fidgets"; the Smiths presumably had not been prone
to plebeian twitchiness. On Sundays there was imminent risk of
an attack of the fidgets when father and mother, daughter and
son rode in Sabbath finery down to morning service in St.
Mark's-in-the-Bowery. Consuelo listened to a stream of whispered admonitions telling her to keep still, sit up and not make a
spectacle of herself.

When she had seen enough of her squirming, Alva undertook
to stiffen her daughter's backbone with a species of orthopedic
corset, into which Consuelo was strapped during lessons with
Fräulein Wedekind. It consisted of a steel rod pressed against
the spine by belts tightened around waist, shoulders and forehead. Writing with it on was next to impossible and reading,
which was the most precious refuge in her life, almost as hard.
Consuelo, looking for the best in everything, came to credit the
device for the compliments she received as a grown woman for
her supernaturally noble bearing.

The same urge to dredge for gold in murky streams led her to
cherish some childhood memories. After church, she and her
brother had lunch with Alva, Willie and perhaps a pair of young
cousins asked in to join them. That was another treat, since on
most weekdays the only contact with her parents came after six
o'clock supper with Fräulein when the two children spent a tep-
id hour with nothing to do but hear the drone of adults talking—
in French, which Willie had learned in Geneva—counting the
minutes until Mother and Father went their separate ways to
bathe and dress for dining. Once the Sunday meal was over,

there was only a Scripture lesson to be endured before boy and girl were set free to play with their building blocks and toy soldiers.

She remembered with fondness roller-skating and riding an old penny-farthing bicycle in the playroom on the same floor of the château as her own bedroom. Young Willie took so many tumbles that Alva warned him the antique machine would be taken away if he fell off it once more. After that, he sat through a lesson from his tutor with not a word about a fractured arm—he had taken another ride and another spill.

Consuelo was in her eighth year when Alva's third and last child was born. On the January night when she and Willie danced at Mrs. Astor's ball, a tightly laced corset had kept her waist demure. Nothing had been said to Consuelo as the expected day approached. She and young Willie were taken for a Sunday walk while Alva went into labor. On their return, they were summoned to the bedroom for a glimpse of the infant son in their mother's arms. Neither then nor later did she offer her daughter any further explanation of the act of love and its possible consequences. The family nurse, called only "Boya," furnished the basis of Consuelo's knowledge of sex and childbirth. God, she said, had sent baby Harold into the world.

The girl was starting to pick up fragments of facts about the universe existing beyond the petit château's white walls and the secluded grounds of Idle Hour. The seigniorial life that Alva aspired to conceded the duty of gentlefolk to concern themselves with the well-being of those who worked for them. Consuelo had exchanged a "good morning" with one of the gardeners when she was prompted to ask the reason for the sadness that shadowed his face. His answer was that his daughter, the same age as she, was a bed-ridden cripple.

The thought of that stunned Consuelo. With permission granted by Alva, she and Fräulein drove to the man's cottage the next day in the pony trap, which she had loaded with toys from her collection. In her first good deed as a lady bountiful, Consuelo gravely presented them to the gardener's daughter.

"I realized the inequalities of human destiny," she remembered, "with a vividness that never left me." For opening her eyes to suffering, she gave credit where it belonged—not to Alva or any Vanderbilt but to Boya, her "sainted" confidante.

* * *

Billy had lost the sight of his right eye, and an uncontrollable twitch afflicted his lower lip, yet age increased his generosity. He gave $100 checks as tips to student waiters when he went on vacation and $100,000 toward shipping Cleopatra's Needle from Egypt to Central Park. Half a million of his dollars were spent building what emerged as Columbia University's Medical School, and he added $260,000 to the million the Commodore had lavished on the Nashville, Tennessee, university which gratefully renamed itself "Vanderbilt."

But the building that attracted Billy's keenest interest was the family mausoleum, once more a project for Richard Morris Hunt, who devoutly fulfilled his clients' fancies. "If they want you to build a house upside down, standing on its chimney," he declared, "it's up to you to do it."

Billy rejected Hunt's original concept for a Gothic extravagance to sit on the fourteen acres of hilltop the old man bought at New Dorp. "We are plain, quiet, unostentatious people, and we don't want to be buried in anything as showy as that would be." He was, however, prepared to pay up to $300,000 for his ultimate resting place.

The architect's second try, a reworking of the Chapel of Saint Gilles at Arles in the French Pyrenees, fared better. Billy, fattened by age where Corneel had been lean, took to his Grecian library, flushed and wheezing but content with the plans for the Romanesque tomb that would be his and his descendants'.

He had a visitor on the afternoon of December 8, 1885. Robert Garrett of the Baltimore & Ohio wanted Billy's thoughts about a terminal Garrett contemplated erecting on Staten Island. Shortly before three o'clock, Willie received a summons to the Fifth Avenue mansion. With his brother Cornelius, he remained through the night, keeping vigil over the body of their father, struck down by a heart attack.

Stockbrokers and bankers, speculators and manipulators also stayed up, some fearing, some hoping for a break in tomorrow's market. John Pierpont Morgan, astute as always, judged correctly that "Mr. Vanderbilt's death will have little or no effect . . . and have so cabled London." On December 9, Vanderbilt shares edged down only a fraction.

When the executors checked the bank deposits and evaluated

Billy's holdings, they were astounded. In the span of ten years, the fumbling ex-bookkeeper had doubled his inheritance from Corneel. The estate was worth more than $200,000,000. Hospitals, churches and charities were remembered in his will to the tune of $1,000,000. Tens of millions more were allotted to provide for every member of the family, but the crux of the document was its twenty-second paragraph:

"All the rest . . . I give, devise and bequeath unto my two sons, Cornelius Vanderbilt and William K. Vanderbilt, in equal shares, and to their heirs and assignees to their use forever." Altogether, Willie had come into $65,000,000. Alva had inexhaustible money to play with. What she wanted most, she decided, was a beautiful new yacht.

When the mausoleum was completed, Billy's remains, temporarily entombed alongside his father's, were reinterred, and Corneel's body was exhumed to lie in the same chapel. For protection against grave robbers, guards were hired, under orders to punch a time-clock every quarter-hour. It distressed Consuelo to realize that neither his charity nor the the shrine overlooking New York harbor memorialized her grandfather. America remembered Billy for the sublime utterance of a multi-millionaire's contempt for his fellow citizens, "The public be damned!"

She accepted the family's word that he said no such thing. Willie *had* been in the party riding with his father in his private palace car on a trip West in the fall of 1882. Billy *had* spoken with a *Chicago Tribune* reporter, John Sherman, and at the same time with a freelance named Clarence Dresser, on assignment for the rival *News*. Grandfather *had* been asked toward the close of the interview whether the Central made a profit on its Chicago Limited, the express service that raced along the tracks linking that city with New York.

"No, not a bit of it," Billy answered, if the newspapermen's notes were accurate. "We only run it because we are forced to do so by the action of the Pennsylvania road. It doesn't pay expenses. We would abandon it if it were not for our competitor keeping its train on."

"But don't you run it for the public benefit?"

"The public be damned! What does the public care for the railroads except to get as much out of them for as small a consideration as possible? . . . Railroads are not run on sentiment but on business principles, and to pay."

Headlines in the *News* the following day focused on·the cussing, whereas the *Tribune* omitted all mention of it. Americans in general, increasingly resentful of plutocrats' arrogance, did not question the truth of Dresser's reporting. Billy hastened to defend himself. "Supposing," he told another gathering of journalists, "that the expression which I am reported to have made revealed my real sentiments. Do people think that I would publish such an opinion? That is not my way, nor was it my father's." Those last words lost him credibility with men who recalled that Corneel cussed worse than a mule skinner.

The family version of Billy's calamitous brush with the press aboard his palace car claimed that at the end of a wearying working day he turned away all but one of a pack of reporters. The solitary young man who was admitted to his presence reproached him, so the story went, by saying, "Mr. Vanderbilt, your public demands an interview."

Consuelo used to avow that Grandfather replied, "Oh, *my* public be damned!" which put a more affable gloss on the encounter. "He was," she said, "not so black as painted." But a little whitewashing could do his reputation no harm.

He had been dead only ten months when the world's largest steam yacht was ready for christening. Not a day had been wasted in placing the order with the Harlan & Hillingsworth yards in Wilmington, Delaware. The blueprints called for a vessel extending 285 feet from stem to stern, which was 15 feet longer than Corneel's *North Star*. Morgan's *Corsair* measured a meagre 165 feet, Gould's *Atlanta* ran to 250, and William Astor's *Nourmahal* 233. Billy had owned not as much as a rowboat.

Alva's sister, Mrs. Fernando Yznaga, rode down with the Willie Vanderbilts and family in their New York Central palace car to swing a bottle of champagne against its bow and send the new plaything sliding down the slip into Christiana Creek. Only one name was judged suitable: this was *Alva*, of fourteen hundred tons burthen, luxuriously equipped, fitted and furnished lavishly yet with the refinement her mistress could afford now. The bills Willie paid topped $500,000.

From Consuelo's point of view, cruising aboard *Alva* was a dubious pleasure, though her father reveled in it and her mother, too, enjoyed seigniorial seagoing. Their voyages took them down to the West Indies, across the Atlantic, and steaming round the Mediterranean. On all these expeditions, Consuelo found things amiss. Her governess and her brother's tutor were always included on the passenger list. That meant every day of sightseeing must be followed by an extra homework assignment. Four or five male guests were the usual complement, since Mrs. Vanderbilt enjoyed masculine companionship as much as she excluded wives and children who could have played with hers. For Consuelo, the sea spelled schoolbooks and unbroken hours of boredom spent staring at the mahogany-paneled walls of a tiny cabin.

The worst trouble lay in the yacht itself; in heavy weather, *Alva* rolled like a tub. The girl lived in queasy terror of storms blowing up, like the gale that promised to sink them as they made for Gibraltar, putting the doctor who always traveled with them hard at work patching up the battered crew.

Some of the shore excursions upset a child who was prey to fears. In the dim light of guides' lanterns in the Pharaohs' tombs, she panicked on seeing bats dangling like clusters of dirty brown rags from the ceilings close above her head. She might have been picturing a parallel with the sepulcher at New Dorp in a comment she made long afterward: It "seemed positively indecent to disturb the dignified seclusion that the mummified kings of ancient Egypt had gone to such lengths to ensure for themselves."

Whatever she said or did, she risked her mother's censure. If she remarked that a different dress might look prettier than the one selected for her, she was rebuked. As she was lacking in all esthetic judgment, she had best mind her own business. "I thought—" she would begin, only to be cut off. "I do the thinking," Alva would snap. "You do as you are told."

Any spark of self-esteem was stamped out in case it set the girl's mind ablaze. At Nice on the Riviera, the Vanderbilts found themselves bombarded with nosegays tossed by elated crowds in the Battle of Flowers. Wasn't the little package of chocolates thrown from some stranger's hand that caught Consuelo squarely on the cheek intended as a tribute to her? Not so, Alva said. "It must have been meant for Harold."

That was the spring when Consuelo first saw Paris, and its

beauty stirred her soul. Even more significant, her mother seemed much happier in France. She retold stories of her ancestry, starting with a citizen of Louis XIV's reign who, in common with fellow Protestants, knew religious liberty under the Edict of Nantes. He sought refuge across the Atlantic in New France in 1685, when the king revoked the law and Catholics resumed the persecution of Huguenots.

Alva skipped ahead to reminiscences of growing up in the bewitching city in the doomed days of glory under Napoleon III before the Prussian siege drove Parisians to eating rats. Her eldest sister, she said, had entered society at a debutante ball in the Palace of the Tuileries when it still stood unscarred by the torches of the Communards.

Consuelo was infected by her mother's rare gaiety. Alva showed more love for mellow brick and weathered stone than for any creature of flesh and blood; and her daughter was eager to share that passion with her. Scenes and scents were imprinted on her memory. The very name of Paris evoked a sense of joy. "The cradle of the freshest thought, the newest fashion, and the latest luxury; the paradise of pleasure seekers; the most attractive jewels that glitter in the coronet of Mother Earth"—she could concur with every word written by another enthusiast of that era.

Paris for her meant the *parfum* of the sticky blossoms on the chestnut trees growing along the banks of the winding river and lining the boulevards that divided the city like a knife cutting slices from a delicious bridal cake. From the Seine's bridges, she watched the blue light shimmering on the water, the patient fishermen, the children waving from the boats that passed sedately beneath her feet.

While Alva combed antique shops and auction galleries for treasures in oils, porcelain and marquetry, her daughter had a brief taste of Eden. She was fluent in the language. She rode the carrousels, watched the puppet shows, and built castles in the sand piles of the Champs Élysées. She could sail a toy boat in the placid pools of the Tuileries, tramp the hillsides of the Bois de Boulogne, and have the most fun of her young life with playmates of her parents' social set. Chubby Waldorf Astor was one and May Wilson, who would be the Duchess of Roxburgh, another.

The memory proved unforgettable. As an old woman, she felt what she called "a sad and tender reverence" for those long ago days. "For the beauty of spring is evanescent and loveliness is a fragile thing."

It was impossible to determine when antagonism sprouted between her father and mother. Consuelo could not fathom why two completely opposite people had ever ventured into marriage. Willie was gentle where Alva was harsh. He was joyful, she was morose. He shied away from trouble, while she liked nothing better to test her strength. But Willie may have given Alva cause to act the shrew.

He was one of the dozen fancy-free millionaires with a taste for womanizing who were victimized by the publisher of *Town Topics*, laced every week with the spiciest gossip in New York. Colonel William D'Alton Mann, who wore a bushy white beard and fed wagon horses the lump-sugar he carried in a frock-coat pocket, had the appearance of a dandified Santa Claus and a predilection for blackmail. A network of informants supplied him with the nuggets of precious scandal. He kept other people's servants on his payroll to report on the peccadilloes of their employers. Ferret-eyed musicians let him know, for a fee, when a romance bloomed or withered on the dance floor. Some of his most valuable sources were disgruntled social climbers anxious to settle the score for being royally snubbed by their betters. What appeared in print was less profitable than the secrets which, he boasted, were locked away in his office safe: the name of an errant wife, the identity of a tycoon's latest paramour, the address of a retreat catering to the illicit pleasures of millionaires and their partners.

Mann's patrons paid him well for including them on his not-to-be-mentioned list. Once they had bought his silence, they were free so far as he was concerned to do as they liked—*Town Topics* would turn a blind eye. Extortion took the form of loans to him whose due date never came. John Pierpont Morgan gained a place on the docket along with Willie and ten others who together contributed $250,000 toward the Colonel's bank account.

Her husband's fancy for other women might have been the lever Alva used to persuade him to give her a present that eventually cost more to complete than the Taj Mahal. Or perhaps it was an impulsion to outshine her sister-in-law Alice, the steely-eyed wife of Cornelius II, who fitfully imagined that she and not Alva had first claim to being acknowledged as *the* Mrs. Vanderbilt.

The year before *Alva* first put to sea, the Cornelius Vanderbilts bought a "cottage"—it contained three floors—and eleven acres of land between Bellevue Avenue and the cliffs at Newport, Rhode Island. Mrs. William K. would not have dreamed of living in a house so humdrum as this ivy-covered, brick-and-frame affair, but she and Willie had no place of their own in that city. When they took their children there for a month or so each season, they had to rent.

Consuelo looked forward to those summers. The old seaport had once seen great fortunes made in the self-perpetuating three-way traffic in which Newport rum was exchanged for slaves in Africa, who were traded for Barbados sugar and molasses, which were shipped back to Newport to be made into more rum. Now the influx of war profiteers' money was earning the little city on Narragansett Bay a reputation as a most exclusive resort. Mrs. Astor's McAllister praised it as "the most enjoyable and luxurious little island in America." Opulent new houses arose like mushrooms on the gentle slopes of the hills above the arc of the inner harbor and the cobbled streets of the old town. On the eastern coast, three miles of cliff walk skirted the walls enclosing Bailey's Beach, where sentinels turned away everyone except members of the club that put up the walls, and their servants, who were restricted to a few yards of sand at the far end.

If they invested enough time and patience, the new rich who spent summers at Newport might be lucky enough to find it a portal to rarefied Manhattan society, but they needed backing from reliable friends to get an invitation to lunch with the best class of people. The sun might be warm and the breeze refreshing, but protocol remained frozen.

What Consuelo liked was the freedom. Local farmers had good reason to be friendly when they sold their fresh meat, vegetables, milk and butter to kitchens where nobody cared how much was charged. The fields were open playgrounds for Consuelo and her select circle of similarly liberated youngsters. In high-button boots, black stockings and pinafore over a long dress, she ran whooping across the countryside, playing white man and Indian. Heirs and heiresses scampered off to picnic in the woods and pick berries in the bushes. As the sun went down, they trailed off home to noble mansions, a band of ragamuffins with clothing torn, legs scraped and faces scratched by brambles. The absurdity of the contrast between pomp and scruffiness appealed to the sense of humor that somehow survived in her.

On fine mornings, she was escorted to Bailey's Beach. In the clubhouse, she changed into a voluminous dark-blue gown with matching, knee-length knickers, black stockings and cartwheel hat to preserve her complexion from sunburn. She was ready not to swim, because she was never taught, but to dunk herself in the cool sea.

Alva had set her heart on being given a cottage at Newport for a future birthday. There was no way for even the plans to be ready by the time she would reach thirty-six next January 17, but she was willing to wait. Once again, she and Willie called on Richard Morris Hunt to prepare the designs. Like her cherished Louis XIV, she had fallen victim to that high-priced affliction, *la manie de bâtir*, fury to build. Above all else, her cottage must exude grandeur. The price was of no consequence, since Willie's money was earning money faster than either of them could spend it, no matter how she tried.

She approved the bulky rolls of sketches and working drawings Hunt submitted one year later. At Vanderbilt expense, he had crisscrossed France to fire his imagination. What he proposed doing on the Newport shore was to recreate the Grand Trianon of the Sun King as it stood in the park of Versailles. He promised it would be the most sumptuous residence ever erected in America. In due course, it was also to imprison Consuelo.

As the excavation got under way, the general contractor, Charles E. Clarke of Boston, took a two-year lease on a harbor wharf and warehouse, where the tons of slate and Italian marble were cut and storage provided for other cargoes of oak and English walnut, wrought iron, steel and bronze, mantels, sconces, pilasters and chandeliers shipped from across the world for the raising of Alva's palace. Human cargoes were imported, too—masons to cut the stone, carvers to chisel the wood, muralists to work in tempura and stucco. She was so pleased with the pace of progress that she had a sculptor, Karl Bitter, create a bas-relief of Hunt and another of Jules Hardouin-Mensart, architect to the Sun King, who labored at Versailles, to be installed on the landing of the mezzanine.

She was too restive to concentrate on any one thing at any time. She turned another project over in her mind, the future of her daughter. Consuelo's namesake was a full-fledged duchess now that her husband George had succeeded his father. And one more American woman had attained the same dazzling rank by marrying another Englishman, the profligate eighth Duke of Marlborough, also called George.

Fat and often frowzy, Lilian Warren Hammersley of New York City was a prize catch nevertheless. This daughter of Commander Cicero Price of the United States Navy had been left a fortune by her first husband, Louis Hammersley. The spendthrift duke had been divorced by his first wife, Albertha, whose standards of rectitude had been set in nursery days—her father was the Duke of Abercorn. Marlborough needed a second wife like Lilian if he was to continue living in accustomed style at his ancestral home, Blenheim Palace, a few miles outside of Oxford. The wedding at the Tabernacle Baptist Church on Second Avenue had been altogether lacking in ducal style. When Consuelo Vanderbilt was married, Alva counted on being able to arrange something infinitely more impressive.

The whole subject was bothersome. "I know of no profession, art or trade, that women are working in today," she once said, "as taxing on mental resources as being a leader of society."

Consuelo grew into adolescence during the four years that elapsed between the conception of the cottage and the opening to the first guests of its three tons of steel-and-bronze entrance doors.

She was strikingly beautiful, consistently repressed and altogether melancholy. She had been confirmed as a Christian at the altar rail of the Episcopal church in Islip, Long Island, which Willie supported but seldom attended. She felt then that if she were to fall in love, it would be only with God. She was saved from offering herself to a convent only because nobody proposed that she might be happier as a nun. In her misery, she rejected luxury. Experimenting with austerity, she tried sleeping in nothing but a nightgown on the bare floor of her room to prove herself worthy of Christ. She succeeded in catching a cold.

She continued to cram her mind with books to stifle her unhappiness—fairy tales, poetry and sentimental novels that had her weeping by the hour. She dabbled in German philosophy as another balm for her sadness, but she was forbidden by Alva to explore the depths of *Weltschmerz*, which was too unseemly a study for an apprentice aristocrat. Governesses still hovered over her. Every weekday morning one of them walked her to two hours of lessons with five other budding heiresses in a private house on Madison Avenue. Willie's brougham and one of the coachmen collected her there in time to go home for luncheon.

It was the only meal she shared with her mother. Places were always laid for Alva's women friends, who were encouraged to drop in whenever they liked. As usual, Alva dominated the hen-party conversation. Discussing art and the treasures the ladies had purchased, spurious or otherwise, gave her the opportunity to improve their minds with her opinions. Consuelo had to sit and listen. A flicker from her mother's eyes was enough to tell her she must not join in.

The cottage was halfway finished when Willie recrossed the Atlantic again in *Alva*, leaving his wife and children in New York. He was following the patterns of other absentee husbands like William Astor, who would be dead within the year. Willie was often away for days at a time. When he returned, there might be a short-lived reconciliation or one of the screaming performances by her mother that Consuelo dreaded. Then man and wife would refuse to speak, and their daughter was conscripted to serve as messenger between them, delivering searing words from Alva for Willie and milder answers in the return direction. The girl learned more about sorrow. She recalled a time of "sinister gloom" when she appreciated this marriage was "a horrible mockery."

Alva, built of steel and mahogany, went to the bottom after a collision in the fog off Martha's Vineyard. Refloating and repairing the $500,000 yacht would cost only one fifth of the original price, but that was not good enough for Willie. He straightway commissioned a replacement, twenty-seven feet longer, from Laird's shipyards in Birkenhead, on England's River Mersey.

From the keel up, *Alva* had been almost 100 percent pure American and launched with American champagne, but the arts and crafts of the Old World were enticing more and more people like Willie.

The cottage just missed being ready for Alva's fortieth birthday. When she did move in with the children, the sentiment underlying the gift to her had turned sour, and Willie was away again. He had sailed for Birkenhead to collect his new two-thousand-ton, full-rigged, sail-and-steam private ocean liner. The name this time was his choice: not *Alva II* but *Valiant*. Monthly upkeep and pay for a crew of seventy-two and a French chef would total $10,000 a month, but the ship was big enough and fast enough to traverse the Atlantic in seven days.

The Taj Mahal, built of white alabaster, was believed to have cost $9,000,000 when the Indian ruler Shah Jahan ordered it as the tomb for his beloved wife, Mumtaz-i-Mahal. Alva's white marble cottage was a $2,000,000 construction job with an additional $9,000,000 spent on its interior.

Unscalable walls around the grounds and sheet-iron lining to the gates were enough to give Consuelo a clue to what might be in store for her, but she could not deny "Marble House" its splendor. The entry doors opened in a grille sixteen feet tall, adorned with gold-plated masks of the boy Apollo, a favorite device of *le Roi Soleil*. Behind them, the hall was entirely paneled and paved with yellow Siena marble. On each wall to left and right hung a Gobelin tapestry whose subjects deepened her gloom. One depicted the Protestant Admiral Gaspard de Coligny about to be massacred on St. Bartholomew's Eve, 1572. The other showed the murder of Étienne Marcel, Provost of Paris, in the 1358 revolt of the Jacquerie. Against the admiral's wall stood an enormous bronze fountain, bedecked with two frolicking cupids. They were decently veiled like all other representations of human anatomy, male or female, which were on generous display throughout the palace. Stucco masks and arabesques of animals and foliage on the ceiling twenty feet overhead added an impression of revelry under stern control.

From this imposing parade ground, a staircase of forty steps, whose wrought-iron railing bore gilt-bronze trophies of mythical battles, swept up to the principal bedrooms. On that second-floor landing, a twenty-seven-year-old Louis XIV in marble competed for attention with a portrait of his great-grandson, Louis XV, done in oils when he was fifteen, which was Consuelo's age this year, 1892.

Alva's boudoir was *la manie de bâtir* manifested in peach-pink rococo. Over each doorway, coy cherubs clasped shields emblazoned with her initial "A" —the frame of her queenly bed was carved with a matching motif. More cherubs played in the carving over the windows and still more around the ceiling mural of a robed and helmeted Athena, goddess of wisdom and war. Damask covered the walls, curtained the four windows, and complemented the bedspread of embroidered brocade. An Aubusson rug covered the floor.

His daughter's sympathy soared again for Willie when he arrived in Newport. His meagre little study at the head of the stairs had a mantelpiece of wood painted to look like marble, a last-minute makeshift after fire had damaged some of the interior stone. He had no complaint to offer; he had something unique—a puny fireplace that burned coal instead of wood, which was a comfort in a dwelling noticeably wanting in its heating arrangements.

His bedroom over the portico was a quarter the size of Alva's, its Louis XVI furniture sober enough for a navy captain's cabin. The only ornamentation was a rinceaux frieze beneath the ceiling whose corners held scallop shells, emblem of the seafarer. This possibly was the one room of the house in which he had been given a free hand.

In the basement kitchens, menservants, who lived on that level, and maids, who were protectively quartered under the eaves on the top floor, worked long and hard through the oppressive heat of August 19. Alva's party that evening would welcome her first visitors to the palace which fashionable Newport persisted in terming a cottage. As darkness came, fog shrouded Bellevue Avenue. Then as the carriages began to trundle up the road, every light of Marble House, gas and electric, blazed inside and out. Alva was enthroned, and everyone must be made aware of it. The maroon-liveried gatekeeper checked in the guests, and Alva and Willie stood inside the portico to welcome them. Whispers of the strife between the two Vanderbilts rustled among the incoming crowd.

The Savonnerie carpet had been rolled off the parquet floor in

the Gold Room, which resembled nothing so much as the interi-
or of a gigantic jewelbox, embossed with figures of pagan gods
and goddesses, nymphs and satyrs. From the chandeliers, cherubic trumpeters stared down at dancers reflected in mirrors
that turned the scene into a carnival of golden light.

Consuelo had been sent up to bed at the usual hour; Alva did
not hold with a child running around among her distinguished
guests. The severe, oak-paneled room at the back of the house
contained no hint of the girl's personality. Her mother had
bought every piece of the dark oak furniture and had chosen every ornament. She had seen to it that everything from the ink-
stand on the writing desk to the silver-engraved brushes on the
toilette table was set precisely in its appointed place by the upstairs maids among the household staff of thirty-six, and nothing
was permitted to be moved to disturb the setting. Nothing of
Conseulo's own was in sight.

But before she went to sleep, she followed a habit formed in
the Fifth Avenue château, where on gala evenings she would
hide behind the balustrade of the musicians' gallery and peep
down at the dinner table, the crystal and gold plate, the adults in
their most pretentious splendor, chatting and laughing and
clinking their glasses. On this night, she slipped along the corri-
dors to the head of the curved staircase and on hands and knees
joined vicariously in the glory.

She had to step up onto a dais before she climbed into the
chilly bed that stood under a baldachin of oak with a canopy and
spread of red silk satin, the same fabric that covered the walls
above the wood wainscoting. All six windows were as narrow as a
Renaissance castle's and so high that she could see only the
murky sky. From the marble terrace under the windows on each
side of the stone mantel, lawns sloped down to the water. She
could hear the waves ceaselessly surging over the rocks that
defied the sea.

It was a room to encourage introspection. The same thought
about Alva returned to her time and again. "It was her wish to
produce me as a finished specimen framed in a perfect setting . . . my person was dedicated to whatever final disposal
she had in mind."

IV

On With the Hunt!

Before the year was over, Alva's title as *the* Mrs. Vanderbilt went unchallenged in Newport as well as New York. Her sister-in-law, Mrs. Cornelius II, was taken out of the running when The Breakers caught fire and burned to the ground. After inspecting Marble House, Cornelius and Alice realized that to compete in the architectural sweepstakes, they would have to follow Alva and go to Richard Hunt. Cornelius laid down one proviso. Their next cottage must be fireproof, erected with a minimum of wood. He paid $5,000,000 in all for the Italianate villa that emerged as The Breakers in a second edition. As a contribution toward capturing the title for Alice, the money went to waste. When this cottage was finished three years later, Alva was no longer a Mrs. Vanderbilt.

Consuelo had nothing to regret about leaving the unhappiness of Marble House that fall to spend most of the following months at Idle Hour. In later life, she was reticent about what happened to her in that "last peaceful interlude," as she termed it. In fact, her heart leaped with the joy of being in love with the most handsome man a girl could dream of.

She was sixteen that winter and Winthrop Rutherfurd thirteen years older. He had inherited his looks from his mother, Margaret, who was a descendant of Peter Stuyvesant, the last Dutch governor of colonial New York. Winty's father, Lewis, supported by Margaret's inherited wealth, was a gentleman astronomer who had earned respect with some remarkable photographs of the moon.

Winty's profession was the law, but pleasure took precedence over a career. Horses and hounds enthralled him; Blackstone and Locke did not. His ambition was to be a good judge of dogs and horseflesh, a sportsman, not a jurist.

The Rutherfurds moved in the most elevated circles of Newport and Manhattan, where a brownstone on Stuyvesant Square served as the ancestral home. Margaret applied a delicate, patrician touch to keep people in their appropriate places on the slopes of society. It was a losing struggle when she had to contend with mountaineers like Alva.

Winty mixed with his own sort when he went fox-hunting on Long Island. Riding to hounds ranked a cut above coaching as a diversion for gentlemen. He had good friends in the young Roosevelts of Oyster Bay, both in Theodore, who would enter the White House as President one day, and in Elliott, a reckless horseman who had a nine-year-old daughter named Eleanor. A note from Theodore to Henry Cabot Lodge mentioned some hazards of hunting: "Poor old Elliott broke his collar bone the third time he was out with the hounds; so did Winty Rutherfurd."

Her cavalier stood five or six inches taller than Consuelo, who was a slender five feet nine. He was so impeccably turned out, so godlike in physique, that the Rutherfurds' neighbor, Edith Wharton, confessed that he had been "the prototype of my first novels."

It must have been Willie who brought Winty and Consuelo together. A happy-go-lucky bachelor of old Dutch family had no place in Alva's matchmaking. It could have been only Willie, sympathizing with his daughter's tedium on other voyages, who invited Winty along when *Valiant* sailed from New York for India on November 23, 1893. A governess, who was trouble enough in Alva's view, was the only other woman on board. There were two more male passengers, one of them Willie's friend, Oliver Hazard Perry Belmont, a distinguished whip of the Coaching Club and son of August Belmont, who conducted the New York banking business of the Rothschilds.

Romance between Consuelo and Winty had a literally stormy opening. *Valiant* was a far better sea boat than *Alva,* but gale winds churned the Atlantic. Going out on deck meant risking a dousing of spray, and she was glad to have his arm to grab to keep her on her feet. By the time the yacht had sailed through the Straits of Gibraltar into Mediterranean calm, she knew that she was more than fond of him.

She was sixteen years old and starved of love from anyone but her father. The veneer of gentility that Alva had applied concealed a nature capable of passionate attachment. Her knowledge of men was minimal, but by the standards she set, Winty was a perfect choice, a knight errant fascinated by her and not her family's fortune, a hero who, best of all, had her father's approval. She was in luck throughout the trip. Alva's attention went elsewhere—she seemed unusually fond of the company of Oliver Belmont.

The party disembarked to spend two days in Cairo while *Valiant* passed through the locks of Suez; then they reboarded for the crossing of the Indian Ocean to Bombay. Seeing India sealed the bond between Consuelo and Winty. The sweltering heat, the dust, the teeming crowds of terrifying humanity drove her to reassess herself. She had always professed to scorn physical comfort, but that had been a pretense. She detested the days when she could not bathe because there was no water to fill a tub. She hated the food that made her stomach churn, compelling her to subsist on tea and toast. A man's protective arm was consoling, and Winty was happy to supply it.

In Lucknow she was struck by sheer terror, her imagination fired by the accounts she had read of the slaughter of British soldiers and civilians that bloodied the place in the Indian Mutiny nearly forty years earlier. She expected a similar fate the night she spent in a hotel bungalow, where the air was foul from the reek of an open drain outside the rear windows. She would never disclose when and how she and Winty first spoke of their love for each other, but there were hints of it happening on that evening of what she described as "lurid memories." The scene was not hard to picture: a frightened girl in need of comforting in a hostile land which stripped away the protections of Vanderbilt wealth, and a savior in a white linen suit who came to defend her.

The rented railroad train that bore the sightseers to Calcutta provided few of the luxuries she was accustomed to in Vanderbilt palace cars, with their sunken bathrooms, gold-plated fixtures, padded furniture, and dining salons serviced by a chef's kitchen. She had not known before how disagreeable a journey by rail could be nor the squalor visible on every side. Nothing had prepared her for this—swarms of biting insects, the heat and dust of the pale brown plains, the din in the stations as other, darker-skinned travelers wrenched at the locked doors of Willie's special car seeking to ride with them. At least, no bullets flew in central India. Only on the distant northwest frontier, in the shadow of the Hindu Kush, were troops of Queen Empress Victoria's Imperial Service exchanging shots with tribesmen alarmed by new British inroads into the mountains they stubbornly regarded as their own.

Consuelo and the others were happy to move back into the serenity of staterooms in the *Valiant,* which had steamed up the Bay of Bengal to anchor in the Hooghly River, while Willie and Alva stayed in Government House, home of the Viceroy. A week of viceregal hospitality at the hands of the Marquess of Lansdowne and his marchioness, who was another daughter of the Duke of Abercorn, left its mark on Alva. Every dollar the Vanderbilts possessed could not buy such pomp and privilege, this army of obsequious servants, the ceremonial, the parades of reverent officers, turbaned soldiers and marching bands. Her goal for Consuelo was brought into sharper focus. She must be married to an English milord as early as possible, and not to a mere knight, baron, viscount, earl or marquess. Since no prince was available, a duke would have to do.

When the girl herself had a day with the younger Lansdowne daughter, Consuelo was taken aback to discover that by her reckoning, her English companion was barely literate, while Miss Vanderbilt looked forward to studying modern languages at Oxford University.

The impact of India was more than the marriage of her mother and father could endure. Neither of them could stomach the thought of each other's company during an interminable voyage home. What set off the terminal quarrel remained their secret. Perhaps it was something as mundane as the climate or the impossible food. Or did Alva unveil to Willie her plans for Consuelo and did Willie say he rated Winty Rutherfurd a better bet for his daughter's happiness?

Consuelo left India unlamenting. It impressed her as a cruel country that subjugated women. She was in love, and Paris in

springtime was a step toward heaven. She lived for the time being with Alva and the governess in a sunlit suite of the Hotel
Continental whose windows looked across to the gardens of the
Tuileries; April tulips would make way for June roses before the
American ladies departed. Alva applied the finishing touches
deemed necessary for her daughter's debut. Polishing her to a
bright gleam called for touring museums, churches and the couturiers' hushed salons on the Rue de la Paix. Consuelo's clothes
were still her mother's business, in line with her axiom, "I
choose them, you wear them." She bought matinee tickets for
the Théâtre Français and the Comedie Francaise, then engaged
a veteran actress of the latter company to give Consuelo lessons
in elocution. Finally, she was ready to make her entrance into
society in the city of love and light.

Alva ordered the floor-length white tulle from Monsieur Jean
Worth. The coiffure, raven hair piled in clusters of curls, was
her idea. She lent nothing from her $1,000,000 jewel collection
to her daughter, who had no *bijoux* of her own. She wore instead a white ribbon around her preternaturally long, slim neck.
One of their carriages took them to the Duc de Gramont's hôtel
on the Rue de Chaillot for this frightening first ball. As a symbol
of virginity, every *jeune fille* was gowned in white. Each of them
sat meekly beside her chaperone until someone came over to ask
for a dance. Her partner must be careful not to hold her too
close or exchange more than a polite word or two before he returned her to the duenna's safekeeping; otherwise fans would
flutter and lorgnettes snap a rebuke. She was afraid she was so
gauche and awkward that nobody could possibly elect to escort
her onto the floor, and that would mark her a wallflower. She
could cope with private humiliation, but it would be torture to
be shamed in public. Her tremors were unjustified. Mademoiselle Vanderbilt would be a magnificent woman one day, but already she was rich and, to at least half a dozen young men, completely irresistible.

One of them who found her so was Jacques Balsan, a twenty-
six-year-old bachelor with a keen eye for a pretty face, heir of a
long line of French industrialists, gentleman rider and devoted
balloonist—rising higher and higher into the sky in a swaying
gondola was the one thing in his life that accelerated his heart-
beat faster than the presence of a charming female. He joined

Consuelo's other self-elected swains in dancing her off her feet. He pictured her as an ideal bride, but he was not among the five men who went to Alva that spring seeking permission to marry her daughter: Consuelo seemed beyond his reach. All but one of the suitors were sent packing by Alva. The exception was His Serene Highness Prince Francis Joseph of Battenberg, who possessed nothing more valuable than his title. His father, Alexander of Hesse, nephew of Tsar Alexander III, had contracted a morganatic marriage with a Polish countess, Julia Teresa von Haucke. Francis and his three equally dashing older brothers could therefore lay no claim to the modest parental estate.

But *Princess* or even *Queen* Consuelo? Alva hurried her daughter off to be introduced to the German princeling, who at the age of thirty-three had yet to find a bride. One fast fading beauty, the Comtesse Mélanie de Pourtalès, was eager to help. The crucial meeting was held in her salon. Entering the rooms, Consuelo felt the familiar surge of anxiety. She had not been thrown before among such lions as these tail-coated diplomats, bewhiskered statesmen and flirtatious boulevardiers, most of whom eyed her like a sacrificial, imported lamb.

At a not quite discreet distance, Alva and the comtesse kept watch as Francis Joseph mustered his charm. The girl sensed intrigue afoot, and it frightened her. She dared not ask questions, but in the course of the evening, one aged Frenchman volunteered some answers, which involved relating something of the Battenbergs' history.

The eldest brother, Louis, a great favorite of Queen Victoria's, was a naturalized Englishman, earning a zealous living as an officer in her navy. The second brother, named Alexander after the father, had just died in enforced retirement at Graz after a tumultuous life that had seen him elected ruler of Russian-dominated Bulgaria at the instance of Tsar Nicholas, only to be compelled to abdicate seven years later. The third brother, Henry, was one of Victoria's sons-in-law, his wife her youngest daughter, Beatrice.

But Francis Joseph, an author of sorts, was at a loose end, waiting for a rich backer to further his ambition to succeed his dead brother as overlord in Sofia. Consuelo, whose knowledge of Balkan politics was as limited as her interest in the prince, found it difficult to follow what the old diplomat was saying. It seemed that the Russians had turned against Bulgaria's present

King Ferdinand, elected after Alexander abdicated, and had denounced him as a usurper. Emissaries from his country had toured the courts of Europe, looking for a replacement acceptable to Russia and the other Great Powers alike. Why not Francis Joseph, bankrolled, of course, by Willie Vanderbilt?

Alva encouraged the fortune-hunting prince to press the courtship, and he enlarged on the scheme to Consuelo. He pictured her as his future queen; she envisaged only another kind of bondage, compelled to live apart from her family among incomprehensible barbarians in a partly Moslem mountain wilderness, giving up Winty in exchange for a pinchbeck crown. The more she saw of Francis Joseph and his Teutonic arrogance toward her sex, the more he repelled her.

She could not yet believe that she was no more than a pawn in her mother's game. Love, in her girlish fancy, would conquer everything, and Winty was her love, the first and only. The letters he sent her made it plain that his feeling for her was equally overwhelming. As yet, he had not asked her to become his wife, but there was no doubt of his intention. He would surely propose at the earliest opportunity, as soon as Alva gave up this absurd business and took her daughter back to America.

Alva did reconsider the qualifications of Francis Joseph. Battenbergs, after all, could in no sense be reckoned a truly royal dynasty. They had no palaces to call their own, no retinues of servants, nothing but their wits and abounding courage. When Consuelo could no longer disguise her feelings, Alva agreed that Francis Joseph was not the man she had hoped for. His search for a sponsor led him nowhere. King Ferdinand ruled in Sofia without interruption until he abdicated in favor of his son Boris in 1918.

Willie had affairs of his own to contend with in Paris. Neither language nor conscience offered any barrier to his alliance with an aristocratic local lady. If rumor was to be believed, he handed over to her the 40,000 francs he won on the Grand Prix races and equipped her servants with new maroon uniforms. Sobersided Cornelius II showed up in a futile attempt to patch the rift between his brother and sister-in-law, but Alva would settle for nothing short of divorce, for which Willie obligingly supplied the grounds. The lawyers filed suit while Consuelo and her mother were disengaging themselves from Balkan plotting.

Since the action was to be heard in New York, whose courts

recognized only adultery as cause for dissolving a marriage, Willie went through the dreary ritual: a rented room, a hired detective, a bribed desk clerk, and a lady of the evening named Nellie Neustretter from Eureka, Nevada, who had turned up in the French capital after abandoning her husband, a San Francisco cigar drummer.

The recent years with Alva had changed Willie. As the New York *World* reminisced, "Six or seven years ago, when W. K. Vanderbilt sat quietly at the roulette tables, leaving much embarrassed when any woman stared at him, he was the despair of all the European hunters of rich Americans." The newspaper made mention of "a young person of Paris who calls herself Liane de Poujy" and the fainting spells she had recently suffered while dining in the restaurant of the Grand Hotel close to the table where Willie and some friends were seated. "That young woman, with visions of such an establishment as none of her rivals ever possessed, was made ill by sheer mental agitation."

The seamy details of her parents' breakup were withheld from Consuelo. She was left to imagine that she and her adored father would always be close. She could not imagine that, on the contrary, she would be put completely at Alva's mercy.

Her mother's next move was to take her to England. Alva had leased a house in the ancient little Buckinghamshire town of Marlow, where a weir and a lock interrupted the gentle flow of the River Thames. Their horses and carriages, a French coachman, and an English footman were sent on ahead. While she waited for her suit to come up before a New York judge, she would make a survey of possible bridegrooms who, if they could not provide a crown for Consuelo, would at least guarantee her a coronet.

More than thirty miles by train from London, Marlow was too remote for use in reconnoitering. She set up field headquarters in Brown's Hotel on Dover Street in the city's fashionable West End. The rooms were dark and dingy, cluttered with equally dismal furniture. Consuelo thought of them as "frowsty in the true English sense" and yearned to be back in Paris, where it seemed easier to conjure up dreams of Winty.

Alva needed another Comtesse Mélanie as a tracker for the hunt. Few women were better qualified than acid-tongued Minnie Stevens, whom she had known for years, and Minnie was willing. Minnie was a daughter of Colonel Paran Stevens, who accumulated American hotels in much the same way as the old Commodore had collected railroads. One of the colonel's earliest coups had been to entice the Prince of Wales and his entourage into staying at the Fifth Avenue Hotel in 1860, soon after Stevens had taken over its management. Mrs. Stevens had starred as Good Queen Bess at Alva's celebrated costume ball, but gentlewomen like Mrs. Rutherfurd persisted in looking down on her as a pushy outsider, and Minnie's marriage to Lord Paget had not softened Margaret Rutherfurd's judgment. In London, though, Lady Paget was cutting a swathe as one of the prince's witty American friends, a select circle that included Consuelo Manchester and Jennie Churchill.

Miss Vanderbilt, naive and bashful, wilted under Minnie's condescending, green-eyed gaze. If she was to be responsible for flushing the quarry, the bait must be made more enticing. Consuelo's new gowns revealed more of her flesh than she had been accustomed to showing, and she did not like that at all. It had not taken Minnie long to suggest a bridgegroom to Alva. Charles Richard John Spencer Churchill, the twenty-two-year-old ninth Duke of Marlborough, ought to do very nicely. He was supposed to be in love with some other girl already, but that should be no obstacle if Minnie and Alva persevered.

The first manoeuvre was to invite him to dine at the Pagets' splendid house on Belgrave Square. Minnie seated bait on her left, quarry on her right, an arrangement that embarrassed Consuelo as much as the low-cut neckline of her dress. The small, slim young man with wispy moustache and intelligent blue eyes seemed to be politely disinterested, though in appearance she lived up to what he had been led to expect. "I hear," he had written beforehand to a friend, "that she is quite good looking."

Other Englishmen attempted to snatch the bait. Two or three approached Alva about marrying her daughter, who was relieved when they were turned away. She was growing a little cynical about her place in the marriage market. What they undoubtedly were after was not her love but her dowry. No overtures came from Marlborough. He had to review his entire position before he went any farther. Consuelo mistook his silence to mean that the danger of her being forced into an Anglo-American entente had abated.

In the absence of the queen, who secluded herself at Osborne on the Isle of Wight or in Balmoral, her Scottish castle, it fell upon her heir, the Prince of Wales, to open and close the London season. When he left to go yachting at Cowes in the early days of August, the parties and balls were automatically over, the mansions were closed, and hosts and hostesses retreated to the country. The time had arrived for Alva, anxious to keep in step, to take up residence at Marlow. Willie stayed on in Paris; the two sons joined their mother. To liven up the house, Alva also brought over one of her sisters, Mrs. William Jay, wife of the Coaching Club's founder, and her daughters, who were younger than Consuelo but would serve to keep her occupied. Consuelo's thoughts, however, dwelt principally on Winty.

In the fall, she was overjoyed to learn that, despite the impending court action, she and Alva were to return to the château on Fifth Avenue. Her mother had decided to face being blacklisted in an era when mention of divorce drove ladies to rise and leave the room. She succeeded in holding on as a leader of society by ignoring all criticism and imposing such stern standards of behavior on Consuelo that they would have daunted a vestal virgin.

She could have no friends except those Alva approved of, attend no party without Alva's consent and then was obliged to give her mother an accounting of every partner she danced with. When at last she blurted out a hint of her feelings for Winty, touching on "his outstanding looks, his distinction and his charm," Alva raked her with scorn. What did a child too immature to select her own wardrobe possibly know about choosing a man?

Winty continued his arm's length courtship under a drumfire of sarcasm. On the morning of her eighteenth birthday, he sent her a single red rose as a prelude to calling at the château. Alva was in the middle of organizing a party to go bicycling, a suddenly fashionable diversion that was ousting the carriages from Riverside Drive. As she and her friends donned their knickerbockers, Consuelo grabbed the opportunity to ask Winty to come, too.

Carriages were summoned to transport riders and machines to Riverside Drive. Ladies and gentlemen settled themselves in their saddles and, depending on experience, either wobbled or sped away. Winty, pumping hard for a special reason, set the pace and Consuelo pedaled furiously alongside. They pulled ahead of the others for a few unique minutes, alone in each other's company, cheeks glowing in the brisk March breeze. Alva, ever suspicious, labored behind, trying to catch up.

Winty proposed marriage as he and his love cycled together beside the white-flecked Hudson. She was happier than she had believed it was possible to be. Of course she would become his wife, she said, but tomorrow her mother was taking her back to Paris and then on again to England.

In that case, he said, their vows to each other should be their secret. She agreed. He would follow her to France, he promised, to have it out with Alva, but meanwhile, she ought to be told nothing. Otherwise she was certain to forbid the marriage. If she persisted in denying their right to become man and wife although his beloved had reached the age of consent today, they would simply run away to be wed as soon as she returned.

It had all been arranged before the two of them slowed down to allow Alva and the rest to overtake them. The tender, romantic music of Richard Strauss wove itself around Winty when Consuelo remembered that day in years to come. To her, he was *Der Rosenkavalier.*

She was aboard ship with her mother four days later when Justice Barrett of the Supreme Court of the State of New York granted Alva her divorce. Willie was already living in Europe, content to assign his railroading duties to the indispensable new president of the New York Central, Chauncey Depew. In and out of a suite at the Metropolitan Club, Willie had called only briefly at 660 Fifth Avenue and Marble House to collect his personal belongings.

The court awarded Alva sole custody of Consuelo, young Willie and Harold, an annual income of $100,000 and a cash settlement whose size was unknown, since the records were sealed. She was also offered both the petit château and Marble House. Rejecting the first because the upkeep would be too expensive, she took over the palace, essential as the setting for the triumph she planned for Consuelo. The judge also prohibited Willie from finding another wife during Alva's lifetime, but that was a pointless penalty, meaning simply that if he married again, it would have to be outside the boundaries of the state.

Other Vanderbilts cut Alva dead from that day on. She was indifferent to their boycott. "I always do everything first," she would boast. "I blaze the trail for the rest to follow. I was the first girl of my set to marry a Vanderbilt. Then I was the first society woman to ask for a divorce, and within a year ever so many others had followed my example. They had been wanting divorces all the time, but they had not dared do it until I showed them the way."

She likewise disregarded insinuations that Willie had done the gentlemanly thing in taking the blame as an adulterer. Whispers linked her with Oliver Belmont, who had a wife in Sarah Whitney. For years he had been around on the yacht, the château, the Newport cottage and Idle Hour, whether Willie was there or not, treating all three children like an attentive uncle on outings to the Polo Field topped off by scrumptious teas. The word went around that Alva and Oliver would be man and wife within a matter of months. She issued a flat denial, then refused any further discussion.

If the question of Winty had come up, Consuelo, incapable of pretense, would have had to confess they were betrothed. She fancied afterward that Alva had no need to cross-examine her when love shone so brightly in her eyes. Alva set out to break up the romance—that was all too obvious.

In Paris, the weeks went by with no sign of Winty, although from his earlier letters Consuelo judged that he intended to arrive there to confront her mother and claim his love for his bride. What had gone wrong? Had he changed his mind about her? Did he feel that she was too young and too gauche for him? Why had he stopped even writing to her?

She had not known despair had such depths. She could do no more than read and re-read his letters, every one of them saved and squirreled away along with the few personal treasures that were not of Alva's selection. Her mother jeered at the girl's dejection. Of course Mr. Rutherfurd had abandoned her, she said; he had the sense to know when he wasn't wanted. The truth was that he had kept his word and turned up in Paris. When he came to the hotel, a servant announced him to Alva, who sent him away, pretending Consuelo had lost interest in him. The letters he wrote were intercepted by Alva and destroyed. The desperate pleas her daughter scribbled to him met with the same treatment.

She was allowed out of captivity only to walk the familiar, hateful round on the treadmill once more, with Alva mounting guard—seeing the sights, attending concerts, being fitted for clothes, going to an occasional ball where she would rather have been a wallflower than the partner of men whose attentions only aggravated her pain.

London was a continuation of distress. Marlborough appeared for a second time to dance with her at the Duke and Duchess of Sutherland's ball. She was so depressed that night that she was almost grateful to him, though they made an oddly matched couple as the top of his head reached no higher than her eyebrows. Either he was emboldened by the apparent change in her or else Minnie had persuaded him, alert to Alva's desire to speed developments while she could still hold on to Marble House and keep Consuelo and Winty apart. The young duke, in any event, had mother and daughter down to Blenheim Palace for the weekend.

Jennie Churchill had first visited there with Randolph a generation earlier. Passing under the weathered stone entrance arch, he had exclaimed with pride, "This is the finest view of England!" Looking at the enormous ornamental lake, stands of thousand-year-old oak trees, and a palace as wide-flung as a sizable village, Jennie could believe him, but, she reported, "my American pride forbade the admission."

Consuelo's American pride was more vocal. It was impossible not to be awed by the beauty of the park that extended for nearly three thousand acres or by the sheer immensity of a building covered by seven acres of rooftop.

Tea on Saturday was served in the state dining room, otherwise known as the Saloon, where logs blazed in twin fireplaces and a silent audience of frescoed figures stared down from the walls and ceiling at Marlborough and his guests, a group so small that it seemed lost in the echoing vastness. The evening was spent in the Long Library, 180 feet from end to end, listening to a recital on the immense Willis pipe organ installed the year before his death by the eighth duke and his pudgy American duchess, born Lilian Price. The painted scroll on its front

was a new touch: "In memory of happy days as a tribute to this
glorious home we leave thy voice to speak within these walls in
years to come when our hearts are still." His widow, whose dollars had paid for the organ, the first electric lights and a central
heating system, had found his words jotted down on a scrap of
The Times.

There were 320 rooms in all, so Marlborough limited his conducted tour to the most magnificent of them, the route defined
by lengths of red drugget that sightseers trod on days when Blenheim was opened for public inspection. On Sunday, he drove
Consuelo around the estate, patently proud of an inheritance
dating back to the start of the eighteenth century, whose preservation he accepted as the most sacred obligation of his life.

She left Blenheim with her mind made up: never under any
circumstances would she consent to be Marlborough's bride.
She would tell her mother about her betrothal to Winty as soon
as she could scrape up the courage, and there was no time for
stalling. The duke would be arriving in New York at the end of
August, which was no more than six weeks away.

Alva whisked her to Marble House immediately after they
sailed home. Lingering in Manhattan would make it too easy for
her to get in touch with her cavalier. She could think of no
means of reaching the man who, for all she knew, had given her
up. The house had no telephone. A mailbox was as inaccessible
as the moon. Every summer day in Newport was as dark as
night. Between Alva and a German governess, Consuelo was
watched every waking minute. The gatekeeper obeyed orders
not to allow her out alone. Any caller who might have acted as a
go-between was told by Alva that her daughter was busy elsewhere, not confined inside.

Consuelo had said an unspoken farewell to Winty when what
appeared to be a chance meeting showed her the truth of his
feelings. He had come to Newport in search of her. He was
there at a dance that Alva escorted her to one night, awaiting his
chance when her mother's attention was diverted to take her
into his arms and whirl her in jubilation around the floor, repeating all that he had promised her before. They must elope;
they had no other choice.

The moment Alva spotted them she bore her daughter away.
Nothing was said until the carriage had rolled through the for-

midable gates and Consuelo had been taken up into the peach-pink bedroom, where the carved and painted cupids mocked her trembling. The words she let flow were the bravest, she thought, that she had ever uttered. They can be reconstructed with little effort of imagination.

"I am going to marry Winthrop Rutherfurd. It's useless for you to tell me not to. I refuse to accept any man you choose for me. I demand the right to choose a husband."

Fury flared about her head. "How little you know about this pitiful choice of yours! Are you such a blind fool that you don't realize he flirts with every woman he sets his eyes on? Have you never heard of his affair with at least one other man's wife? Do you imagine he's interested in you and not the money?"

Consuelo's silence acted like kerosene on the fire of Alva's rage. "Why do you think I forbid you to entangle yourself with this man Rutherfurd? I will tell you. Because insanity runs in his family. And why do you think he is not already married? I can answer that, too, though you're too green and dewy-eyed to appreciate what I'm saying. He is impotent—incapable of fathering a child."

It was the girl's turn to explode. "You are lying and scheming, and I don't believe you. He isn't mad. There's nothing wrong with him. I am going to lead my own life and marry Winty."

"You shall not. You will do what I tell you to do. I have already made the choice. You are to marry the Duke of Marlborough. That is not my wish. It is my order."

The harshness of the command set the girl sobbing, but she could not abandon the fight even if neither weeping nor words would mollify her mother. "Then I shall run away to be married. I am eighteen, remember. You can do nothing to stop me."

"There is one thing to be done, I promise you. I shall make sure you do not leave this house until you learn to obey."

"How ridiculous! I shall simply escape and go to him."

Stress thickened the accents of the South in Alva's voice. The drawl was dominant now as she spoke, slowly and deliberately. "If you succeed, I shall shoot him and not hesitate about it. I will shoot and kill him to prevent him from ruining you. I shall hang for it, and my death will be on your hands."

Consuelo ran out the door and around the corner up the long hall to her own austere room. Through the eastern windows she could see the pale pink light of another day tinting the gray clouds above the sea and hear the shrieking of awakened gulls. She felt incredibly aged, "as if all my youth had been drained away." She had fought with all the strength she possessed and gone down to defeat under her mother's ultimate weapon, the thrust of guilt. Now the girl's emotions were seeping away. In the arid absence of feeling, it seemed to her that she was a mere husk, worthless to anyone.

She was left alone for hours, watching the sky brighten as the hidden sun moved higher across Marble House. Sleep was out of the question. The unused writing table tempted her, but if she addressed a letter to Winty, the servants would only hand it to Alva. The whole house was unusually quiet. The room behind hers was empty; young Willie was away on his sailboat. No breakfast tray arrived. No tap sounded on her door.

After Winty, the man she longed for most was her father, but he, too, was out of reach, at sea aboard *Valiant*, ignorant of her suffering and its cause. If she were able to communicate with him, what good would it do? He had lost too many of his own battles with Alva to have a hope of winning this for his daughter.

The afternoon brought a visit from the English governess. Miss Harper, normally unruffled, was in a flutter as she opened the door. Mrs. Vanderbilt, she said, had been taken gravely ill, and her doctor was expected. Then, after more hours of solitude, an evening caller expanded on the story. Her aunt, Mrs. William Jay, a house guest here as she had been at Marlow, came to scold, not to sympathize. The message she relayed from Alva was in effect this:

"Your mother has had a heart attack, and you are responsible. You must know that she will never allow you to marry the other one. She assures me that she means what she says and she will kill him if you do."

"Do you think it possible that she will ever change her mind?"

"Never!" Mrs. Jay had no illusions; she knew Alva too well. One more scene like last night's might be her last. The doctor had given that warning, Mrs. Jay reported.

Consuelo could think only that she was compelled to make another choice. Not between Winty and Marlborough but between her personal happiness and her mother's life. She accepted everything said to her as true; too trusting to be skeptical, she realized only later that the tale of the heart attack was a fiction. Under the terms put to her, she had no option. She was defenseless against Alva's attacks. Guilt annihilated her.

She had a request to ask of Mrs. Jay: would she be good enough to let Mr. Rutherfurd know that Consuelo must not see him ever again?

On August 23, Marlborough and his cousin, Ivor Churchill Guest, the future Lord Wimborne, landed in New York on their way to Newport. On the duke's arrival, under a sailor hat with a red and orange ribbon, Alva had the gates of Marble House opened to allow her friends a Sunday inspection of her catch. They turned up in droves, surprised, as one visitor observed, to find not "a big, strapping Englishman with a loud voice but, instead, a pale-faced, frail-looking lad with a voice devoid of that affected drawl peculiar to the English, and as soft as a debutante's." His white flannel suit and boutonnière intrigued the company as much as his witticisms, murmured so quietly it was hard to hear him.

On Monday night, Alva's good friends, the Wilsons, had the country club transformed into a bower of pink American Beauty roses for a fancy dress ball they held there in his honor, preceded by dinner for sixty-five. Georgia-born Richard T. Wilson had added to his family's finances first by selling blankets to the Rebs, then, during the reign of the carpetbaggers, by buying up Southern railroads at bargain prices. Some Southerners, less forgiving than Alva, would not speak to him. Marlborough escorted Consuelo, with Alva their chaperone. He was noticeably amused by favors presented in the cotillions—calico lampshades, Dresden figurines and wickerwork baskets.

Alva did much better than that at her fete on Wednesday. The newspapers agreed it was the most expensive, most beautiful gathering ever seen anywhere, surpassing even her celebrated costume ball. She had personally bought the $5,000 worth of cotillion favors in Paris. Every etching, fan, mirror, and watchcase was a memento of the years of Louis XIV, tagged with a medallion embossed with a picture of Marble House.

The lace-trimmed white satin gown she selected for Consuelo had once been the girl's grandmother's, worn by her when she was Phoebe Desha, a belle of Mobile. Tonight, Consuelo stood pale and impassive beside her mother, welcoming guests as they streamed into what looked like an arboretum of palm trees, ferns, hyacinth, hollyhocks and lotus flowers with flocks of artificial hummingbirds, butterflies and bees suspended among the blossoms. Marlborough's attention was not entirely concentrated on his hostess and her daughter. With Mrs. Jay at his side, his head turned whenever a pretty face passed by.

Young Dick Wilson, not the duke, led Consuelo in the first cotillion to the violins of Mullally's Casino Orchestra, which alternated through the night with a Hungarian *tzigane* band. Midnight supper was served by bewigged footmen in maroon coats, black knee-breeches and patent-leather shoes with gilt buckles. Thirty-five small tables had been set up for the repast on the marble-floored courtyard on the ocean side of the house, where hundreds of white silk Chinese lanterns swayed in the offshore breeze. A second meal was due three hours later.

No other Vanderbilt was to be seen. Cornelius II and Alice stayed in their just completed new cottage, a $5,000,000 conglomeration of Caen stone, marble, wrought iron, chimney stacks and gingerbread, the new version of The Breakers.

In Marble House, the throng expected at any minute to hear a drum roll and a cymbal crash heralding the formal announcement that Consuelo and Marborough were engaged. They were disappointed, and in their disgruntlement some told each other that the girl the duke was really after was Gertrude, daughter of Alice and Cornelius II.

The sadness they had seen in Consuelo's face prompted a comment that circulated through the cottage colony that summer of 1895: "A marble palace is the right place for a woman with a marble heart." *Town Topics* concluded that "Winty was outclassed. Six-foot-two in his golf stockings, he was no match for five-foot-six and a coronet."

BOOK TWO

V

The Wedding of the Year

The sturdy traditions continued unbroken: the rich got richer, the poor got poorer, and poverty bred violence. That spring, the United States Supreme Court had declared federal income tax unconstitutional and ordered every dollar collected to be refunded. In the White House, Grover Cleveland reluctantly agreed to receive John Pierpont Morgan after the bulbous-nosed banker had said that if he were rebuffed he would let the country go bankrupt. Face to face with the President, he consented to avert disaster by raising a private loan for the government of $62,000,000 in gold at 4 percent.

Between two and three million Americans had lost their jobs in the wake of the financial panic of 1893 that saw many a railroad wiped out and the Atchison, Topeka & Santa Fe exposed for defrauding the public of $7,000,000. But the Vanderbilts' empire, in which Morgan had a large stake now, escaped serious harm. The young American Railway Union was convalescing from the wounds inflicted by a court injunction banning it from interfering in railroad affairs after it boycotted all Pullman cars out of sympathy for workmen of the Pullman Palace Car Company in Chicago, locked out when they struck against a cut in wages. The union's Eugene V. Debs was sent to prison, where he started dipping into the works of Karl Marx.

Unrest was polarizing the nation, and 750,000 workingmen went out on strike. Earlier in the year, eight thousand New York streetcar drivers and conductors mobbed trolley cars, and days of rioting in Brooklyn brought in the state militia to open fire on the strikers. Twenty thousand tailors in the sweatshops of New York struck for better pay. So did the tinplate workers of Pittsburgh, miners in West Virginia, and laborers on the New Orleans levees, where whites fought blacks, leaving dead and wounded.

Evil times stirred turbulence between ethnic groups. A rabble of Italians attacked black miners in Spring Valley, Illinois. The citizens of Walsenburg, Colorado, lynched two Italians who murdered the local sheriff, and the pattern was repeated in Florida and Kentucky. Boston Irish took to the streets for a shootout with the police. In Chicago, other Irishmen gathered in a "physical force" convention that collected funds to buy guns and ammunition to oust the British from Ireland.

Marlborough stayed on for another week in Marble House, ensconced in the best guest room on the second floor, with its eighteenth-century marble chimney piece, made-to-order walnut furniture in the style of Louis XV, and a portrait of Mademoiselle de Blois, fathered by Louis XIV out of wedlock but subsequently legitimized. Since Willie kept *Valiant* clear of Newport Harbor, Alva had to persuade John Jacob IV, Mrs. Astor's only son, to take Consuelo and the duke out for a day's yachting. He did not much care for it; he had no stomach for the sea.

Every morning Alva paraded her daughter and her nobleman in an open carriage to the Casino to greet the beau monde, the ladies in flowery organdie, the gentlemen in crisp white linen. A luncheon party followed, given in her astonishing dining room, where dark pink Algerian marble lined the walls and one more portrait of Louis XIV peered down on solid bronze furniture, made in Paris, with chairs of such weight that the legs were fitted with casters to enable the footmen to slide them under the guests' hindquarters. A dinner or a ball occupied every evening. Of all other Vanderbilts, only Willie's younger brother, Frederick William, spared time for Marlborough. Oliver Belmont, also recently divorced, lingered in the wings.

Consuelo and her mother could not bring themselves to be more than polite to each other. Intimacy between mistress and slave was scarcely to be expected. The girl sought compassion from her governess, the quiet English spinster, who raised her spirits with visions of public service. In England, she said, Consuelo might use her position as a great lady to help others, the unfortunates who existed at the foot of the pyramid, the luckless ones who knew the torments of hunger and despair.

The thought of it scurried through her mind on the evening Marlborough proposed. In tails and white tie, he chose the gloomiest room in the house to ask his long postponed question. The Gothic Room was designed like a museum piece in cold stone and carved wood to house a collection of medieval miniatures and crucifixes, with a statue of Saint George slaying his dragon and windows filled with somber stained glass. He would do his best, he declared, to be a good husband. Her answer was preordained. When she looked back over the years, she recalled no feelings of emotion, no exchange of kisses. She ran to her mother with the news and broke down in tears when her brother Harold, just turned eleven, said the duke was interested only in her dowry. She had no answer to that.

A gossiping servant may have spread the word, which Alva immediately denied, but on the day of leaving for New York she ordered the gatekeeper for the first time to let passersby step through onto the stone-paved drive where, under his supervision, they might stand at a respectful distance to admire Marble House and its fountain, whose water gurgled from three tragic masks hewn from stone. Her plot had worked; Consuelo was engaged.

In Manhattan, the Duke of Marlborough and Ivor Guest put up at the red-brick Plaza Hotel opposite Central Park. They would soon be off on a prenuptial trip to Niagara Falls, one of the sights the duke wished to see while he was in a country to which he vowed he would not return. Reporters tracked him to his rooms. Was he engaged to Consuelo Vanderbilt? Why, yes, he replied; as a matter of fact, he was. They sped uptown to the new house Alva had taken at No. 24 East Seventy-second Street, next door to Colonel and Mrs. Jay's. She and her docile daughter would know little peace until the wedding was over.

She gave Consuelo no freer hand in selecting the trousseau than in finding a husband. Appreciating the value of publicity like the rest of her kind, Alva graciously allowed artists from

Vogue, which had been founded three years earlier with Cornelius II among its stockholders, to sketch every item. A November issue would picture everything from the embroidered cambric lace lingerie to the high-collared Worth dress with four layers of Brussels lace flowing over white satin and a full court train embroidered with pearls. Alva had such confidence in her plans that she had ordered it during their last stay in Paris. She had no qualms about disclosing the total cost: $3,000.

The bride-to-be flinched to read elsewhere that garters with diamond-studded clasps would be holding up her white silk stockings; that was a journalist's invention. She winced again to learn that when Marlborough was faced with paying $250 duty on a package of jewelry from England after it was opened in customs, he had that wedding gift returned to its sender.

But the humor that lurked in her bubbled up when Marlborough ran foul of the law. On a rented bicycle, he was coasting down a hill in Central Park with his feet up on the frame when Policeman Sweeney sprinted after him, yelling that he was breaking the rules. "I was not aware such rules existed," said His Grace coolly, but ignorance did not save him from arrest.

The British legation in Washington fumbled its defense of him. "I cannot blame the duke for feeling sore," the spokesman sniffed. "You see, matters are conducted so differently with us. You, in your great republic, have far less regard for personal liberty than we have."

In London, *The Gentlewoman,* a magazine pored over by more housekeepers and ladies' maids than its title indicated, set its seal of approval on Consuelo. "There is nothing of the 'new woman' in her disposition, and she detests knickerbockers and divided skirts . . . She has no opinion on women's suffrage, women's rights and the Irish question."

"New women" on both sides of the Atlantic were sisters in frustration in the struggle for the right to vote. American suffragists had been aggrieved when Congress rejected their petition to be included in the Fourteenth Amendment of 1868 ("No State shall make or enforce any law which shall abridge the privileges and immunities of citizens") because "This is the Negro's hour." The movement itself had split into a New York group led by Susan B. Anthony and a Boston faction that followed Lucy Stone. The Supreme Court had ruled that neither the Fourteenth nor the Fifteenth Amendment of 1870, securing equal rights for white and black, encompassed votes for women. In the British Parliament, Prime Minister William Ewart Gladstone had announced that women must be "thrown overboard" lest they "overweight" and sink his 1884 Reform Bill adding more males to the ballot lists.

The Gentlewoman's information fell somewhat short of the mark. The makings of a "new woman" were coming together within Consuelo. The pressure on her increased when Alva commanded her to return every present from her father's side of the family. She was permitted to call only on Grandmother Maria, the only other Vanderbilt to receive an invitation to St. Thomas' Protestant Episcopal Church, who promptly refused it.

Willie breezed into town to take up his usual suite at the Metropolitan Club in plenty of time for the ceremony, originally set for November 5. Marlborough objected to the date. In his country, that was Guy Fawkes Day, when bonfires blazed and fireworks thundered to commemorate the Roman Catholic conspiracy to blow up the House of Lords on that day in 1605, when King James I was due to open Parliament. An anonymous letter tipped off the authorities; Fawkes, the gunpowder expert, was seized, tortured, and executed. Marlborough succeeded in having the wedding postponed for twenty-four hours in the interest of good taste.

November 5 was devoted, instead, to the matter of the dowry. The duke's solicitor, George Lewis, who served his clients counsel and a cup of tea simultaneously in his London office, had come over to handle the negotiating. There was no greed on one side and no stinginess on the other, which made for a smooth settlement. Willie wanted his dear and only daughter to be properly provided for.

The contract drawn up between "the Most Noble Charles Richard John, Duke of Marlborough, of Blenheim Palace, in the County of Oxford, England, party of the first part, and William Kissam Vanderbilt, Esquire, of Oakland, in the County of Suffolk, New York, of the second part" gave Marlborough life interest in a trust fund established from a portion of the Vander-

bilt holdings—"the sum of two million five hundred thousand
dollars in fifty thousand shares of the Beach Creek Railway
Company, on which an annual payment of four percent is guaranteed by the New York Central Railroad Company." If the
duke died first, the annual $100,000—twenty thousand pounds
in English currency—would go to Consuelo, who with her husband was to receive an additional $100,000 a year from Willie,
worth at least five times that sum in our current money market.
The newspapers overestimated the size of the gift by $1,500,000.

While a crew of fifty workmen strung garlands from the
church's ninety-five-foot dome, paneled every foot of the inside
walls with white and pink roses and fixed four-foot-tall flam-
beaux of palm and flowers to the pews, Alva suffered eleventh-
hour tremors. Perhaps her daughter's meekness was a pretense,
disguising her resolution to escape to Winty. She kept her eyes
on Consuelo thoughout the final dinner with the bridesmaids,
each of them handpicked by Alva, which the Jays gave at their
house next door; besides being a luminary of the Coaching
Club, Colonel Jay served as Alva's attorney.

Alva had no cause for apprehension. Her threats had worked
so successfully on her daughter that not a spark of rebellion
glimmered in her. Everything seemed to be happening at a great
distance away, making her only a placid bystander, disinterested
in the outcome of events. She would have liked to explain to her
brother Harold her reasons for her meek submission, but the
task of finding the right words was too burdensome to bother
with. At least her father, wiser than she about Alva's nature,
would sense the truth without being told.

She felt thankful for Marlborough's absence when he was off
on his sightseeing tour; that spared her the effort of seeing him
and listening to his sardonic opinions about America and Americans. She had no hope of changing his thinking or his habits; he
was too set in his ways for that. But she vowed to herself that
neither would he change hers. He had promised that he would
be "a good husband," whatever that implied, and she would
have to be content with his vow.

Alva still could not believe that any child of hers could be so
docile. Surely her daughter must make a final attempt to assert
herself. On the morning of the sixth, she posted a footman at
Consuelo's door to keep her in and everyone else but her maid

out. Willie was barred from the house until it was time to take
his daughter to church. Alva had a last-minute hitch to contend
with: the orchids from Blenheim's greenhouses had not arrived.
A three-foot-wide bouquet of them was rushed around from a
florist's. Alone in her misery, denied even the company of her
governess, Consuelo could not check her tears. She wept as the
maid dressed her, and she went on weeping.

Outside the house, a crowd of two thousand romantics overflowed the sidewalks and jammed the street. Every window in
the neighborhood with a view of Alva's front steps was filled with
spectators. Halfway down the block toward Park Avenue, wom-
en watched through opera glasses for a sight of the bridal party.
In front of the church, where a closed awning stretched from
the doors to the Fifth Avenue curb, thousands more had been
gathering between Fifty-second and Fifty-seventh streets since
breakfast time, some armed with camp stools and field glasses,
others perched precariously on stoops and railings. Two hundred police wrestled to keep the avenue clear. "There was no
undue pushing or hauling and no suspicion of clubbing," one
reporter was happy to see.

The ceremony was scheduled to begin at noon, but on Alva's
instruction the organist's recital commenced at ten-fifteen with
Beethoven's "Fugue in C." A sixty-man symphony orchestra under the baton of Dr. Walter Damrosch would take over later for
the climactic march from *Lohengrin.* The first guests, invitation
cards ready in their hands, scrambled for positions by the still
locked doors.

Using a less conspicuous side entrance, a cluster of clergy arrived for the tying of the nuptial knot. The Right Reverend Codman Potter, Bishop of New York, had a few words with the
Right Reverend Abram Newkirk Littlejohn, Bishop of Long Island, who had baptized and confirmed Consuelo, and then a
few more with the Reverend Waldo Burnett from Southbor-
ough, Massachusetts, once the chaplain at Blenheim. The rec-
tors of St. Thomas', St. Mark's, New York, and St. Mark's, Long
Island, awaited their turn.

The Four Hundred plus hundreds more squeezed into the
pews. Mrs. Astor came, attended by half a dozen of her clan.
Oliver Belmont sat with his parents and brother Perry. New
York's millionaire governor, Levi Morton, and his wife won a

cheer from the crowd at the door—their daughter Edith was one of the eight bridesmaids in white satin who were gathering downstairs at No. 24 East Seventy-second Street; Colonel Jay's daughter Julia was another. Upstairs, the bride and her maid worked together to sponge away the tears that refused to stop flowing from her puffed-up eyes.

The double-barreled knight, Sir Julian Pauncefote Pauncefote, Britain's Ambassador to Washington, was ushered in with his lady some minutes before the bells chimed the hour and a maroon carriage, its coachman and groom both bedecked with bunches of white chrysanthemums, deposited Alva and her two sons at the curb. Buxom and stately in blue satin and Russian sable, she steeled herself into calm as she took her place on the center aisle. On one side of her sat young Willie in a frock coat with a top hat under his arm; on the other, little Harold in a black knickerbocker suit with an expansive Eton collar. To be late might lead the congregation to fancy that something was amiss. In fact, she had left the house in a turmoil with the bride not yet to be seen.

As soon as Alva's carriage had turned the corner of Seventy-second Street, Willie's dashing coupé brought him around from his club. Without glancing at the crowd, he darted through the doorway and up the stairs for a few minutes' seclusion with his daughter. Inside the church, the orchestra filled in the lull with more selections while Dr. Damrosch watched for the flick of the sexton's white handkerchief to signal Consuelo's arrival. The minutes dragged on. Alva was in torment. Had her plan miscarried after all? Marlborough, in his new American frock coat, waited in the vestry as self-assured as ever, chatting with Ivor Guest, his supercilious best man.

Neither father nor daughter recorded what they said to each other during their twenty minutes together. He loved her enough to be tempted to offer her his help in running away; he could have lived down fresh scandal now that the Vanderbilts were firmly set at the peak of society. But they were both afraid of Alva's reprisals if she were to be mocked. Whatever Willie said, he did not disappoint Consuelo, whose affection for him never faltered.

She lowered the tulle veil under the wreath of orange blossoms, grateful that it reached her quivering knees. They went down, hand in hand, to join eight fretful bridesmaids, each adorned with a diamond butterfly, gifts from Consuelo. She had been given diamonds by both her father and her fiancé—a tiara from Willie, a belt from the duke. Alva, in a rare act of abnegation, had presented her with every string of pearls received from Willie, one of them once owned by Russia's Empress Catherine, another by Napoleon III's Empress Eugénie.

The white handkerchief fluttered, and the conductor's baton set the beat of the wedding march. Consuelo's strong fingers tightened on Willie's arm to slow his grim stride toward the altar. It must not seem that he was in a hurry to get it all over. Guests in the front pews saw that under the Worth gown her shoulders trembled. Marlborough's eyes glanced everywhere but at her as a choir of fifty voices started singing, *O, perfect love, all human thought transcending, Lowly we kneel in prayers before Thy throne!*

As soon as Bishop Potter had pronounced the benediction, the duke and his new duchess filed into the vestry with Willie to sign the contract, witnessed by Sir Julian and the British Consul General. Before the ink was dry, her father was off through a back door. Alva did not want him at the wedding breakfast for one hundred and fifteen, served at home among another forest of potted palms. At her circular table in the dining room she preferred to have less expendable people like Mrs. Astor, Governor Morton, Bishop Potter, Sir Julian and her unmarried sister, Armide.

The bride changed into a dark traveling dress, but the groom retained his frock coat when they left the house for Idle Hour. A handful of rice in the back of his neck sent him leaping into the carriage after Consuelo. A pale blue satin shoe missed its target but tilted the coachman's cockaded hat. Through the panes, Consuelo saw her mother standing behind a window curtain, weeping, and she wondered why. Hadn't Alva accomplished everything she had set out to achieve? The one ambition left for her surely was to marry Oliver Belmont. He was part Jew and five years her junior, which meant nothing to her; he had rank, charm, good looks and money, all of which meant a great deal.

Willie had chartered a boat to carry the pair to Long Island City. There, a palace car, its interior another exercise in floral artistry, was coupled to a locomotive and the tracks cleared all the way to Oakdale. Consuelo sat tensely on the edge of a plush-upholstered swivel armchair opposite her husband. Honesty compelled her to take this first opportunity to tell him the truth about her feelings toward him. She could not live with deceit.

"I am sure that we shall both do our best to make the other happy, but there is something you must believe. Our marriage was my mother's idea, not mine. She insisted on it, even though there was another man who wanted me. She made me turn him away."

Marlborough—always "Sunny" to his intimates—paused in the task of opening the pile of telegrams of felicitation that lay on his lap. "Really? I take it he was an American. I don't see much point in discussing it any farther." He resumed reading the messages on yellow paper, handing over most of them to her without comment, but one deserved to be read aloud. Not even a duke heard every day from Her Majesty Victoria, Queen of the United Kingdom of Great Britain and Ireland, Empress of India.

Lights blazed and log fires crackled to welcome them to Idle Hour, where servants would provide the only company. All in all, it was a peculiar honeymoon, bringing her bittersweet memories of Willie's presence there with her and her brothers, distant days of happiness that sharpened the contrast with the disturbing present. It was strange to sleep in Alva's room while Marlborough occupied Consuelo's bed in her old room next door. Instead of being dominated by her mother, she sensed that she was now to be ruled by a husband who was little more than a stranger.

In exactly one more week, he would celebrate his twenty-fourth birthday, but much more than half a dozen years separated them. He was imbued with pride in almost two centuries of family power and prestige; her generation of Vanderbilts was the first to be accepted from birth as scions of society. He was familiar with the physical contacts appropriate to this night. She was untutored, reluctant, fearful in the knowledge of her total innocence. Man and wife had perhaps just one thing in common: the element that might bind them together was missing in each of them. They had no love for one another.

Dressing in her well-publicized Parisian lingerie, she felt, as she recalled, "like a deserted child." She yearned to be back in the time before her mother's scheming made the girl feel suddenly old. She refused afterward to say more about that aspect of the contrived marriage than, "In the hidden reaches where memory probes lie sorrows too deep to fathom." The chasm between duke and duchess seemed unbridgeable.

He did not want to live at Blenheim until it had been restored to glory. The bills for the work that had to be done to make good years of neglect would be easier to pay now. They must wait until the spring before he could install her as mistress of his palace. He would overcome his queasiness, if he could, and they would sail in a little cargo steamer from New York to Genoa. He would like to see as much of the world as he could on his first extended absence from England.

His valet and her French maid, Jeanne, completed the party of four, the only passengers aboard. The Atlantic was as cruel as could be expected in November, leaving Sunny too ill to enjoy any part of the crossing. He fell into predictable fits of gloom so dark that she was impelled to paint the brightest possible pictures of their future to dispel his dread —or was it his hope?—of dying.

They had to abandon the ship at Gibraltar. Henceforth for his sake they must go by land, starting with a tour of Spain. Consuelo's energy by this time was spent. In an age when few doctors appreciated the links that psychiatrists detected between unhappiness and lethargy, the problem was diagnosed in simple terms: she had outgrown her strength.

In wintry Madrid, she discovered that not only American matrons vied with each other for social recognition. Lord Rosebery, Gladstone's successor as leader of the Liberals who had been cast out of power last June, was there to enjoy an audience with Queen-Regent Cristina at the Palacio Real. He had lost his wife, the former Hannah Rothschild, eight years earlier and had toyed with the idea of courting the Prince of Wales' youngest daughter, Victoria. After meeting Consuelo with Marlborough at the British Embassy, Rosebery became the first man in her new life to be captivated by her nervous charm. Determined not to be overshadowed by any Liberal statesman, Sunny set about obtaining invitations to the palace for himself and his bride. She thought she acquitted herself adequately in the presence of the widowed queen, dropping the triple curtsey that court protocol demanded. But what impressed her more that day was a distant glimpse of the ten-year-old lad who would reign as Alfonso III, the last king of Spain in her lifetime.

A train carried duke and duchess into the sunlight of Monaco, where her education in the ways of a world she knew nothing about was advanced a stage further. The smiles some of the elegant women accorded him from other tables in the hotel restaurant told her that they knew her husband. She had never seen such seductive creatures, beautifully clothed and exquisitely made up. Who were they? All he would say at first was that she must not so much as look their way. But who *were* they? He finally supplied a grudging answer. They were *demi-mondaines*, on whom every respectable woman should turn a blind eye. She had naively imagined that Sunny had entered their marriage as innocent as herself. She knew better now, and the knowledge was painful. Even the sunshine could not lighten her heart.

They were in Rome for Christmas. The music of church bells and the bustle in the streets increased her longing to be home again, with her family reunited by some impossible magic so that her father could be there, too. She had grown so wan that Sunny thought it advisable for insurance to be written on her life. The doctor who examined her was "brutal" in her opinion; a thorough medical inspection was a novelty to her. The policy was withheld; he concluded that she would be dead before the coming summer ended.

She had no wish to die. Any amount of misery was preferable to annihilation. She had a Vanderbilt for a father, and though the present generation was not as rugged as old Corneel, there wasn't a namby-pamby among them. The Smiths of her mother's side had produced Alva, who matched the Commodore in fortitude. Given enough time, Consuelo would work out a life for herself, she felt sure. A mauling at the hands of a lone Italian doctor could not convince her that she was doomed. Her emotions had suffered a battering in marriage, which must be the explanation of her physical weakness. The only sensible thing to do was to seek another doctor's opinion.

The London specialist who was hurried over rejected the diagnosis. If she obeyed his prescription for complete rest, strength would slowly return. Her desire to bear a child would have to be deferred. Marlborough, anxious for a son, must also be patient. She thought of motherhood in terms of joyfulness rather than duty. Among the Vanderbilts, only the Commodore had been smitten with a sense of dynasty. Billy had split the fortune into halves, and both her father and Uncle Cornelius were continuing the process of fragmentation.

The rest cure was spasmodic at best. They left Rome for Naples, then on to Alexandria and Cairo for a trip up the Nile. The double standard of morality dividing men and women irritated her whenever it evidenced itself. At Pompeii, her health had improved to the point where she resented being excluded from the dark chambers where guides permitted only males to inspect the flaking murals and venereal figurines. She took to her cabin in a Nile felucca not from physical weakness but in preference to watching a troupe of belly dancers, though she thought afterward that she would rather have liked to have seen the one who cut short her performance by waggling herself overboard.

In January, she heard the expected news—Alva was the new wife of Oliver Belmont. No Episcopal minister would unite two divorcés, but William L. Strong, the Republican banker who had been elected mayor of New York on his pledge to clean up the city, was happy to perform a civil ceremony at No. 24 East Seventy-second Street. Young Willie and Harold were the only Vanderbilts present, and no Belmonts appeared at all. Then the newlyweds entered one of Alva's maroon carriages—she retained the Vanderbilt color for her servants' livery, too—to drive to Grand Central Terminal and board a train for Newport. Now as well as Marble House, she had Oliver's "Belcourt," another seaside château, designed by Richard Hunt, in which to entertain her followers. In his offices above the station, Willie was glad it had been a quiet wedding. Like the rest of the family, he felt notoriety had gone far enough.

The younger honeymoon couple reached Paris too early for the white blossoms to have burst on the chestnut trees, which softened the impact of those remembered days in the city when Consuelo expected to be married to Winty. There was shopping to do, and she did not know how to handle it, having bought nothing on her own account in all her years so far. Sunny volunteered to advise her—and proved to be as dictatorial as her mother.

Monsieur Worth in person greeted her at his premises on the Rue de la Paix. He had itched to dress up this young American heiress in greater splendor than the clothes Alva put her into. Among the gowns pressed on her was one of blue satin with a train of ostrich feathers; she knew the color was a poor complement to her olive skin and the style absurd for a girl of eighteen.

Since Willie had promised to pay for everything, Sunny proceeded to restock the Blenheim linen closets and his personal wardrobe. What his duchess needed was jewelry. She gathered that his father, the eighth duke, had ravaged the family heirlooms to pay his debts. His first step on inheriting the title in 1883 had been to sell off much of the Blenheim collection of master paintings, rare books and Oriental china. He had picked up a useful £87,000. from Her Majesty's government, which was loath to see Raphael's "Anside Madonna" or Van Dyck's "Charles I on Horseback" fall into alien hands. The Paris Rothschilds bought three Rubens, and a Sebastiano del Piombo went to the Reichsmuseum in Berlin. The remainder he consigned for auction. Five years later, when he had his wife Lilian Hammersley's inheritance to draw on, he was often back as a customer in Christie's sales rooms, attempting to fill the gaps caused by his profligacy.

His son had to start afresh in assembling a jewel collection worthy of the Marlboroughs. His stepmother, the dumpy dowager duchess, regarded what was left behind by her dead husband as hers. The day would come when she, too, had an auctioneer knock down jewelry, silver plate and objects of vertu to the highest bidder.

One of the bibelots her husband rated worthy of Consuelo and the future line of duchesses was a collar made up of nineteen rows of pearls with diamond clasps which, despite the length of her delectable neck, chafed her under the chin whenever she wore it. She also had to admit to herself that the tiara her father had given her resulted in crushing headaches. Apart from a strand or so of pearls, jewelry did not appeal to her. Enormous rings were shunned because she was self-conscious about the size of her hands, the single disproportioned part of her body. But so far as her husband was concerned, she left France for England with him in March equipped with the jewels, furs and wardrobe he considered indispensable for a duchess.

On their interminable honeymoon, she had tried to establish

ties of intimacy with him, though he was so toplofty about America and Americans that she had to check her indignation. "He had a way," she said later, "of talking as if we were all Red Indians." When she saw the throng of his relatives waiting for them at London's Victoria Station, she foresaw that the frail bonds linking her with him might soon be severed. She was, she realized, as utterly alone among strangers as Robinson Crusoe. She could speak the language even if she could not count the change with its bewildering pennies, shillings, florins and half-crowns, but to make herself clearly understood, she would have to adopt their mode of speaking, quietly and fast.

At dinner that evening, she began the task of getting to know the people she had to think of as family. With her mother-in-law, she hit if off right away. Albertha, a tight-corseted Victorian grande dame, was Lady Blandford, since she had divorced the eighth duke while he was still the Marquess of Blandford, a few months before he succeeded to the dukedom. By birth she was a Hamilton, and the Hamiltons had borne titles since the sixteenth century. By blueblood standards, Consuelo learned with amusement, the Marlboroughs were of comparatively recent pedigree. Albertha did not mince her words as she grumbled about having been kept from seeing Sunny's wedding because he was too stingy to buy her a steamship ticket.

She was shrewd, gay and, in her daughter-in-law's opinion, scarcely literate. She did not share Sunny's disdain for America, but she was a pillar of ignorance. At the moment, London and Washington were wrangling over the location of the border between Venezuela and British Guiana. American antagonism ran high after President Cleveland invoked the ever convenient Monroe Doctrine and warned England to keep her hands off Central America. There was genuine horror of a war between two nations speaking the same language. Albertha could not make head or tail of the fuss; in her firm belief, Americans lived in constant danger of being scalped by redskins.

Another diner, Lady Sarah Wilson, a cousin of Sunny's, obviously considered Albertha a fool and Consuelo an interloper. The girl sensed she was being patronized, which she was not prepared to accept from anybody. She was acutely conscious of being better schooled than any haughty noblewoman and determined not to be quashed. Marriage had made her English in legal fact, but in her heart she felt she would forever remain a democratic American.

She was happy to start an alliance of sympathy that evening with a carrot-haired young man who had been born unexpectedly early in a little downstairs room at Blenheim in 1875. Winston Spencer Churchill, whose father had died of syphilis only a year ago, was asked later whether his mother, Jennie, had been at a ball in the Long Library or out shooting in the park when she went into labor. "Although present on that occasion," he joked, "I have no clear recollection of the events leading up to it."

From what Sunny had off-handedly told her in advance, Consuelo knew that this cousin with whom he had often played as a child was her husband's closest friend; yet they were so utterly different in makeup that it was hard to understand why. Winston, at twenty-one, was training at Sandhurst Royal Military College, eager for a commission in the Fourth Hussars. She was fascinated by his bouncy exuberance, his plain determination to savor life to the full, where Sunny, the epicurean, maintained distance between himself and virtually everyone, herself included.

She felt decidedly uneasy in Winston's presence at first. Currently he was next in line after Sunny for the dukedom, which he would inherit unless she proceeded to do what was expected of her and bear a son. Sunny's Uncle Randolph, Winston's father, had left a pile of debts and an estate of less than £76,000. Aunt Jennie, Winston and his brother Jack were perpetually short of cash. In the performance of her wifely duty, Consuelo would probably keep them in that strait. She felt relieved that for the present she had not created obstacles in a fast-growing companionship with Winston by becoming *enceinte*.

Sunny's grandmother, another dowager duchess of Marlborough, thought otherwise when Consuelo was introduced to her the following day. "Are you in the family way?" was one of a host of probing questions. It was imperative for Sunny's wife to have a son to save the dukedom from falling to "that little upstart Winston." Consuelo shouted confused reassurances into the old woman's ear trumpet.

The subject of pregnancy was touched on only lightly during her next visit. The little Duke of Abercorn, Albertha's brother, chairman of the British South Africa Company and a member of the Prince of Wales' household, was fascinated by the sable lining of Consuelo's coat. Ringing for his valet to fetch a similar ducal garment for comparison, he was crestfallen to discover that hers was the more luxurious.

A concluding stop took her to meet another of Sunny's aunts, Lady Lansdowne, who resided appropriately enough at Lansdowne House on Berkeley Square. Willie and Alva had been her guests when she had been an imperious vicereine of India, which she took to be justification for her to coach their daughter on the finer points of noble behavior. Hansom cabs, for instance, were not suitable vehicles for a lady to ride in, nor was a stroll along Piccadilly to be undertaken without a companion. The teenage duchess would also be well advised to familiarize herself with Debrett's *Peerage of England* and so learn precisely where everybody of consequence fitted into the universal scheme of things.

The girl's manner was bashful, but under the surface she decided it was all a bore, an archaic means of breeding snobs and perpetuating snobbery. She had not had the willpower to oppose Alva, but even before she moved into Blenheim Palace, she protested in silence against the manner of life it exemplified.

On the last day of March, Sunny had her put on her sable-lined coat to take the Great Western Railway train from Paddington Station to Oxford, to change there for the seven-mile run on the Marlboroughs' Blenheim branch line to the miniature royal borough of Woodstock.

The little stone station stood almost directly across Oxford Street from one set of the park's gates, but Sunny wanted his bride to proceed in splendor through the Triumphal Arch, built to the order of the first duchess after her husband's death in 1722.

Sunny had declared a holiday for Blenheim's workers, and twenty thousand sightseers streamed in from the surrounding countryside for a peek at Consuelo. Arches of flags and foliage spanning the main street and cobbled marketplace made the centuries-old town as lively as a county fair. When the train carrying bride and groom, servants and luggage, pulled in, she saw a red carpet spread, on which stood the mayor together with the dignitaries of the town corporation.

Coming out of the building with their escort, she noticed that well-scrubbed Blenheim laborers had unhitched the horses from Marlborough's carriage to haul it by hand to the palace doors. Down the gentle hill leading to the town center, the crew had to pull back on the ropes to slow the pace. She would have preferred a ride less feudal in spirit and less arduous in fact, but her nervous smiles brought rounds of cheering. They turned into High Street with its rows of Carolinian and Georgian fronts, passing Number 29, where Oliver Cromwell was reputed to have stayed during England's Civil War.

The mayor in his befurred tricorn was waiting again for them there. The town clerk unwound a parchment scroll to read a proclamation; the mayor made one speech, Marlborough another. A delegation of schoolchildren, with the day off from classes, filled her arms with flowers. Then His Honor the Mayor irked her by reminding Her Grace the Duchess that the first of his kind took office in Woodstock before Columbus sailed for the Indies.

The brass-helmeted fire brigade, whiskers freshly combed, pulled their wooden-wheeled engines into place at the head of the line. The band of the second volunteer battalion of the Oxfordshire Light Infantry struck up a march. A platoon of the Ancient Order of Foresters fell into step behind them, followed by a detachment of employees from the estate. His Honor and his fellow burgesses preceded an honor guard of county yeomanry, and finally Consuelo and Marlborough were on the last lap of their journey.

The procession wound past Chaucer's House, once inhabited by the poet's son, and around the sharp left turn to the Triumphal Arch, hidden away out of sight at the end of town because at the time of its erection one obstinate smallholder refused to budge. Bugles, drums and clashing cymbals echoed across the lake, and the parade reached the palace's East Gate, seventeen tons of ornamental metal set among stone lion heads, wreaths and laurel. High against the sky, the duke's standard, fleur-de-lis on a field of white, had been raised to announce his return.

Carriage and marchers pounded over the stones of the Great Court up to Blenheim's main front steps. Another small army waited there in segregated groups—butler and chatelaine, chef and kitchen maids, valet and footmen, housemaids and laundresses, coachmen, grooms, tenant farmers and gardeners. Each contingent had a speech to deliver and more flowers to present. Bows, bobs and curtseys welcomed Consuelo to her new home while the wind threatened to blow her hat away. "A large company subsequently sat down to lunch," *The Illustrated London News* reported, "and the day closed amidst brilliant illuminations and general rejoicings."

"I suddenly felt distraught," the mistress of Blenheim remembered, "with a wild desire to be alone."

VI

A Lucifer of a House

Understanding Sunny would have baffled her even if she had loved him. In the absence of that emotion, he was an enigma. The delicately made young man cloaked himself in middle-aged dignity, though he looked little older than a schoolboy. Appearances seemed to count for everything with him. Like her mother, he respected a show of magnificence more than minds and souls and the passions that drove lesser men and women.

He lived as if encased in reverence for the past; yet the more she learned about his own sad childhood and youth, the more she was puzzled by his regard for times gone by. His father, George, the eighth duke, had been too absorbed in his own pursuits to spare much thought for his family. George was one of "those wicked boys," as the Prince of Wales called them when George was constantly in the company of the underemployed, pleasure-chasing future king.

George dissipated the prince's friendship as well as the £ 37,000 a year that Marlborough property should have brought him. It was all very well for him to claim that women were the only worthwhile prizes in life, but he overstepped the mark by stealing the wife of Lord Aylesford—"Sporting Joe" to the prince's set—while her husband was tiger-hunting with His Royal Highness in India.

Sunny was five years old when the prince denounced George as "the greatest blackguard alive" and refused to have anything more to do with him or his brother Randolph. After Lady Aylesford bore George's child in Paris, he decided that he did not want to marry her after all and turned his eyes on his brother's wife, lovely Jennie. Sunny grew up in the shame of knowing George was an outcast from royal society and a lecher, despaired of by his father, John, the seventh duke, a pillar of Conservative politics.

He was a schoolboy when his mother finally divorced George, who soon took in his brother and sister-in-law to make Jennie the temporary mistress of Blenheim. Half a decade later, Sunny learned of his father's second marriage, to Mrs. Hammersley with her $100,000 a year and $5,000,000 fortune. A New York magazine remarked, "Everything His Grace of Marlborough brought with him was clean except his reputation."

Yet he was a scholar as well as a rakehell. Urdu was one of the languages he spoke. He wrote for magazines, experimented in chemistry and counted himself a genius. While his second duchess fed her spaniels chicken fricassee with macaroons and bedded them down under satin blankets, he used some of the new money to install a laboratory on an upper floor of Blenheim. He also accepted a job as chairman of the City of London Lighting Company, which increased his appearances in the House of Lords, leading a movement to combat the government's monopoly of the telephone system.

Consuelo felt moments of pity when she learned how Sunny inherited the dukedom. He was a student at Trinity College, Cambridge, four days short of his twenty-first birthday, when the news reached him. His father had taken on a new mistress in Lady Colin Campbell, who had ambitions to go on the stage, and to persuade the editor to publish an acticle she had written, he contributed some thoughts on "The Art of Living," to Frank Harris' magazine, *The Fortnightly*.

On November 9, 1892, he went upstairs to bed, bright and cheerful, looking forward to tomorrow's board meeting of the lighting firm. At half past eight the next morning, his valet went into the room with the usual cup of hot chocolate and found George dead. Randolph moved swiftly to deny the distraught widowed duchess' call for an inquest, but *The Times*' obituary lacerated George:

"The late Duke was his own worst enemy, and by the scandals

of his private life—which became public property through more than one divorce suit—he threw away the certainty of attaining to a position of great influence in the country. He had a large share of that ability which has been so conspicuous in his younger brother; some persons say, indeed, that he was the cleverer man of the two . . ."

So Sunny, just short of legal manhood, had been forced to leave the university, to be jettisoned into an ocean of trouble. He bore responsibility for restoring the Marlboroughs' reputation along with their amazing palace, the only one in the kingdom owned by anyone but the reigning monarch. He had followed his father's example in seeking an American bride to augment the money it would take. "Life opened up for him" when his father died, Cousin Winston said.

Consuelo found the imprint of an earlier predecessor everywhere at Blenheim. The spirit of Sarah Jennings, the first duchess, was almost tangible in the east wing, the only section of the palace habitable during her lifetime. Sunny felt a powerful attachment to the voluptuous, golden-haired ancestress who had been called "a torpedo in petticoats," born in 1660 to a reputed witch in the market town of St. Albans, Hertfordshire.

In her husband's judgment, no other duchess, and certainly not Consuelo, could compare with Sarah. "Hers," he wrote later, "was a dominating character which, for the last thirty years of her life, lacked scope for action, and therefore asserted itself violently in the narrow field left open to it. But in the last resort it is not as a mother, nor even as a wife, that she must be judged. She belongs to history. No woman not of royal rank has ever held before, or is ever likely to hold again, such a position as was hers during the critical years of the early eighteenth century, when the maps of Europe and the constitution of England were in the making."

At eighteen, Sarah Jennings had made a great friend of thirteen-year-old Princess Anne, the meek, unhappy younger daughter of the then Duke of York; he was the second surviving son of the beheaded Charles I, and his elder brother reigned as the present Charles II. The man Sarah picked as a husband was aquiline-nosed John Churchill, a captain in the company of which the duke was colonel. Some historians considered her the explosive force in his pyrotechnical career.

When the Roman Catholic duke became King James II five years afterward, the Churchills' fortunes soared, though they were avowed Protestants like Anne, who had been left to choose her own faith. It was Lord Churchill whose brutal troops put down the Duke of Monmouth's armed rebellion against the king. By then Churchill had already served the new monarch on a mission to Alva's idol, Louis XIV, and spoke openly of resigning if James should establish Catholicism as his kingdom's religion.

Though he continued to enjoy his pay and privileges, he became one of the first to make overtures to the Protestant Dutch prince, William of Orange, promising to bring over his king's army should William see fit to invade England. The moment he did, at Brixham, Devon, in 1688, James sent Churchill against him with five thousand men. During the night before what seemed to be imminent battle, the scheming general crossed into the opposite camp. The Dutchman was proclaimed joint sovereign of Great Britain and Ireland with his wife, Mary, eldest daughter of the king he had deposed, and Churchill emerged as Earl of Marlborough. Why he took the name was a minor mystery, explained perhaps by his mother's ties with the Ley family, which had produced earls of Marlborough until the title died out a decade earlier.

Churchill soldiered in the Netherlands and in Ireland, but William distrusted him. He was thrown into the Tower of London, charged with treason for keeping in touch, as a kind of insurance, with the exiled James, who was living in France with King Louis' blessing. Marlborough had, in fact, disclosed to his late master his new master's plan to attack Brest in the ceaseless contest with the Catholic French. The evidence against him was inconclusive and, probably with Sarah's intercession, he was set free, but stripped of all appointments.

Who was to follow William to the throne of England was one of a multitude of constitutional problems to be worked out between king and Parliament. A Declaration of Rights settled the succession on Anne *after* William, her sister Mary, and their children. But Mary died first, followed by William as the result of a fall from a horse, and they left no heir. In April, 1702, Anne was crowned queen. The reign of this dull-minded, luckless woman would be one of the most brilliant in the annals of England, and nobody's star shone more brightly at first than John and Sarah Churchill's.

Sarah and the queen treated each other as sisters, calling each other "Mrs. Freeman" and "Mrs. Morley." A third party of the charade was Mrs. Masham, otherwise Abigail Hill, a cousin whom Sarah introduced as a poor relation into Anne's service. The new attendant's soft-spoken manner was altogether different from the termagant Lady Churchill's.

Less than two weeks after Anne's coronation, Marlborough was off again to war, commanding the united armies of England and Holland against the supposedly invincible French. As a reward for recapturing fortresses on the Rhine, on the Neuse and at Liège in an inconclusive campaign, Anne raised him to duke on his return home and awarded him an annual £5,000 for the rest of her life; Sarah was pressing her hard.

King Louis was bruised but far from beaten. Next year, his generals scored enough successes to encourage them in 1704 to march alongside the Danube in a bid to seize Vienna—Austria, too, was fighting the Sun King. Malborough applied his superb sense of strategy to divine the enemy's intention and hurried his troops to intercept the French and their Bavarian allies.

Louis' cavalry and infantry outnumbered the forces of Marlborough when the two armies met on August 13 near the Bavarian village of Blenheim—"Blindheim" to its natives—on the left bank of the river. But mounted on a white horse in a scarlet surcoat, the duke outmanoeuvred the Sun King's regiments, leaving nearly thirty thousand of their number killed, wounded or drowned, and the river's blue water ran purple with blood. The victory, won at the price of 670 British dead, was sealed by the capture of 11,000 soldiers, a hundred cannon and two hundred battle standards as trophies for his queen. The sun was beginning to sink on ten years of French military triumphs.

Consuelo never had been taught history in terms of kings and queens and of riches won in war, not by trade in stock certificates. She could have found little to enthrall her in any account of historic bloodletting. The building of Blenheim Palace, however, was a subject that intrigued her. How did it happen that the private rooms were so cold and cheerless, the closets so dark and airless, the bathrooms so few and the kitchens so remote that the food got cold before it was served? The petit château had been infinitely more elegant and comfortable, though she did not care to press the point.

In gratitude to the duke, Anne gave him the whole manor of Woodstock and a grant of £240,000 toward erecting a house there. It was an act of monumental generosity, when she allotted only £30,000 to be shared among all her officers and men who had lost their horses in fighting the French. For her gift to Marlborough, she charged a quit rent: one standard "with the flower de luce painted thereupon" to be presented at Windsor Castle on each anniversary of the Battle of Blindheim, a custom that survived through Consuelo's day up into present time.

To the west of the tiny town lay a game preserve, enclosed within a wall seven miles long by Henry I, who early in the twelfth century built, or possibly rebuilt, a hunting lodge there which became a royal palace. By order of Sarah, it was to be totally destroyed and its stones used as rubble for the Grand Bridge across the lake created from marshland by damming the trickling stream of the River Glyne.

"I mortally hate all grandeur and architecture," declared Sarah, who took on supervision of the construction when her husband was engaged in fresh encounters with the resurgent armies of France at Ramillies, Oudenarde and Malplaquet. Her deeds belied her words as a thousand workmen labored to give effect to the grandiose dreams of John Vanbrugh, playwright turned architect, who intended to raise a palace that would rival Versailles. The original estimate of £100,000 was left in shreds, but that was not Sarah's doing. It was Vanbrugh who was afflicted like Alva with *la manie de bâtir.*

"The chief point to remember," wrote a latter-day chronicler in words that sounded like Sunny's, "is that Blenheim had first to be a monument to the Queen's glory; and this within the limits of contemporary conventions which insisted on symmetry, formality and a disposition of state rooms—ante-room: drawing room: bedroom—from which there could be no deviation." Its symmetry was one of the wonders of the place, as Consuelo discovered. At a certain spot within the palace, it was possible to peer through one keyhole and view nine more, so perfectly aligned were the doorways.

"I made Mr. Vanbrugh my enemy," Sarah recorded, "by the constant disputes I had with him to prevent his extravagance." She was shocked by his proposal to include a covered walk for servants and appalled by his bridge, which contained thirty rooms fit for living in, some with fireplaces and chimneys. She declined to pay extra pennies to the carters whose wagons mired down in winter mud fetching stone from the quarries in Wychwood Forest.

Five years passed, and Blenheim was nowhere near finished. On his campaigns, Marlborough was busily accumulating souvenirs to adorn his future home, one of them a thirty-ton bust of the Sun King pried from the gates of Tournai. Sunny put the best possible light on the time-honored practice of what might have been condemned as looting if done by the common soldiery. "He felt that his fame would be the special heritage of his descendants," Sunny explained, "and he determined that they should be in a position to maintain it. For them he saved money, and for them he collected pictures and tapestries in his travels through Europe." The Louis XIV furnishings of Blenheim that Consuelo admired were antiques of unquestionable provenance, which was rarely true in the mansions of Manhattan.

The efficiency of John Churchill, former pageboy, received less tangible recognition; he was made a prince of the Holy Roman Empire, a title his heirs would hold in perpetuity, as well as Prince of Mindelheim in Swabia. Since Sunny was therefore a prince, Consuelo was an indubitable princess, which was a bonus to gladden her mother's heart.

Sarah and her husband had known personal sorrow in the death of their only surviving son. The seventeen-year-old Marquess of Blandford, whose name was a courtesy designation, caught smallpox at King's College, Cambridge. The Marlboroughs were left with four daughters. The eldest, Henrietta, was Lord Godolphin's wife; the next, Anne, was married to Charles Spencer, Earl of Sunderland; both the others would have dukes for husbands. To ensure there would be subsequent dukes of Marlborough, an obliging Parliament passed an act settling the dukedom on John Churchill's daughters and their progeny.

Fresh grief stuck Sarah and John when the flow of Anne's bounty dried up. Sarah was enraged to find that her cousin, Mrs. Masham, had usurped her place as queen's favorite, partly because Mrs. Masham was easier to get along with than Mrs. Freeman, whose temper had not been improved by her continual clashes with Vanbrugh. Sarah had been de facto paymistress of Blenheim until now in her post as Mistress of the Robes and Keeper of the Privy Purse.

Party politics also played a hand in the Marlboroughs' fall from favor. They were Whigs, but Mrs. Masham had surreptitiously served another cousin of hers, Robert Harley, as well as Anne, and plotted with him to weaken the Whigs' influence with her mistress. Sarah forced a final interview with the queen she had teased and tormented for so many years. Her tears and scoldings did no good. She was compelled to surrender her key of office to the now detested Mrs. Masham. The calculated humiliation of the Marlboroughs began.

All work on Blenheim stopped. Craftsmen and artisans who had gone unpaid for years downed their tools, leaving stone half cut, wood half carved and ceilings half stuccoed. Everything except £20,000 of the bounty had already been spent, and unpaid bills mounted to £45,000. Lawsuits were filed to get them paid. Though Sarah had labored like a pack horse to press the completion of what she called a "wild, unmerciful house," she had failed. The only way to finish the job would be to skimp on the interior and put up Marlborough's own money, £60,000 of it, which no man as provident as he was in a hurry to do.

Duke and duchess took themselves off in voluntary exile to Europe in the fall of 1711 and came back the following August, the day after Anne's death, surrounded by quarreling servants; James I's great-grandson now reigned as King George I. Four more years elapsed before it was resolved who was to pay and how much it would cost for the abandoned palace to be made habitable; Marlborough would carry the financial burden. Only then did carpenters, masons, plumbers, carvers of stone and wood, glassmakers and farriers return to work. At that time, there was no serviceable entrance into the family quarters.

Sarah had little affection for the product that was far from complete when the Marlboroughs moved in after fourteen years of waiting. She blamed the preponderance of interior stonework for stirring up her gout. Other critics of the day were equally disapproving. Blenheim, they said, was "too rhetorical, too declamatory." The palace "is not out to charm; it is there to strike with awe." It was "a Lucifer of a house; pride and ambition are its keystones." Alexander Pope in a poem on the subject wondered, "But where d'ye sleep, or where d'ye dine?" Consuelo reached her own conclusions. "It is strange that in so great a house there should not be one really livable room." She kept that opinion to herself for the present; Sunny worshipped Blenheim and all it stood for.

The first Marlborough lived long enough to spend only two summers residing in his monument. Then his eldest daughter, Henrietta, inherited the title and Sarah, the dowager duchess, aged sixty-two, spent twenty-two years of widowhood attempting to magnify his glory. His portrait had been painted before, so she commissioned Thomas Rysbrack to carve a marble bust of him and a statue, larger than life, of her fickle benefactress, the late queen. The Triumphal Arch went up, but that was not enough for Sarah. Picking over any number of sketches, she selected the design for a lead statue of him to stand on a pillar nearly 130 feet high overlooking the park, with its back turned on Woodstock. It would be known as the Column of Victory. The unending task of building the house that was simultaneously citadel, palace and memorial continued.

Consuelo had never seen a place displaying so many mementoes of its previous proprietor. The first duke knelt before Britannia in the mural on the ceiling sixty-seven feet above the tessellated marble floor of the Great Hall. In and out of armor and with and without his family, he peered out of paintings on the walls. He sat on his white horse in enormous tapestries that hung from ceiling to wainscot in all three State Rooms. Even the yard-long silver centerpiece for the dining table in the Saloon depicted Marlborough at Blenheim.

It was something of a tradition, she found, to assess the virtue of the seven other Marlboroughs who preceded Sunny on the basis of what they had achieved for the palace rather than by their accomplishments in politics, the arts or public service. The good ones added to Blenheim's treasures, the bad subtracted from them, the indeterminates left things much as they found them.

Most of the palace remained a shell in the days of Henrietta, the second duchess. She left no heir, so the third duke was her nephew, Charles Spencer, son of her sister Anne, fathered by the Earl of Sunderland. Consuelo caught the connection. "Sunny," short for "Sunderland," was a nickname passed down in the family like the rest of its possessions.

Charles Spencer did well by leaving three sons. The eldest, George, duke number four, was a definite plus, a doctor of literature, Fellow of the Royal Society, and bosom friend of King George III. This duke expended a fortune on pushing the palace closer toward completion, buying furnishings left and right and engaging the landscape architect "Capability" Brown to bring into existence the lake and copses of trees that turned nature into an artifact of fervid imagination. Another of his hired specialists, Sir William Chambers, built a new town hall for Woodstock in 1766 and the Temple of Diana, where Sunny's cousin Winston would one day ask for the hand of Miss Clementine Hozier. The town escaped being degraded into a kind of backdrop; Capability Brown, forever inventive, put forward a scheme, which was not carried out, for adding medieval battlements to the park walls and to every house of Woodstock within view of the palace.

Number four, duke at twenty, lasted for fifty-eight more years. He was a gem collector; a patron of the arts, having Romney paint his portrait in Knight of the Garter regalia; and a producer of amateur theatricals in a theater erected in the East Court to seat audiences of two hundred. Old age brought on eccentricity; he spoke not a word for three years, refusing to see all visitors, including Lord Nelson, hero of Trafalgar. Sunny had odd ways of his own, especially in his flamboyant wardrobe. His wife wondered if this was yet another aspect of the inheritance.

Number five, another George, who looked extraordinarily like number one, concentrated on expanding the gardens of flowers, cedar and cypress which his father had laid out by Brown's waterfalls downstream from the lake, complete with fountains, a small bridge and a Swiss chalet. George also retrieved "Churchill" as the family name, for stronger identification with the most memorable of the Marlboroughs. It did not help. Some of Blenheim's treasures in furniture and paintings had to be sold to settle his debts, but he finished in sad financial straits, confining himself to a few rooms to keep expenses down.

The sixth duke, again a George, was a spendthrift, too, but in the following generation the pendulum swung toward improve-

ment. Number seven, like his duchess a close friend of Queen
Victoria, was forced to sell off more family heirlooms to enable
him to take up Disraeli's offer of the viceroyalty of Ireland at a
salary that covered only half the outgo; they wanted to remove
their blackguard son, Sunny's father, from London to Dublin to
shield him from ostracism after his shabby treatment of Lady
Aylesford.

Number seven had shown a desire for public service singular-
ly lacking in his forebears. Consuelo realized that Sunny had
similar ambitions as she talked with some of the people he invited to Blenheim. His duty, as he interpreted it, was to uphold the
best traditions of aristocracy, notably the Marlboroughs'. Consuelo resolved to do whatever she could to help him, strange as
the whole concept of a rigidly divided society was to her, a displaced American who had no personal cause to question the
myth that in her native land hard work automatically led to
riches.

Her explorations started when her mother-in-law, Albertha,
took her to be presented at court at the end of May. Nothing but
a brand new state coach would do to carry them to Buckingham
Palace. Sunny accordingly bought one, gleaming red, with
three sets of matching livery—for the bewigged coachman and
two powdered footmen—embroidered in silver thread with twin-
headed eagles, Sunny's insignia as a Holy Roman prince.

Marlborough House, built by Sarah on crown land in St.
James', served these days as home for the Prince of Wales and
his Princess Alexandra. Without a base in London, Sunny made
do by renting a makeshift place on South Audley Street. The
next time Willie's generosity overtook him, the Marlboroughs
would build their own pied-à-terre, a $2,500,000 abode called
"Sunderland House."

Her bridal gown was recut with the prescribed low neckline
for wearing when she paid her respects to Wales and his wife,
permanent understudies for the sequestered Queen Victoria.
With the help of the Swiss ladies' maid her mother-in-law, Lady
Blandford, had engaged for her, the young duchess encircled
her narrow waist with Marlborough's diamond belt and set Willie's tiara upon her upswept hair. If her head ached under the
weight of it, there was no sign on her solemn face as she entered
the palace ballroom—which was nowhere the size of the Long

Library at Blenheim—to the music of a military band perched
up in the musicians' gallery.

The immense white train of her dress rustled over the parquet
when she advanced toward the red-carpeted dais on which
prince and princess sat enthroned. Consuelo sensed a different
kind of rustling—of curiosity about her—as she drew closer, her
eyes pausing briefly on the fat figure of Wales, then fixing on his
graceful wife. Alexandra, diamond choker hiding the scar on
her neck, encouraged her with a smile, and Consuelo gleamed
with pleasure. "She simply swept the board," another woman
who was present acknowledged afterward.

The ritual looked easier than it proved to be. She was required
to do no more than curtsey to each of the Highnesses in succession, and then, because no one's back could ever be turned on a
royal personage, she must retreat in reverse, looking neither left
nor right, after a page had scooped up the train and folded it in a
single swift motion over her extended right arm. To trip or stum-
ble would be an offense more unthinkable than riding alone in a
hansom cab. American competitiveness carried her through.
She managed it all without a flaw, as delighted with herself as
Cinderella at the ball.

Albertha's praise was sincere but maladroit: "I must tell you
that no one would take you for an American."

Her daughter-in-law, buoyed by success, chose this moment
to speak up for herself and her country. She was tired of hearing
Americans being referred to as though they were all aborigines.
She admired this stalwart old woman with the delicate hands
and tiny, tight-laced waist, but Albertha must be made to understand that Consuelo was not forever to be patronized.

"I suppose you mean that as a compliment, Lady Blandford,
but what would you think if I said you were not at all like an En-
glishwoman?"

"Oh, that is quite different."

"Different to you, but not to me."

Albertha recognized the point. She liked to see spirit in a girl,
and she received more attention from her daughter-in-law than
from her son, who seemed to have no more feeling for his mother than for the memory of his father, holding them equally responsible for a disrupted childhood. When Sunny wished to
confide in an older woman, he went to Albertha's sister, the

Marchioness of Lansdowne, once vicereine of India, who continued to treat Consuelo like a curious species of butterfly introduced into the Marlborough collection.

The Marlboroughs spent the season in London through the end of July, doing the weekday rounds of parties, fetes, receptions, dinners and balls at the majestic houses of the aristocrats which, she thought, did not really compare in true elegance with their counterparts in Paris. Devonshire House, Lansdowne, Montagu, Apsley, Holland, Grosvenor—the dukes, marquesses, earls, barons, baronets and knights who, with their ladies, comprised the kingdom's Four Hundred made the circuit night after night; governed by rules of decorum that decided what they wore, what they said and their thinking, too; dining off silver and gold plate; twirling around on the dance floors in polkas and waltzes until they were dizzy because to reverse was regarded as outré, with weary flunkeys in white wigs and silk knee-breeches on call from start to finish.

She adapted herself easily to the pattern set for women of her status. In the morning, she squeezed herself into a black riding habit of fashionably tight cut to canter an immaculately curried horse along the tanbark of Rotten Row. In the afternoon she returned to Hyde Park, gowned in ruffled organdie with parasol to match, to ride aimlessly to and fro in a carriage until it was time to demonstrate her fealty by pausing at Grosvenor Gate to watch Alexandra out for her daily airing in a sparkling barouche.

Sunny decided his duchess deserved a vehicle of similar style. On its slender springs, it swayed so ferociously that a trip in it was an ordeal for anyone prone to travel sickness. Consuelo, a good sailor herself, ventured to infringe the code outlined by Lady Lansdowne by taking a hansom cab for shopping expeditions. Sunny's other new toy, a hooded phaeton, was too grand for such mercantile outings. When he rode in that behind a pair of thoroughbreds, he wore a gray top hat and a white gardenia, and he expected her to dress in equal splendor.

They were guests, of course, at the mansion that, carrying their name, had come to typify the apex of the pyramid. Marlborough House and the people with entree there enjoyed influence, authority and high old times with Wales, whose tastes ran from baccarat to beauty in women. The prince, the most popular man in the kingdom, was also one of the happiest that summer. His racehorse, Persimmon, won the Derby, his stable was on the way to earning him nearly £30,000 in stake money, and he had an engaging new friend in Lady Dudley.

The timing of Consuelo's introduction to the Marlborough House set was auspicious. Last December, His Royal Highness had been horrified at the prospect of his nation and the United States going to war over Venezuela. Like most of his country-men, he believed that England had shown almost exaggerated goodwill toward Americans, but in Washington Cleveland had threatened to use force if necessary to keep British fingers out of the transatlantic pie.

"There was evidence," the year's *Annual Register* declared, "of a stern determination not to forego any national or treaty rights if it could be shown that our claims on Venezuela were honest and justified." The prince answered an invitation from the New York *World* with a Christmas Eve cablegram to its pro-prietor, Joseph Pulitzer: "I earnestly trust, and cannot but be-lieve, present crisis will be arranged in a manner satisfactory to both countries and will be succeeded by same warm feeling of friendship which has existed between them for so many years."

Britain did not officially recognize the boundary commission set up by Cleveland, but the prince was not slow in his response to Consuelo's charm. In the middle of June, he moved as usual into Windsor Castle for the best part of a week for the racing at nearby Ascot. Sunny rented another house across the road from the track, ordering the state coach and team of four to be deliv-ered to the stables so that, like the prince, the Marlboroughs could arrive at the course in proper style.

They were asked to lunch with him and the princess in the royal pavilion, and they risked their feet being stepped on in the crush of other lords and ladies who, under gray top hats and flowery parasols, crowded the Royal Enclosure, anxious to see and be seen. It seemed to Consuelo that, falling into line with the rest of the women, she did little else all day but change her clothes and have the maid refix her hair to meet the demands of the timetable and the capricious weather. Wales thought the time had come for her to dine with his mother, the queen, tucked away within the castle walls, and spend a night in a Windsor bedchamber.

The printed invitation, giving the duchess something less than forty-eight hours' notice, produced an undemocratic flutter in her youthful heart. It offered an option which Mrs. Astor's McAllister withheld when he gave anyone entree to the Mystic Rose. "A dinner obligation, once accepted, is a sacred obligation," he insisted. "If you die before the dinner takes place, your executors must attend the dinner." Anyone who dared be out of town when summoned to meet Her Majesty could simply have the invitation returned to the Master of the Household.

One of Sunny's Churchillian aunts rehearsed his wife in what a duchess must and must not do in the presence of the doddery, seventy-seven-year-old Victoria. Her hand was to be kissed and her responding kiss accepted on the forehead. She was to be spoken to only if she opened a conversation. At no time could she be given a view of the back of one's neck. A nod of her lace-capped head must be looked for as a signal that one's time with her was up.

Consuelo was chilled to find the dumpy little woman in widow's weeds stood no taller than her breastbone. Kissing the plump hand meant dropping a curtsey so deep that the girl wondered how she could ever rise out of it without stumbling. She hoped—irreverent thought—that the diamonds in her coiffure would not "scratch out a royal eye."

Her impressions of the evening were strictly personal. Sunny would not appreciate hearing that she rated the dinner depressing and Victoria overwhelmed by self-importance and the desire to dominate. The queen and Mrs. Astor were like sisters in that regard.

The prince wished to see more of Sunny and his American bride. He kept himself busier than usual that fall, superintending arrangements for young Tsar Nicholas' impending state visit to the queen at Balmoral. But once the emperor and his family had arrived in the imperial yacht, Wales was excluded from the talks she had with this Russian husband of her granddaughter Alix and the queen's prime minister, Lord Salisbury. So the prince, reverting to his normal schedule for November, went off to Sandringham House, his wind-blown retreat in the East Anglian wilds of Norfolk, and invited Sunny and Consuelo to spend some time with him there. She dreaded the thought of it. Country house parties were a diversion that took a lot of accustoming oneself to. Over too many weekends this past summer,

Sunny had as many as thirty guests, most of them strangers to her, filling every Blenheim bedroom. Since she had no secretary, the job of writing and handling all the invitations was a burden in itself, but Sunny believed such wholesale entertaining was an essential part of her education as duchess.

Planning a house party was not unlike walking through dark woods booby-trapped with spring guns. As hostess, she needed to know about her guests' romantic entanglements to assign them convenient bedrooms. When nobility descended on her, she must be sure to seat them at table in strict order of rank lest they felt an affront to their dignity. She had to see to it that enough males were asked down to provide every unattached female with an escort, eager or otherwise. There were menus to be prepared for three meals a day, the French chef and English butler to be coaxed into grudging cooperation with each other, servants to be pacified when they sulked about the extra load of work falling on them.

Sunny gave her a minimum of help or encouragement. He was as slow to praise and as hasty to criticize as Alva. Running and financing the household was a woman's business; his function as husband was to supervise the estate. But he would no more permit her to have anything done to modernize the plumbing than he would let her strike a match to light a fire. One reason she disliked house parties was her embarrassment about Blenheim's chronic shortage of bathrooms. She could not get used to the squabbling between ladies' maids as they manouevred, towels and sponges at the ready, to reserve precious bath time for their impatient mistresses—or the sight of tubs being hauled in front of bedroom fires with accompanying hot-water pitchers, towels and soap.

Sunny, on the contrary, looked forward to being at Sandringham, where shooting was a way of life. Every clock was set forward by half an hour to provide more daylight for the prince and his guests, assisted by platoons of beaters, to bang away with shotguns for an annual kill of thirty thousand partridge and pheasant, every bird tended like a battery hen by the keepers. Sunny, a first-class shot, was constantly out at Blenheim after pheasant in the park and snipe and wild duck on the lake. On one ear-splitting day, he and four other hunters accounted for five thousand rabbits. He would be in his element at Sandringham. Consuelo wondered how she could possibly stand at attention from Monday afternon until Friday morning, which was what appeared to be demanded of her.

All the people there were bound to be much older than she; they always were. Jennie Churchill, a frequent guest of the prince's in the past, had pictured in advance what her niece should expect. Wales and the other sportsmen would be off to the coverts straight after breakfast, leaving the women to form little cliques and dawdle over writing letters, thumbing through magazines, tinkling with the grand piano and gossiping ceaselessly until dusk brought His Highness and the other men home, trailed by a wagon toting the day's toll af game.

The Marlboroughs' excursion started badly. At Paddington Station, Consuelo's maid, one of a bevy of Blenheim servants sent on in advance, lost one of her mistress' bags with a sentimental collection of inexpensive jewelry. When the newspapers reported the incident, Sunny, for reasons unknown, denied that it had happened. But once she arrived under the prince's roof, Consuelo found things improved.

For all its inchoate size and tasteless architectural mixture of Tudor, Jacobean and Victorian stonework and red brick, Sandringham made a cosier home than Blenheim, though its owner, chatting alternately in English, French and German, let nobody forget that he was "Your Highness." His wife, deaf as she was, proved much more approachable. Consuelo found warmth in this butterfly of a woman who took her up to her incredibly cluttered suite to show her some of the dresses she had consistently saved since her girlhood.

The young duchess tried a day following the guns in a carriage to luncheon in the marquee set up some distance from the house, where vintage wine and hot and cold dishes took the edge off the prince's robust appetite. As a means of escaping the small talk of most of the other woman, the day was a success, but when it came to an afternoon of sheltering behind hedgerows when the thunder of the breech-loaders started up again, she counted the minutes until she could get back to tea and a blazing log fire. She was too tender-hearted to watch without a tremor as birds crippled by shot fluttered to earth, beating the ground with shattered wings.

Teatime called for changing out of tweeds into the most elab-

orate gowns that money could buy—a different one for each session. Gloves were mandatory for every lady. Led by the prince
in black tie and jacket, the freshly scrubbed and laundered
males joined the party to listen to a string orchestra play Strauss
and Offenbach for a full hour. What she heard from Wales during their stay encouraged her. With superb adolescent assur-
ance, she rated him "the best informed person in the kingdom."
Perhaps she was biased by memories of stern Fräulein Wedekind
and Francis Joseph, the scheming German princeling, or of Paris in the era of Winty, but she was delighted to gather that the
prince, too, preferred the French to the Germans from whom
he was descended.

Bridge tables, the billiard room and the bowling alley were
available to fill in time if there was any to spare before the next
event of the day, dinner, served at precisely nine o' clock, Sandringham time. In the interval, ladies and gentlemen awaited
their turn for a bathtub, and maids laid out their mistress' attire
for the evening: a new gown, of course, a tiara, jewels, and
gloves to be buttoned to the elbows. Places in the parade into
the tapestried dining room were as rigidly ordered as a procession of Catholic clergy bearing the Pope aloft around St. Peter's
Square.

"Although no uniforms were worn at dinner," Jennie Churchill had related reassuringly, "this was a ceremonious affair,
with everyone in full dress and decorations." The host was a
stickler for punctuality in everyone but his notoriously tardy
wife, so the table was cleared after exactly one hour. The moment Consuelo and the other women followed the princess into
the drawing room, footmen hurried in with cigars and brandy
for the men. They would linger for only thirty minutes; Wales
was always impatient to get back to the ladies.

Pure chance may have saved Consuelo from becoming the
target of more concentrated attention. He was looking for a new
mistress to replace Frances, the strikingly beautiful heiress of
her grandfather, the late Lord Maynard, whose obliging husband was Lord Brooke. Her part in Wales' amours was coming
to an end after ten years now that she had turned Socialist. Pregnancy would soon save Consuelo from being pursued by him,
and by the time she was through with childbearing, he had
found what he wanted in the Honorable Mrs. George Keppel,

aged twenty-nine, who satisfied his needs for the remainder of his life.

He played cards for the rest of the evening now that baccarat had lost its hold on him. The rounds of bridge sometimes lasted until the early hours of the following morning, but woe betide anyone who retired before the princess. He was, Consuelo concluded after listening to him, "a shrewd man of the world." She left Sandringham with the comfortable feeling that in his wife she had found as close a friend as ever could be made of royalty.

Her education in the rituals of the English had progressed a pace or so. But her mood was not entirely joyful. The prince wanted still more of the Marlboroughs' companionship. He would be arriving at Blenheim, he said, to get in some shooting toward the end of November. It was a prospect to overawe any hostess, most particularly a girl of nineteen.

VII

Crosses of Gold

Her mother-in-law would be able to help her cope with the details of protocol. She would know best what to do about entertaining, feeding and housing the prince, though she had a fanciful sense of humor that needed to be held in check. At a past dinner party, Albertha had served slivers of laundry soap along with the sliced cheese. When Lady Aylesford was carrying the eighth duke's child, Albertha had a miniature baby doll substituted for the customary poached egg under silver cover on his breakfast tray.

The first order of business was to draw up a list of suggested guests and submit it for the prince's approval; there would be more than two dozen visitors in all. Along with his wife, the prince proposed bringing his eldest daughter, Maud, and Prince Charles of Denmark—a Danish Navy officer, a first cousin and her husband since last July. Because the youngest daughter, poor, lonely Victoria, went everywhere with her possessive mother, she would be arriving, too.

Who should the other guests be? Jennie Churchill would certainly fit in if she could be persuaded to come down and interrupt her casting around for a new man to marry. It might have served young Winston a good turn if he could be there, and Consuelo would have someone close to her own age, but he was off soldiering in India. Henry Chaplin, one of the prince's staunchest companions, was a safe bet; the two had a lot in common, including a taste for gambling.

Consuelo was learning, at a speed that sometimes surprised her, how to pick a path through the brambles of royal society, using published guides to the peerage and the *Almanach de Gotha* as maps. The Viscount Castlereagh, future Marquess of Londonderry, was entered on the roster. "A pedigree of full twenty-four descents," cooed one of her gazetteers, "a great territorial inheritance and a name interwoven with the historic events of the counties of York and Durham" entitled him "to a very high place on the roll of nobility of England . . . The head of the family at the time of Henry V was Sir Piers Tempest of Bracewell, who served under the monarch at the battle of Agincourt." Castlereagh, his arteries as hardened as his opinions, eyed her as if she were a toothsome imported bonbon, but the prince would not find fault with that.

She could distinguish without hesitation between the two George Curzons, one already a viscount, the other a rising star of the Foreign Office, married to Mary Leiter, daughter of a Chicago speculator; this George would one day be viceroy of India and first Marquess Curzon of Kedleston.

Both Curzons were eligibles, to be added to the list without risk of deletion, together with one more plain "Mr.," Arthur James Balfour, silken in speech and manners, who served as First Lord of the Treasury and Tory leader in the House of Commons; the prime minister was his uncle, Lord Salisbury, who had originally employed him as his private secretary. For the present, at least, the prince and Mr. Balfour got along famously well together. The fifty-year-old politician had put in an earlier appearance at Blenheim along with a hundred other members of Parliament attending a Tory garden party organized by Sunny. After luncheon in the Great Hall, the party sallied out onto the terrace of the Great Court, a ready-made stage, for a round of speeches delivered to the throng of the faithful that had gathered to cheer.

Consuelo became an instant devotee of the scholarly, sophisticated Englishman, an archetype of a class that thought of a seat in the Commons as something to be passed from one generation to another, like part of the family estates. She had never met anyone like Balfour, whose spoken words sounded like literary masterpieces and who hid his cleverness under a disguise of refined indolence.

"When I think of him," she declared, "it is as of some fine and disembodied spirit." For his part, he appeared to think of her the way a kindly uncle regards a winsome young niece. She felt secure in his company. He was a man she could learn from and respect.

Half a dozen or so other lords and ladies with time to spare for a week of doing little else but going gunning for game or staying indoors by the fire rounded out the list drawn up by Consuelo and forwarded to Marlborough House. Though no complications arose, her misgivings increased as the November days slipped away and another tally of details to be dealt with grew longer instead of shorter.

She and Sunny would have to abandon all their ground floor rooms to the prince and his entourage and squeeze themselves somehow into cramped quarters upstairs. Sunny had spread himself by bringing a team of cabinetmakers over from Paris to carve and gild the new woodwork paneling of the State Rooms, copied from *boiseries* of Louis XIV's bedroom at Versailles. One of them, embellished with yet another tapestry and Seeman's portrait of the first duke, would have to be converted into the prince's bedchamber with the introduction of a washstand, commode, water jug and towels. Sunny regretted that the French decor he had commissioned was rather out of scale; his wife marveled at the intrusion of the unseemly articles for the royal toilet among boule furniture on the Savonnerie carpet. But what had been good enough for Louis was presumably acceptable by Wales.

She braced herself by remembering she was an American, the daughter of a country created by pioneer women toiling alongside their men in field and forest, sod hut and log cabin. Inch by inch, it seemed that in local elections at least they were finally winning the vote; Idaho granted them that right in this year of 1896. She had probably heard from Alva about the first dabbling of her toes in politics.

Oliver Belmont's money financed *Verdict,* a new satirical magazine like *Judge* and *Puck,* with a similar colored cover and zeal for reform. Its articles hammered away at the Vanderbilts as evil monopolists. It hated Grover Cleveland but reluctantly endorsed the spellbinding William Jennings Bryan's protest that "you shall not crucify mankind upon a cross of gold." The Nebraskan editor had won the Democrats' nomination for the presidency, then lost this November's election to the Republicans' William McKinley, who had a campaign chest of $3,500,000 and other cash reserves to draw on.

Verdict had only a brief span of life. Its final issue contained an editorial expressing Alva's new liberalism: "Be pure, and your government will be pure; be brave, and it will have courage; be free, and freedom will abide in your high places and descend therefrom the rabble least among you. Be dogs, and you will have dog government—a kennel, a collar, a bone to gnaw and a chain to clink." Though her brainchild suffered a premature end, her influence on her daughter continued strong.

Only a trickle of letters came for Consuelo from relatives across the sea. One of the *divertissements* she had planned was a ball at which neighbors who passed Sunny's screening might be presented to the prince. This particular attraction on the program had to be canceled. No cablegram arrived from New York to tell her that Grandmother Vanderbilt was dead; Consuelo saw the news scrawled on a news vendor's placard on a London street. In court circles, the period of mourning was determined by the doleful queen, who had worn black for thirty-five years in memory of Albert, her prince consort. The duchess sent a confidential cable to Willie in New York, seeking his objective opinion on whether the royal visit should be called off. He recommended a tactful compromise: cancel the ball and hold a concert in its stead.

There was no question of her going back for the funeral of the kindly old woman she had dearly loved; no steamship could arrive in time. All she could do was order flowers for the day her grandmother was laid to rest in the New Dorp mausoleum. Willie may have told her that his mother left an estate of $1,100,000, most of its income derived from funds which reverted now to the trust controlled by Willie and Cornelius II.

Wales and his coterie came down from London by special train, with servants clustered in third-class compartments and monogrammed leather trunks piled to the ceiling of the luggage van, but not the ladies' jewel cases, which were clutched in the hands of their maids. Sunny waited at Woodstock Station along with a detachment of the Monday evening crowd that would raise loyal cheers along every yard of the way to the Triumphal Arch. The route was decked with the same flags and bunting that had served at Consuelo's homecoming. The fire brigade, with the brass of their helmets and the fittings of the hand-drawn pumper polished bright, turned out again as the honor guard. This time, the mayor and corporation tramped alongside the carriages in a demonstration of the profoundest respect. At the arch, a porter stood holding his silver-knobbed red-corded ceremonial staff as if it were a halberd and he were about to join battle against the French at Agincourt. The princess' non-stop smiles and an occasional hand flick by the prince were all the re-ward the throng expected. Blenheim's Grand Avenue was agleam with its newly installed electric lights. On succeeding days, men of Woodstock would march with torches flaming to pay obeisance to Wales.

It was not that Consuelo felt disloyal, but so much of what she had to do seemed to be effort wasted. She had to dress almost as grandly as for a ball before she went down to breakfast, timed on the dot of nine-thirty to conform with the inflexible princely schedule. Lunching with the men up in the park at North Lodge meant changing into country tweeds and sturdy shoes. Tea at four-thirty required a third change of clothes and a subsequent session in the Long Library, whose depleted shelves Sunny was slowly refilling, where they listened to an organ recital or a con-cert by the Viennese orchestra he had hired in London. No cos-tume could be worn more than once. Counting dinner gowns, this had involved buying sixteen new outfits for the four days. Heiress though she was, the expense irked her.

Dinnertimes had the merit of being relieved of their custom-ary tedium. When she and Sunny dined alone in the echoing Saloon, they sat opposite each other at either end of the expan-sive table, while footmen had a stipulated sixty minutes in which to serve eight courses—two soups, two kinds of fish, an entrée, meat, game, savory and fresh fruit. Sunny would pile his plate, then sit back brooding without touching a mouthful. The si-lence between them might last for fifteen minutes, before he took a bite and grumbled that it was cold. She eventually grew so weary of the delay before she could ring the bell to interrupt the butler, engrossed in a novel behind the service door, that she took her knitting in when they sat down to dine.

Ordinarily, if they had guests, she would be obliged to sit

flanked by the most distinguished males in the company, more often than not graybeards who either disturbed her with flattery or bored her with tales of their own exaltedness. Having the prince at her side for two meals a day made for a different kind of tribulation. What he liked best as an accompaniment to vintage wines and French cooking in generous portions was the spice of scandal; she regretted being too unworldly to have succulent morsels of gossip to share with him.

Alexandra presented no such problem. The princess, fifty-two next month, was so girlish in her ways that she might have been Consuelo's age. She bubbled over with gaiety, twitting her enchanted hostess with an account of the perils she faced in the duchess' surrendered bedroom, tripping over the polar bear skins on the floor and stumbling up the little ladder to climb onto the dais and slide between the satin sheets.

This was one friendship that thickened in the course of an otherwise horrific week. Another was with Arthur Balfour, who found killing birds as distasteful as killing time. He brought his typewriter with him for work in his room every morning until the hour arrived for him to borrow a bicycle and pedal his way to lunch. When he posed in the group photograph that was a required souvenir of royal visitations, he stood out in the ranks as the only gentlemen not wearing a sporty little cap or a regal Homburg, or armed with a Malacca cane or a shooting stick.

Friday's concert had swelled into a reception for more than a hundred, the women in full bloom of diamonds, the men in uniform or courtly knee breeches. Consuelo awoke in her upstairs hideaway exhausted before she even tackled the day's agenda, wondering perhaps whether, once the guests had gone, she could steal twenty-four hours uninterrupted in bed as she had at the close of her first London season. She must find an opportunity this morning to go over the guest list with Wales to see whom among the county families he cared to have introduced to him. Just as Alva had filled Marble House, the State Rooms must be graced with orchids from the eighth duke's hot-houses, which in the heyday of his life had been an art gallery containing Titian canvases, subsequently sold to pay his debts. The hour-long chore of working out the order of procession into supper with the aid of her little printed table of precedence had to be tackled to take into account tonight's new recruits. And she still dared not be late for breakfast.

* * *

She survived. The mistress of Blenheim had circles under her eyes which only a common actress could have disguised with makeup, but to the end she carried off the day as though she had been handling similar situations since the prince was a chubby nineteen-year-old bachelor going to the ball held for him in New York at the Academy of Music on Fourteenth Street, where two thousand uninvited guests forced a passage through the barriers ahead of time and the floor collapsed. Commodore Cornelius Vanderbilt had sat on the arrangements committee for that riotous affair.

Sunny, forever concerned with embellishing the Marlborough name, hit on an idea for giving the prince a truly royal Saturday morning send-off. The summer garden party had been devised to ease the young duke's road into a career in politics. The departure from Blenheim was likewise contrived to win extra marks from the man who by any odds would soon be king of England. Sunny put on his full dress uniform as an officer in the Oxfordshire Hussars—dark, gold-frogged tunic; breeches of Mantua purple, which was the Churchill family color; Hessian boots with pink heels; and a plumed shako.

With peruked and powdered manservants standing by, Consuelo bade *au revoir* to prince and princess as they were helped into the Marlboroughs' cumbersome daumont behind a team of four matched grays, the standard color for Blenheim horses. With Sunny in the saddle of another and an escort of uniformed cavalry bringing up the rear, the cavalcade set off on the ride to Oxford railway station.

Consuelo hoped entertaining could be suspended until Christmas and Sunny's relatives came upon her. The faraway end of the social spectrum deserved more of her attention, she thought. The vast estate was studded with villages and hamlets steeped in antiquity. Aborigines of the Stone Age had fished local steams using chips of flint as hooks. Roman slaves had dug clay here to shape pottery for their masters. Norman invaders established the feudal values that had never changed; the measure of a man's status was the amount of land he owned.

Village life went on at the pace of the days when those holding title to the entire countryside evicted peasants in uncounted thousands to enclose the land for sheep, whose wool earned the biggest profit of any crop. Steam engines did the threshing now, but laborers still worked ten hours and more a day with sickles and scythes, paying rent for ancient stone cottages that lacked running water.

Compared with other communities on the estate, Woodstock was a metropolis in miniature, with its rows of shops and trim Georgian-fronted factories up the lanes turning out ladies' gloves and jewelry forged from steel. Consuelo preferred going out along the graveled walk that wound through Lower Park to a little lodge and a swinging gate opening on Bladon, a village no more than a speck on a survey map.

She found a dressmaker there to sew many of her everyday dresses—the more spectacular gowns admired by Sunny continued to be bought in London and Paris. Women and children invariably dropped a curtsey as she passed, while menfolk tugged off their caps with a "Good day, Your Grace," a title that still sounded odd to her. In a sense, they were part of Sunny's birthright, expecting nothing better for themselves in his lifetime. Radical politics to them were as unknown as a place at a king's banquet. The duke paid each the same few shillings a week as any other noble landlord, but they were looked after if illness disabled them, and when they wanted extra pennies, he encouraged them to enter the park to saw and chop storm-stricken trees for sale as firewood. Sunny, they told each other, was a *proper* duke.

Consuelo tried her hand at introducing modest changes. Leftovers at Blenheim were traditionally carried to a side table in the Saloon for the reigning duchess to squash into empty biscuit tins for distribution to the hungriest families in the villages. No attempt had been made before to sort out the mess: fish, meat, vegetables and desserts were mashed in together. She instituted the practice of separating each item on the bill of fare. It was little enough, but it was a beginning, and Her Grace won the blessings of the needy.

The obligation to visit poverty-stricken homes brought her a kind of contentment. The contrasts could be harrowing when she ducked her head under the doorway of a lopsided cottage where dim daylight filtered in through leaded windowpanes to greet an old woman huddled in a shawl by a chilly hearth. Outside lay some of the loveliest landscape in England, cloud-dappled sky, green fields, towering trees, peaceful rivers and, usually, a trim garden of roses, hollyhocks, larkspur and sweet william clustered against the cottage walls. America was a land on a different planet.

The fourth duchess, Caroline, whose portrait by Reynolds hung in the Green Drawing Room, had endowed almshouses at the turn of the eighteenth century. There Consuelo found an old blind woman on whom to lavish a measure of her frustrated love. Sara Prattley liked the Bible read to her. Since she was hard of hearing, Consuelo was thankful for the elocution lessons from the actress of the Comédie Française. Mrs. Prattley's favorite was the gospel of St. John. Consuelo came to know every word, eyes pricking as she recited, and her audience of one repeated after her, "He answered and said, A man that is called Jesus made clay, and anointed mine eyes, and said unto me, Go to the pool of Siloam and wash; and I went and washed, and I received sight."

The American girl with the ringing voice, whose long legs carried her with the delicacy of a deer, became a wonder among the villagers. The only flaw they could find in her was gullibility: this lady bountiful was apt to be taken in by any tale of woe, and her gifts sometimes went to those who did not deserve them. A later generation still sang the praises of the legendary Consuelo and what she did for Sara Prattley, when both of them were long since dead. The duchess considered that she reaped greater benefit from their hours together. "I felt the peace of God descending into that humble home, and I was happy to go there for the strength it gave me," she said.

At Christmas, she went from house to house with toys for the children, blankets and parcels of clothing made up for the elders. Inside the palace stood Christmas trees for schoolchildren's parties, and teas as fine as those served to aristocrats were given for the grown-ups. In summertime, she brought in roundabouts and opened the grounds for a children's fair. In Bladon three-quarters of a century afterward, the oldest of the inhabitants reminisced about days when she handed them little bags of candy and lifted them up for turns on the merry-go-round.

After a lonely first Christmas at Blenheim, she moved with Sunny into a house he had rented in Melton Mowbray, Leicestershire, an Early English town of a few thousand people, justly celebrated for its pork pies, Stilton cheese and fox hunting. Sunny was a lover of the chase, a daring horseman who would take any fence to stay ahead of the field. Cousin Winston recalled times when they were out together with the Quorn, Bicester, and Pytchley hounds: "I strove to follow his lead as far as possible and with far humbler aspirations." Sunny, in hunting pink, rode like a man possessed.

Consuelo was not in his class on horseback. She would rather canter around Blenheim on a calmer mount than a quivering hunter. At Melton Mowbray, all she could do was follow the chase over rutted pastures in a careening buggy. Before they left Woodstock, she had learned she was to fulfill her most important duty as duchess: she was carrying Sunny's child.

When Sunny had enjoyed enough of the Quorn for the time being, he returned to his palace. The dissatisfaction they shared with each other was coming into sharper view. If frost curbed his hunting, he took himself off to London or for an occasional fling in Paris. In solitude, Consuelo caught up on her reading, which was melancholy. The rationalized gloom of Friedrich Nietzsche and Arthur Schopenhauer, forbidden to her by Alva, suited her present mood, even if studying German philosophers branded her a bluestocking among Churchill women. She did not mind; she was beginning to feel more sure of herself.

Alva sailed to England to be there for the birth of her first grandchild, delivered by an urbane obstetrician, whom she berated as utterly inept, in a made-over drawing room of Spencer House, the eighteenth-century London mansion of another branch of the family of the fifth duke, who had renamed himself Churchill. It might have been guilt over her suffering daughter that led Alva to fancy she detected an icy presence of a ghost at the bedside. For the comfort of John Albert Edward William Spencer Churchill, Marquess of Blandford, born on September 18, 1897, his grandmother ordered a sumptuous gold-and-blue cradle with draped lace canopy to be sent from Venice. As soon as he could crawl, his mother had him sculpted in bronze.

"Albert" and "Edward" were imposed choices, unavoidable since the Prince of Wales, another Albert Edward, volunteered to be his godfather. "John" was for the first Marlborough, "William" for Willie. Consuelo did not care at all for "Albert," but it was as "Bertie" that her son lived his life. Like a prince, he was christened in St. James' Palace, where a smiling Willie stood in the congregation.

The man she continued to admire above all others looked much too youthful, she thought, to be a grandfather and happier than she had ever seen him. He had found a new hobby, infinitely more appealing than working in an office. On the death of Grandmother Vanderbilt, who frowned on betting and race tracks, he quickly registered his colors: black cap and white jacket with a black hoop on the sleeves. His two-year-olds ran poorly the first season, so he crossed to France to buy a whole training stable and the 2,900-meter track that went with it at Saint Louis de Poissy.

He staffed the place with American stable hands, jockeys and trainers, ready to challenge even the Rothschilds, whose entries at Longchamps, Saint Cloud and Maisons-Lafitte were invariably odds-on favorites. Much more material to his daughter was the fact that he had taken an apartment on the Avenue des Champs Élysées. Instead of being removed from him by three thousand miles, she could see him anytime she was in France.

Childbirth came close to killing Consuelo, narrow hipped and physically fragile. She had lain drifting in and out of consciousness for a week, aware of little other than a sense of accomplishment. She was still convalescent when Sunny met Gladys Marie Deacon, aged sixteen, visiting from Paris, her birthplace, where she lived with her mother and sisters.

She pronounced her name to rhyme with "glade is." She had huge blue eyes, a profile like Helen of Troy's and a past she would choose to suppress. Her father, Edward Parker Deacon, a Boston millionaire, had shot and killed her mother's French lover in a Cannes hotel bedroom when the child was eleven years old. Pardoned by President Carnot after spending a year in prison, Deacon regained custody of his daughter and promptly placed her in a convent. The following year, close to the time Consuelo was aboard *Valiant* with Winty Rutherfurd en route for India, Mrs. Deacon kidnapped Gladys, and her father brought suit to win her back.

Now, back with her mother, she was a junior belle of La Belle Époque, studying in France, Germany and the United States, outwardly carefree and precociously cosmopolitan, intellectual and elegant. Gladys captivated Consuelo when Sunny brought her into view. His duchess felt certain that she and this rare adolescent would be the closest of friends.

A new clique of servants was added to the household hierarchy. An English nanny presided over the nursery with the help of an undernurse and a French nursery maid. Nanny, Consuelo was pleased to discover, was something of a treasure. English nobles, male and female alike, took misery in childhood for granted. They liked to exchange accounts of the horrors they had endured behind nursery doors, telling how they were slapped, pinched and locked into closets for punishment by tyrants in starched aprons who were all smiles in the presence of a parent. They appeared to believe such Spartan treatment built character.

Blenheim's Nanny vented her spite on her French assistant, not on the baby she referred to without fail as "the marquess." It required Consuelo's skill as a diplomat to preserve an *entente cordiale* when Nanny complained that the maid would have to go because she was a typical, smelly, unwashed Frenchwoman. The truth turned out to be that she resented having Nanny stand over her whenever she climbed into a bathtub.

Sunny had one response to fatherhood that bewildered his wife as Bertie grew to be a little boy. The duke's affection for his son was restrained, as in the majority of his class who wanted to have as little as possible to do with a child until he was at least fourteen. But he broke the rules by refusing to chastise Bertie. "My father bullied me," he explained, "and I am not going to bully him." Discipline was Consuelo's unsettling responsibility.

The next winter followed the pattern of the first. The Marlboroughs went up to Melton Mowbray. Consuelo could not hunt because she was due to have another child. She had borne Sunny an heir; it would be prudent to have what she joked about as "a spare." Back alone once more at Blenheim, she walked for miles along the paths around the lake and up between the glorious beech trees and the avenue of huge elms, planted in triplicate on both sides of the Grand Avenue that stretched from the Ditchley Gate to the Column of Victory. There were nearly two solid miles of them, supposed to represent the embattled armies as they faced each other in the glorious Battle of Blindheim. Age and weather had taken their toll. Sunny was set on replacing every imperfect tree, predicting, as he noted in his forestry record book, that the avenue would be "the finest in Europe by the end of the twentieth century."

He undoubtedly wished his second child could be born on Marlborough property, but Sunderland House was not yet in being. Thirteen months after the heir, the "spare" entered the world in Hampden House, London, where the fussy little Duke of Abercorn and his sable-lined overcoat resided. Abercorn was pleased to vacate and rent out the house for Consuelo's confinement. The baby was christened "Ivor" for the best man at his parents' wedding and "Charles" for his father.

With two sons alive and well in Nanny's charge, Consuelo considered she had fulfilled her responsibilities in motherhood: she would have no more babies. She had been, in Albertha's words, "a little brick," and the little brick hoped to sample a few of the available pleasures as soon as she was well enough. One of them was to ride with the Quorn for a day's hunting during the annual winter pilgrimage to Melton Mowbray.

Garbed like a fashion plate in *The Illustrated London News*, she mounted her hunter with the feeling that she must test herself against her husband and make him realize that she had willpower to match his. It might be the most fearful ride of her life, but it had to be done to prove something that was not yet tangible. Waiting for the huntsman's horn and the music of hounds was like listening for the first crack of rifle fire. She could not make out whether it was tension or the biting cold that caused her trembling.

Suddenly, she heard the cry, and Sunny was off at a gallop, ducking to dodge the overhanging branches of a tree as he took the first fence. She urged her horse after him in a leap over the same high rails. And so it went, with Consuelo close on Sunny's heels, satisfied with her place there because she had no hope of overtaking him. Staying with him would be enough. The run across fields and fences lasted so long it set a record for the season. Consuelo, barely recovered from childbirth and exhausted by the pounding of the saddle, surely prayed for the fox to find momentary refuge in a covert so that she might pause to regain her breath. But he kept running until her strength failed. She had no choice but to rein in and watch riders and hounds pull away from her. She had not succeeded totally in what she had attempted, but she gave herself high marks for the effort. Hunting, she concluded, was not really a pastime for her. Reading to improve her mind was perhaps a better way to outdistance Sunny.

That winter, she provoked her husband into open anger. The Marlboroughs were still in Leicester when reports from Sunny's agent told of hunger in the villages around Woodstock. On her own initiative, she instructed him to offer work at Blenheim to any man willing to work repairing the roads; their pay would come out of her own pocket. Sunny flared up upon discovering what had been done behind his back, but she was no longer a model of meekness. It was ridiculous, she said, for him to accuse her of showing signs of Socialism. She had acted as she did simply because her conscience could not tolerate such stark contrasts between their riches and other people's poverty.

She did not think of herself as a Socialist or any other kind of "ist." She had no deep-rooted belief in politics, only in individuals, and her religious faith was a matter of intense personal feeling, not paying lip service to a creed. Prayers every morning before breakfast at Blenheim stirred her sense of the ridiculous. As the palace clock rang out the half hour after nine, every servant within earshot stopped whatever was being done indoors or out to hurry into the chapel, where the Anglican curate waited to start the service. She recalled many mornings that she scurried in still fastening the last buttons on the sleeve of a blouse while the maids and menservants assembled in the pews discreetly lowered their eyes as if in silent prayer.

The chapel itself was a vainglorious monument to the victor of Blindheim, who was buried first in Westminster Abbey, then reinterred in a chapel tomb beside Sarah after her death in 1744. The white marble sarcophagus which she thoughtfully commissioned ahead of time occupied most of one wall, though it was no match for the Vanderbilt mausoleum on Staten Island.

It depicted John Churchill in the toga of a Roman emperor, flanked by Sarah, robed like a Roman matron, and their two sons, young John, dead at seventeen, and Charles, who did not survive infancy. Old Corneel, with his grandiose bronze memorial at Grand Central Terminal, would have liked Sarah's idea of having the group of four figures attended by History, holding a quill in her hand, and Fame, clasping a trumpet, while the tomb itself crushed the daylights out of Sarah's adversary, Envy, shown as a puny dragon. An apprentice believer in the rights of women, as Consuelo was, would note that of John and Sarah's four daughters there was no mention.

Sunday afternoon service was more formal, with schoolgirls in starched petticoats and schoolboys with hair soaped flat walking up from the villages to provide a choir. To the mistress of Blenheim, God seemed closer in Bladon's almshouses, especially by the fireside of Sara Prattley.

Feelings that had been numbed by a forced marriage were returning to life. Her resolve to get things done was no match for Alva's; yet because strength responds to strength, respect for her adamantine mother began to come back. She could not forgive her, but in the name of mercy she was willing to try. Alva for her part was eager to make amends and at the same time resume shaping her daughter's thinking. Presents arrived in a steady flow—the most useful was an electric runabout in which Consuelo could take off alone without ringing for a horse to be saddled or a carriage prepared when pressures in the house grew unbearable.

Trouble simmered in South Africa in the summer of 1899. The Boers of the Transvaal demanded independence from England, which claimed to be the paramount power, and their neighbors in the Orange Free State sympathized with them. Three days before Ivor's first birthday, the Dutchmen in both territories declared war on the British, and Sunny itched to be off to join the colors like other gentlemen of his caste. The enemy, mounted on hardy ponies, knew every inch of the terrain. They hemmed in the town of Mafeking and invaded Natal, forcing every British outpost to pull back into Ladysmith, which the Boers also besieged.

Half of England felt uneasy about soldiers of the queen being employed under the fumbling general Sir Redvers Buller against farmers seeking their freedom, but the duke, a Tory to the fingertips, knew where his duty lay. Repeated British failure in the field earned the contempt of other nations eager to possess Transvaal diamonds and gold. France, Russia and Germany were looking for means of capitalizing on England's predicament when Kaiser Wilhelm descended on Blenheim.

Like the government itself, Sunny gave him credit for defying public opinion in Germany at a time like this. Wales took the same view and personally arranged every ceremonial detail for the emperor, a nephew who rattled him, to visit the queen at Windsor and stay for a while at Sandringham. The wives of Wales and Sunny shared an opposite sentiment. The princess chuckled when she heard that the kaiser proposed to bring three valets and a barber to her country home. "Ach, the fool!" she exclaimed when she discovered that the barber had an assistant in tow whose exclusive job was to apply curling irons to the imperial moustache.

Possibly she infected Consuelo with her assessments of His Imperial Majesty, though Her Grace had reasons of her own to resent his presence. She was kept in suspense about who should attend the Blenheim luncheon. Consuelo wanted to pack the Saloon with other guests, drawn from noble neighbors who deserved the singular honor of sitting down with the disdainful German. Sunny, in hussar's panoply once more, would ride escort to the daumont when it met him at the station. Consuelo was led to expect the Empress Augusta Victoria would accompany the kaiser, and Alexandra the prince. The table had already been set with the gold service and every place assigned in the necessary ranking order when a telegram from Windsor stated that the royal party would consist of men only. She conducted a mad scramble to reshuffle the seating arrangements before setting out in the carriage to welcome the Kaiser, Wales, and his younger brother, the doughty Duke of Connaught.

Men of distinction were an intolerable nuisance that day. Sunny would not listen when Consuelo suggested he ride in the carriage with her; Wales refused to sit next to his nephew; and over lunch Wilhelm displayed nothing but his own conceits. If she had heard from Alexandra about the assistant barber, she must have been relieved that he, too, had not been brought along to service his master's bristling upper lip.

But evidently the emperor approved of the day. His standard fluttered over the palace, he unburdened himself of a lecture on the Battle of Blindheim, and the German music played on the eighth duke's organ delighted him to the point of asking the organist over to Berlin. Consuelo, nevertheless, dismissed him in her mind. He struck her as arrogant, devoid of a trace of charm and "no more than the typical Prussian officer." She could not take to Germans.

Cousin Winston, who wanted to smell gunpowder, too, was already in South Africa, not as an army officer but a reporter for the *Morning Post*, when Sunny packed his array of uniforms and sailed for Cape Town, to go on from there to the fighting front with the Oxfordshire Hussars. Consuelo never mentioned regret over their parting, and neither did he. He won mention for courage in the official dispatches, and she overlooked that also. She had left Blenheim for the present and rented a London home for herself in Warwick House close by the Ritz.

Field Marshal Lord Roberts had been put in command of the outwitted British forces. Under him, Sunny made the march from Bloemfontein, capital of the Orange Free State, into Pretoria while Winston drove a four-horse wagon. "I well remember his wrath," Winston wrote, "when I told him one day that had he not been a duke, he might at any rate have earned his living as a jockey. He protested with vigor and warmth that he could have kept himself going with an old curiosity shop."

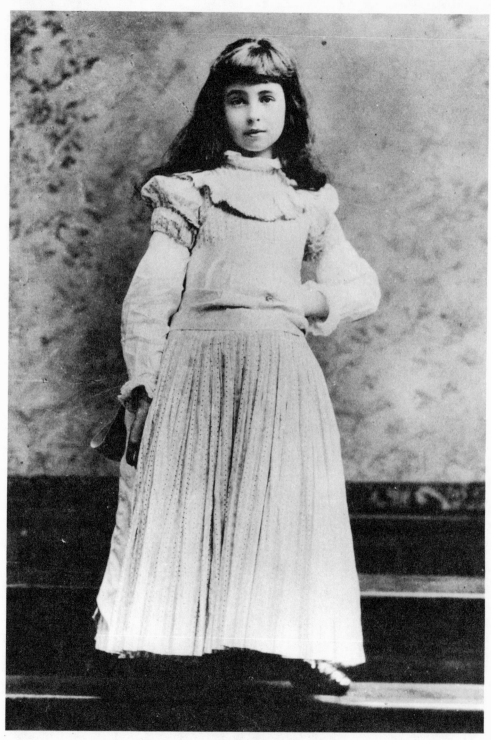

Consuelo at age ten *(Brown Brothers)*.

Alva Vanderbilt at her fancy dress
ball, 1883 *(Brown Brothers)*.

William K. Vanderbilt, 1900
(Brown Brothers).

The William K. Vanderbilt house, 660 Fifth Avenue *(Brown Brothers)*.

The white-and-gold salon at 660 Fifth Avenue *(Culver Pictures)*.

Marble House, Newport, R.I. *(Preservation Society of Newport County Photos).*

The Ballroom at Marble House, *(Preservation Society of Newport County Photos).*

Consuelo in 1894. Detail from a portrait by Carolus Duran *(Culver Pictures)*.

"Sunny," the ninth Duke of Marlborough, at the time of his marriage to Consuelo, 1895 *(Brown Brothers)*.

The ninth Duchess of Marlborough *(Brown Brothers)*.

The wedding of the year, 1895, as drawn by T. Dart Walker *(Culver Pictures)*.

Spectators gathered along Fifth Avenue to catch a glimpse of the wedding party *(Brown Brothers)*.

Consuelo leaving St. Thomas' Church after the ceremony *(UPI)*.

Blenheim Palace (courtesy *His Grace the Duke of Marlborough*).

First State Drawing Room at Blenheim Palace. On the right wall, the Carolus Duran portrait of Consuelo (*courtesy His Grace the Duke of Marlborough*).

Consuelo with her two sons, Lord Ivor Spencer Churchill (left) and the Marquess of Blandford, 1900 *(Brown Brothers)*.

Sunny with Ivor and Blandford in the Great Hall at Blenheim *(Brown Brothers)*.

The Marlborough family, painted by John Singer Sargent (*courtesy His Grace the Duke of Marlborough*).

Consuelo at the coronation of King Edward VII, 1902 *(Brown Brothers)*.

Sunny as mayor of Woodstock *(Brown Brothers)*.

Sunny addressing a political rally at Blenheim *(Brown Brothers)*.

Consuelo received by the guard of honor of tramway men at the opening of a hall for the Tramway Brotherhood, Kensington, 1908 *(Culver Pictures)*.

Consuelo visiting the slums of Southwark, 1919. On her right, the future Edward VIII, then Prince of Wales.

Newport, 1914. Consuelo with O. H. P. Belmont *(UPI)*.

Alva, Mrs. O. H. P. Belmont, addressing a suffragist rally at her Newport house, 1914; Consuelo at far right *(Brown Brothers)*.

Colonel Jacques Balsan,
during World War I.

Consuelo and Jacques Bal-
san in their Sutton Place
apartment, 1950s (courtesy
Valentine Lawford).

Consuelo in her Southampton drawing room, 1960 (© 1963 by Condé Nast Publications, Inc., courtesy Vogue; photograph by Horst).

VIII

Cracks in the Shell

It had promised to be such a gentlemanly war, affording as much sport and as little peril as an afternoon of polo. Routing the Boers had been forecast as a walkover. The newspapers spoke of these crude, bearded malcontents as if they were merely flies to be swatted. Sunny, like every other officer bound for the front, could take with him his valet, groom, coachman, and personal servants, along with hampers of his favorite delicacies, cases of wine, his horses, and shotguns to get in some big-game hunting during off-duty hours. His circumstances were exceptional in one respect, however. For the past year, he had held the appointment of paymaster general, which could have kept him at home if he had wanted to stay.

Soldiers of the Queen had been expected to eat their first Christmas dinner away from home in Pretoria; she sent out chocolate specially stamped with her image for the anticipated celebration. Instead, the fighting on the sun-baked African veld had turned into a messy, uncouth ordeal, a great and costly conflict by the standard of the day, adding £250,000,000 to the national debt, taking its toll in nearly eight thousand Britons slain in action or dead of wounds, plus thirteen thousand more killed by disease. A column of men in pith helmets and bright tunics crisscrossed with white webbing made easy targets for mounted bands of sharpshooters who, with Mauser rifles, attacked like Indian war parties and were off and away before they could be pinned down by return fire. The cost was felt more because there was little glory to be won whatever the outcome.

The march Sunny and Winston took part in was an exhausting business. Loss of wagons to the Boers spelled half rations for the British some days. On reaching Pretoria they were chagrined to find that "Oom Paul" Kruger, burly president of the newly declared Transvaal Republic, had fled, carrying off his government's archives and an unknown amount of Boer gold.

Humiliation in the field produced the usual ungentlemanly responses. No right-thinking officer like Sunny would question the need for cavalry to sweep the countryside clear of every family that might harbor hostiles, burning down farmhouses, cramming women and children into concentration camps where epidemics raged and mortality was heavy.

Much more than six thousand miles of distance separated Consuelo from her husband. She saw the war with an outsider's eyes. Americans regarded the Boers as kin to themselves, free people fighting against oppression by forces greatly superior to them in numbers, equipment, and firepower, just as the British had been at Lexington, Bunker Hill and Valley Forge. Alva probably relayed some of the gibes currently popular in New York: "The surprise party is the chief amusement of the Boer social season" . . . "The Boers are good billiard shots—they are great at reversing the British."

The compassionate duchess could not support the war, but she could work with women similar to herself to temper some of the suffering it inflicted. She had not joined in a group effort of this sort before Jennie Churchill enlisted her help in raising funds to equip an American hospital ship to be sent out to Cape Town.

She invariably felt secure in confiding her marital problems to this sprightly American aunt, counting on her support regardless of the fact that the birth of Bertie had ousted Winston as heir to the dukedom. Jennie, although perennially hard pressed for cash, bore no grudges. Her niece was vastly impressed by her talents—the way Jennie threw herself headlong into a new cause of this sort like a diver plunging off a cliff; her almost professional skill as a pianist; the sparkle in her magnificent gray eyes as she related a risqué tale passed on to her by her old friend the other Consuelo, Duchess of Manchester. But this Consuelo had no desire to emulate her aunt. As an exuberant American in the Marlborough House set, Jennie had been, in her niece's words, "mistress of many hearts," including that of the prince himself. Consuelo was far more finical. She envied Jennie's joie de vivre, but Consuelo would seek fulfillment in other ways than giving and receiving sexual favors.

The paucity of medical services on the battlefields was scandalizing England. A fellow American, William Lehman Burdett-Coutts, who adapted the social climbers' habit to his own purposes by marrying an aged British heiress and exchanging his name for hers, described the scene on the spot: one underpaid army doctor for every hundred wounded, no nurses, male orderlies robbing patients in their beds if they were lucky enough to have one and not be laid on the floor in stretchers, men "dying like flies for want of attention," a death rate of over 20 percent at one pestilential hospital.

Consuelo spared time and money for the cause, but Jennie went further. The young woman she had recruited knew that Sunny's aunt had motives beyond altruism. Jennie wanted to sail aboard the ship to find Winston, at large with a price on his head after escaping from a Boer prison camp. Equally important, she was desperate for a glimpse of her adoring fiancé, Lieutenant George Cornwallis-West, the Princess of Pless' younger brother who was with the Guards. Consuelo felt no similar urge to see Sunny.

She was altogether too rich, too fastidious and too timid to resort to Jennie's brazen overtures to a millionaire shipowner from Baltimore, Bernard Baker, who without bothering to consult his fellow directors handed over an old cattle boat for conversion into a sea-going hospital. The American ladies formed a committee, which met most days to press ahead in accordance with a formal resolution they had concocted: "That the American women in Great Britain, whilst deploring the necessity for war, shall endeavor to raise among their compatriots in America a fund for the relief of the sick and wounded soldiers and refugees in South Africa. It is proposed to dispatch immediately a suitable Hospital Ship, fully equipped with medical stores and provisions, to accommodate 200 people, with a staff of four doctors, five nurses, and 40 commissioned officers and orderlies." They were seeking to collect $150,000 for the vessel they decided should be rechristened the *Maine,* a singular choice, since the United States battleship of that name had gone to the bottom of

Havana harbor at the start of the Spanish-American War in 1898.

It was the ladies' hope to man the *Maine* entirely with their countrymen and have her sail under both the Stars and Stripes and the Union Jack. However, they ended up with a majority of Britons among the ship's complement, and though the queen consented to provide a British flag, President McKinley wanted no part of the enterprise. Jennie supplied Old Glory and rounded up a Chicago meat-packing heir, Allison Armour, to shop for provisions at the Army & Navy Stores. The whole affair was decidedly her show. Consuelo was not quite ready to become such a highly visible public personality, but it was a move in that direction. It nudged her into realizing, as she said, that "opening bazaars and giving away prizes could be successfully done by a moron."

She followed Jennie's example in one other respect while Sunny was away, now serving along with a group of fellow dukes on the staff of Lord Roberts, for whom he worked as assistant military secretary. Consuelo was less shy than she had been about being attended by attractive young men, though intimacy with none of them was closer than arm's length.

With Roberts in command, it seemed that victory was finally guaranteed as his spectacular advances continued and he sent a flying column to relieve besieged Mafeking. The news reached London on a May night when she had a theater date with an army officer whose name went unrecorded. The town celebrated as it never had before. The streets were awash with men, women and children, singing as they linked arms and danced for joy. Straw hats and wide-brimmed chapeaux were kited toward the sky, to be grabbed and worn on heads nearest to where they landed. Strangers exchanged kisses, bands played, pubs ran out of beer, parades formed by spontaneous combustion, and hastily scrawled banners hailed the field marshal and his triumph. On the way back to Warwick House, her carriage got trapped in the exultant throng. She imagined she might have been hauled out as an acolyte in the all-night frolicking but for the presence of her stalwart protector.

In the fall, when Sunny left for home together with Roberts and others of his entourage, the war was generally believed to be over. The two Boer republics had been annexed, and British troops occupied their capital cities. Consuelo perhaps agreed with a comment in *Life,* a magazine that ran in competition with the Oliver Belmonts' *Verdict*: "A small boy with diamonds is no match for a large burglar with experience." The insurgents had no munitions factories or any other obvious necessities for continuing organized resistance.

Salisbury's Conservative government called an immediate election to capitalize on the presumed victory and strengthen its hand in the anticipated peace talks. But the Boers were no ordinary warriors, as Winston, another homecomer, recognized. The breakup of the enemy's regular army left the British forces without a target to attack. The rebels led by Botha, De Wet, De la Rey and Smuts fought on as guerrillas for almost two years more before the two Boer republics were incorporated into the British Empire.

The duchess applauded Winston for running for Parliament as a Tory convert, out to win the sooty Lancashire town of Oldham, teeming with cotton mills and iron foundries, for his party in what was dubbed "the khaki election," khaki being the new shade of uniform adopted for the protection of troops whose original scarlet had proved an easy mark for Boer riflemen. His half-American cousin was not starchy like Sunny, but free and easy, bursting with enthusiasm for anything he tackled. He also nourished a certain sympathy for the Boers, which was lacking in the duke.

Yet Sunny was tolerant and openhanded so far as his relatives were concerned. In his view, it was unthinkable for a Churchill to wander too far astray. He put Winston up in a London flat, forked out £500 toward his expenses and took Consuelo with him to go vote-gathering in barbarous Lancashire.

The campaign was as murky as the color of the army's new battle dress, but she was entranced to listen to this spry young man's speeches whipping up enthusiasm among audiences five or six thousand strong, two and three times a day, and to share the cheers that greeted them when she rode beside him in an open carriage. The essence of Tory policy was to smear the opposition with the slogan, "Every vote for a Liberal is a vote for the Boers," but she forgave him that, just as she excused his boyish boast, "I have suddenly become one of the two or three most popular speakers in this election." He was anxious for every scrap of help the family could give him. He even interrupted his mother's Scottish honeymoon with Cornwallis-West to bring her into the fray.

Churchill romped to victory in the balloting which his party had counted on to wipe out the Liberals; yet, in fact, the Tory majority shrank by eighteen, and if its slogan meant anything, 2,105,518 Britons had voted for the Boers, 2,428,492 in favor of the Conservatives. Consuelo predicted great things for the latest member of Parliament from Oldham who labored so hard over his set speeches in the House of Commons, prompting Arthur Balfour's lofty comment that he carried "heavy but not very mobile guns."

Consuelo's husband and his red-headed cousin were no more alike than a borzoi and a bull terrier. One held himself aloof from everyone, including his wife; the other grabbed hold of life in public and private like a joyful puppy tasting its first marrow-bone. Winston appeared to nurse no grudge against Consuelo for having snuffed out his chances of inheriting the dukedom even if Bertie in later life hedged on this point, writing, "I doubt if he hankered much for the place itself. Much as he cared for Blenheim, it would not have appealed to him to go down in history as its owner. He had other and better ideas."

Winston thought of Consuelo as "one of the most gracious and charming of women." She was tied in marriage, discontented but invulnerable. He had lost his heart to "the most beautiful girl I have ever seen—bar none." Pamela Plowden's father was the British Resident in Hyderabad when Winston met her there as an army officer. The romance had just wilted with his discovery that she was involved with two other men. "But there is no doubt in my mind," he said, "that she is the only woman I could ever live with."

Under the shady, open-sided marquee set up under the cedars on the lawn away from the house, Consuelo would sit absorbing Winston's words whenever he came down as a summer guest. Reading books or the morning newspapers was nowhere near as edifying. He talked endlessly—about his need to remedy his lack of education as a Harrow schoolboy, about history, literature, and above all politics. He had already written two books based on his experiences in the army, and he planned a biography of the father he revered. By comparison with Sunny, bolstered by

Vanderbilt money, his cousin was a starveling. Perhaps, she thought, that partly explained Winston's boundless energy, which Sunny had in only limited supply.

Warm afternoon were interrupted to lob lackadaisical balls across the tennis net or take out a rowboat for a leisurely pull around the lake before a maid laid an al fresco tea table with mounds of home-grown fruit, bowls full of clotted cream, jam scones, and frosted cakes baked that day. Sometimes the men would get up a cricket match with a servant or two added if necessary to make up the opposing elevens. Consuelo was slow to get the hang of a game that entailed so much dawdling and changing of ends, cries of "how's that?" and "jolly well done, sir!" She was content to sit under a parasol in a deck chair chatting, relieved when the last wicket had fallen and it was time to retire for tea.

Winston inspired her. He had an inkling that the system to which he belonged was entering an era of radical change. It was no longer enough for an aristocrat to fancy he had a divine right to hold his head high and stare down his nose at the crowd. Much as he regretted the passing of the tradition that had sired him, he would not swim against the tide like Marlborough. Consuelo, with no love for the products of the system, agreed to make her first formal public speech.

She would go to Birmingham to address a club made up of blind men, some of them victims of industrial accidents, others of the war, outlining to them what could be done by way of technical training to find them paying jobs. She wrote and rewrote every word in advance, with Winston serving as editor and mentor. There was no quarrel with Sunny; he and she trod separate paths that rarely converged. Winston's praise warmed her soul, but she was stricken with stage fright when she got up to speak, the peerage's most wistful and willowy duchess.

She told herself that this audience of unfortunates would not question her motives in coming or the honesty of her beliefs, as ladies of her own circle were apt to do. Standing there as straight as a plumb line, she sensed approval from these sightless men. The applause when she had finished rang in her ears. She was an instant convert to public life, even if repeating such appearances turned her knees weak and her throat dry. For the first time in her life since she bore her sons, she had achieved something on her own account. One more crack was opening in the shell.

Blenheim retained its hold over Sunny's heart and mind. Preservation of the sacrosanct past counted most with him, not adjustment to the uneasy present or preparation for the indecipherable future. He had no need to offer himself as a candidate for election. His hereditary seat was there in the House of Lords if he chose to go up to town, as he occasionally did, to express a thoughtful opinion on the state of the nation. His sense of responsibility to fellow men focused on Woodstock, the inhabitants of rural Oxfordshire, and landowners in general. Workaday life in towns and factories was unknown territory. Big business he found equally unintelligible and uninteresting. He could not envisage sitting behind an office desk or degrading a lustrous name as a figurehead on a board of directors like some of his peers. He was being spoken of as the next Viceroy of Ireland, his grandfather's old appointment, but Sunny did not pursue the matter any harder than he did afterward when he was being considered for a similar appointment in Canada. His world was centered on Blenheim.

The task of exalting the palace inside and out was his paramount duty. He commissioned white marble busts of himself and Consuelo from the American Waldo Storey, to stand on fluted columns in a corridor leading off the Great Hall—an excellent likeness of the duke, an unrecognizable duchess. At a later date, he would have himself done again in bronze by Jacob Epstein, another transplanted American for whom Consuelo sat, too.

Sunny acted as though sensing that time was running out for the ninth duke and duchess to be memorialized as man and wife in stone and on canvas for future generations of Marlboroughs. He appreciated the exceptional honor when the Prince of Wales, as King Edward VII, conferred the Order of the Garter on him—the monarch placed maximum value on this award, which he subsequently refused to bestow upon the Shah of Persia or the King of Siam, much as his ministers begged him to, on the ground that these rulers were "infidels," not Christians.

Soon after Sunny had the right to the robes of a Knight of the Garter, he had himself portrayed in them for a family portrait with his wife, their two sons, and a Blenheim spaniel, a rarer species than the King Charles breed, distinguished by a brown spot on the crown of its head. The choice of artist was automatic—still another American cosmopolite, as apparent evidence that, in spite of iciness between himself and Consuelo, he bore her countrymen no ill feelings. The towering, chain-smoking John Singer Sargent, Royal Academician, was renowned for his paintings of society women, among them the Duchess of Sutherland, the trio of Wyndham sisters, Lady Ian Hamilton, and the former royal light of love, Lady Brooke. He had even managed to make Lilian, the American eighth duchess, look halfway presentable in a gilded frame.

He arrived from his studio on Tite Street, Chelsea, to be told by Sunny that he required a picture of matching proportion to Reynolds' huge 1778 canvas of George, the theatrical fourth duke, with his duchess, their six children, two spaniels, and a whippet. The problem of spreading out four figures and a dog to fill the space nonplussed Sargent, but Sunny would accept no argument—the two paintings must be sized for balanced effect.

The artist had another ticklish situation to contend with. Consuelo stood inches taller than her husband, who had no desire for the disparity to be emphasized. How to disguise the fact? Sargent posed the four of them on a flight of shallow steps, the duchess higher than Sunny. He dressed her in black after a Van Dyck in the palace collection and accentuated her slender neck by prohibiting her usual string of pearls. A Churchill relative grumbled that without them the duchess appeared *undressed*.

She took the two boys with her innumerable times for sittings in the Chelsea atelier, watching intently as an incisive portrayal of a queenly young woman with a self-centered husband emerged on the easel. Sargent had a stock reply to other people's accusations that he was a satirist: "I chronicle; I do not judge." The completed portrait was a subtle study of a marriage gone cold, but what the family dwelt on was the day frail little Ivor bounced off Sargent's sofa and broke an ankle.

Outdoors at Blenheim, Sunny embarked on the titanic labor of undoing the handiwork of Capability Brown and giving tangible form to the dreams of Vanbrugh. The elms were replanted along the Great Avenue; the Great Court, extending as large as a town square on the palace's north side, was stripped of its grass and completely paved with hundreds of thousands of stone blocks. He toyed with Vanbrugh's idea for erecting another enormous gate and colonnade as a fourth wall of the court. He gave up on that, but he wanted something more arresting than conventional formal gardens of brick walks and evergreens trimmed into the fantastic shapes of topiary to flank Blenheim east and west.

Only one man possessed the essential combination of talents as architect and landscape gardener, the Frenchman Achille Duchêne, who specialized in restoring dilapidated châteaus to glory. Sunny kept him busy for decades. They started in the east by devising a series of interlinked decorative pools with spurting fountains and a robust mermaid, another design by Waldo Storey. This was comparatively plain but expensive sailing compared with the western end, where the terrain was difficult. Sunny was not daunted. They would alter the scenery by building up vast terraces studded with fifteen more pools with five fountains jetting from them, the whole concept resembling a gigantic medallion in an oriental carpet.

It would make a perfect setting for one of the first duke's keepsakes, a heroic column supported by river gods, the work of Giovanni Bernini, creator of the Barberini Palace and the colonnade of St. Peter's, Rome. If the money held out, Sunny intended to reconstruct the Great Parterre on the southern exposure, terraced gardens of flowers and trees stretching as wide as the palace itself and reaching out for nearly half a mile from its walls.

Infected with the fury to build, Willie was pouring $6,000,000 of his New York Central dividends into a new Idle Hour after the original was devastated by fire while his elder son, Willie II, was honeymooning there with Virginia Fair, otherwise known as "Birdie," daughter of the late Senator Graham Fair, who left $15,000,000 accumulated from the Comstock Lode. What was more important to Willie were his race horses—he was engaged in assembling the finest racing stables in France. In this year, 1901, he bought a dozen brood mares with foal from Julius and Max Fleschmann and sixteen brood mares with yearlings elsewhere in the United States. His colors would earn him $53,000 next season. Among his boon companions was the Frenchman Jacques Balsan, still single, growing more handsome with the passage of the years—and still eager for the company of Consuelo on her visits to her father.

Consuelo's budding concern for the poor and the deprived did not deter her from personal extravagance. She was, after all, Alva's daughter, brought up in total disregard of expense. She read everything from Edith Wharton and Henry James to the radical Sidney Webbs and H. G. Wells, whose novels were scented with Socialism, but she stayed clear of the iconoclast Thorstein Veblen of the University of Chicago and his *The Theory of the Leisure Class*. She wasn't prepared to swallow his thesis that the rich, whom he probed with the scalpel of irony, advertised their superiority over the rest of mankind by their conspicuous spending, making leisure itself more enjoyable to them by their parading it in public.

She belonged to the caste that believed "more expensive" naturally meant "better." Her money was spent on the things of quality with which she like to be pampered—exquisite furniture, porcelains, oriental carpets, and paintings, not omitting portraits of herself. She was as pleased to sit for an artist as he was to have her as a model of grace and meticulous refinement. Paris enticed her like a candle flame in the darkness. There she could go racing with Willie, enjoy a free hand on shopping expeditions without Alva or Sunny bullying her, choose her own escorts to the parties that attracted her every evening, explore the environs of Bohemia with Gladys. She was always sad to leave.

In Paris, she posed for Paul Helleu, whose drypoint etchings and soft pastels made a woman look as tempting as a Gibson girl. He masqueraded as a melancholy Lothario, but the impression he left on her was that he was "too sensitive" for the part. She was surprised when he asked not a single franc for the likenesses that, with furs at her throat and feathers in her hat, gave her the air of a French coquette. She stopped going to him when she found he was engaged in selling the pictures to admiring strangers.

She had already become a ripe apple waiting to be plucked in at least one other artist's fancy. Boldini, the Italian, painted in the manner of a magazine illustrator with swift, melting line and splashy palette. He was so notorious a woman chaser that she extracted his promise in advance that he would not lay hands on her. As she sat in his studio, striving not to move, she laughed to see the chubby little man wrestling to check his impulses and keep his pledge. His portrait enchanted her. She thought it would look well in her dining room, but for familial reasons it would have to be enlarged to include her son Ivor.

She was on safer ground posing for Ambrose McEvoy, an Englishman, companion of Augustus John and a society favorite with his paintings of upper-crust patrons in oils and in line and wash. The succession of sittings demanded to produce three sensitive portraits of her brought no invitation to romance.

Sunny was not blind to Consuelo's beauty or the attraction she had for other men, though he was as silent on the subject as on most other things in her company. He chose an odd moment, she thought, to talk about it, possibly because death was in the air. In the dusk of a January evening, Queen Victoria died at Osborne with Alexandra beside her, clasping her hand. Draped in black from head to toe, Consuelo rode with Sunny in a Great Western Railway special to the private siding in Windsor for the funeral in St. George's Chapel.

"If I die," he brooded, "I see you will not remain a widow long."

When the ceremonies were over, he saw fresh substantiation for his thinking. In the castle chamber where refreshments were served, enthusiasts swarmed around his wife, whose charm with the veil thrown back from her face no layers of sepulchral clothing could hide. Married or single, men competed to make their mark with a young woman still as slender as a debutante. Curzon, now Lord George and viceroy of India, was one, and Balfour, soon to succeed Salisbury as prime minister, another. For the moment Herbert Henry Asquith, the anti-Boer Liberal Imperialist, preferred her company to that of his garrulous and domineering wife, Margot. At the heart of the crush of statesmen, ambassadors, Cabinet ministers, courtiers, admirals, generals, and plenipotentiaries, Consuelo was the lodestar at the wake.

The new king, growing fatter and more irritable every day, continued to show favor toward the Marlboroughs. In no rush to be crowned—the coronation was scheduled for June of next year—he made the improvement of British relations with Germany a priority. His nephew in Berlin, Kaiser Wilhelm, had forecast that before the twentieth century was halfway over, England might be squeezed out of India and the Near East by Russia and the United States. Tsar Nicholas, in the kaiser's opinion, was an incompetent bankrupt, but avaricious American financiers would be happy to lend him money to expand his empire in Asia. The kaiser proposed a bargain: if the British navy would help make Germany a power in South America, and never mind the Monroe Doctrine, the German army would protect Britain's overseas possessions from this Russo-American threat.

With a possible Anglo-German alliance in mind, the king encouraged the kaiser to send his eldest son and namesake, Crown Prince Wilhelm, on a late summer visit to study life in England and stay at Blenheim. Consuelo and Sunny found themselves jettisoned into a week of international intrigue. Gladys Deacon, something of a fixture under the Marlboroughs' seven-acre roof, was another guest in the largely unoccupied guest rooms. Pop-eyed young Wilhelm courted the twenty-year-old belle from the minute they caught sight of each other.

Their hostess rated him vapid and fatuous but eager to please, which was of no consequence, since the niceties of protocol barred her from trying to cool his ardor. Warning her girl friend about the risks inherent in international flirtations did no good; Gladys' vanity was massaged by his attentions. All Consuelo could do was smile at the plight of the prince's companion, Count Paul Metternich, tormented with doubt about how long he would last in his brand-new post of ambassador to the Court of St. James'. As a chaperon, he was out of the running. Keeping track of His Imperial Highness was impossible when the count had contracted a stiff neck on top of his *tic douloureux*.

Gladys' lightning coup was complete when as a token of his intentions her suitor presented her with a ring, a first-communion gift to him from his mother, the Empress Augusta. There was no refusing him when he asked if he might personally drive Sunny's majestic coach-and-four to Oxford station on the day of his departure, though he had never handled so large a team. Perched on the box beside him as punctilio demanded, Consuelo was tensed to grab the reins if the grays bolted. Sunny dispatched a mounted groom as advance guard, tooting on a brass

horn to give warning of what was coming down the road behind
him. Wilhelm panicked the count by fixing his eyes for most of
the journey on the serene Hellenic face of Gladys, bracketed between Sunny and Metternich on the rear seat. They all survived
with nothing worse than near misses as they passed farm wagons, pony traps and other better managed equipages. Wilhelm
was still gawking at Gladys as the train pulled out for Paddington.

A momentary chill settled over Anglo-German relations when
his parents learned what was afoot. Through a courtier, the kaiser wrote to Consuelo, asking her immediate help in retrieving
the ring, a tricky assignment. So far as Gladys was concerned
the ring was hers to hold on to, a deserved tribute to her charms.
Perhaps the gift could lead to something more substantial, even
a marriage that would make her a princess. Consuelo was neces-
sarily firm. Gladys must do as she was told and disabuse herself
of impossible dreams. "It was," said Consuelo, "a foolish and
completely futile conquest." Gladys bowed to imperial indignation. There would be future conquests as facile as this.

In an age when reporters must apply for information at the
servants' entrance, not a line about the blighted romance appeared in British newspapers, but in Paris a year later *Le Matin*
got hold of the story. By then, the king's opinion of his nephew's
scheme had soured. Edward VII was proving much fonder of
the French again, and Consuelo could cease pondering whether
the Marlboroughs had unwittingly taken another hand in
changing history.

During the winter after Wilhelm's punctured romance, the
duke and duchess traveled to Russia to welcome in the New
Year according to the calendar of the Orthodox Church. It was
a social, not a diplomatic mission, but they would not set off for
St. Petersburg without the king's approval, and his delightful
friends the Marlboroughs would be asked for an accounting of
their expedition to satisfy his hunger for every scrap of information on the international scene. Sunny fussed over preparations
for the journey in the same irritating, pernickety fashion as
when he was outfitting her for her role as his duchess. She must
buy a new wardrobe of Paris fashions and more lavish jewelry in
order to hold her own among the Russian nobility. To guard her

treasure trove, a detective must be added to the retinue of friends, valets and ladies' maids who would accompany them and their monogrammed trunks.

Kaiser Wilhelm had come close to the truth in describing the tsar as a bankrupt. In the matter of hard cash available, the Vanderbilts outweighed the Romanovs. Nicholas' private coffers were usually empty. On his $12,000,000 a year he had to maintain seven palaces, a staff of fifteen hundred, his railroad train, his yachts, five theaters, hospitals, orphanages, homes for the blind, and the imperial ballet, traditional supplier of mistresses for the tsar and his uncles, sons, and nephews. Thanks to Willie, Consuelo and Sunny each enjoyed the same annual $100,000 that Nicholas allowed every grand duke in his family.

Russia depressed Consuelo from the start with its interminable winter nights and dreary landscape blanketed with constantly falling snow. Wherever she traveled, Paris was the measure of any city, and the avenues of St. Petersburg fell short of that mark. She stifled in their archaic, airless hotel suite, awaiting the day she would be invited inside a Russian household instead of to embassy parties, where diplomats of all nations fawned on her, even the misogynous Count Lamsdorf, the tsar's foreign minister.

She found herself caught between two worlds opposed to each other like a nutcracker's claws. She wore her pearls, tiara and white satin belted with diamonds to venture her first mazurka in the arms of Grand Duke Michael, brother of the tsar, under the sparkling chandeliers of the Winter Palace—and on the snow-laden pavements outside the markets she saw shabbily clad women standing in line for food. She philandered with bemedaled aristocrats, typically autocratic and imperious, and she thought of the beggars who shivered in rags on the icy streets.

She learned at one exclusive ball that Nicholas would be her companion at supper. In the six years of his reign, he had dashed the hopes of Russian liberals and challenged dissenters like the exiled Vladimir Ulianov, who called the tsar "Nicholas the Hangman" and himself "Lenin," to overthrow the monarchy. "I shall maintain the principle of autocracy," the new tsar had said, "just as firmly and unflinchingly as it was preserved by my unforgettable dead father." Over the soup and caviar, stur-

geon and game, Consuelo, unabashed, spoke up in favor of reform to soft-faced Nicholas, the only man alive who could set
the wheels in motion.

Why didn't he give his country a taste of democracy? Because
this land of his was not ready for it, he replied. She was interested in the working of his Cabinet. She gathered that he had none
and ascribed that to his dread of men stronger than himself, a
common failing among despots, she thought. He had another,
less debilitating weakness which he shared in those days with
other royalty: might he exchange photographs with Consuelo as
souvenirs of this evening? All in all, she concluded he was "pitiful." She never did meet his wife, who was Alexandra's niece,
the Tsarina Alexandra; Consuelo faulted her for being antiso-
cial in her domination of him.

The Marlboroughs spent some days sightseeing in Moscow—
another city hopelessly inferior to Paris in the duchess' assessment—and then, without regret on her part, returned to a London soon to be brimming over with everyone of note in the
Almanach de Gotha arriving to see Edward crowned in Westminster Abbey.

Duke and duchess went into rehearsal for their performances
in the ceremonial, he as Lord High Steward who would carry
the crown itself on a crimson cushion, she as one of the quartet
of ladies, each of them a duchess, chosen by Alexandra to bear a
canopy over her head as called for in the ritual. Consuelo's common sense warned her that the two rear bearers were bound to
trip over the long trains of the pair in front, a point overlooked
by the overawed organizers. A meeting in council yielded the
remedy: four pages would pinch hit for the ladies until the
queen was seated, at which time the awning would be handed
over to the duchesses.

The June 26 coronation was designed to be a pageant surpassing anything any Briton alive had witnessed. The climax would
be followed by a great procession of kings and queens, emirs and
maharajahs. They provided a curtain-raiser in their early appearances on the streets of the city in their state coaches with escorts of cavalry. In the first part of the month, the Marlboroughs
were deluged with invitations to dine and dance every night at
Buckingham Palace, an embassy or one of the town houses of

their caste. Then at a palace banquet for two hundred guests held seventy-two hours before the day of the ceremony Alexandra made her entrance without the king. He had been groaning for the past week, "I will go to the abbey though it kills me." Now he lay upstairs in bed, awaiting tomorrow's operation for perityphlitis, which his doctors knew could not be postponed. The next day's dress rehearsal in the abbey was transformed into a service of prayers; his life was in the balance.

Recovery came about so fast and smoothly that his crowning was reprogrammed for August 9. It would be shorn of much of the intended glamour and most of his fellow sovereigns, who had made their way home, but it would be British to the core. Consuelo that morning had the foresight to anticipate the needs of the day ahead: a bar of chocolate slipped into a pocket of her fur-trimmed, red velvet robes to quell her appetite during the five hours or more spent on a hard, wooden chair, a headpiece fitted into her tiara so that it would fit snugly when all the duchesses donned theirs in tribute a second or so after Alexandra was crowned.

This duchess, an iconoclast, was amused by the spectacle of some diminutive noble lords swamped by the moth-balled robes of some huskier ancestors. She smiled to see others whose ancient coronets slid down to their chins, but the fanfare of silver trumpets and the voices of the choir filled her with a different feeling. She thought her idol, Alexandra, had never appeared lovelier than in this dress of gold-embroidered Indian gauze as she knelt to be anointed under the canopy which the duchess was helping to hold.

She was aghast when a trickle of holy oil from the spoon in the Archbishop of York's trembling hand ran down the queen's unwrinkled forehead. It was only afterward that Consuelo learned this was no accident. Alexandra supplemented her thinning hair with a wig; she had begged her anointer in advance to make sure some of the liquid touched her body, not merely the *toupet*. At the instant the crown was lowered onto her coiffure, she had no more loyal subject than Consuelo, who sensed patriotism for England surging through her bones. The feeling was soon gone, replaced by puritanical dismay at the realization that the throng revered Edward as though he were *God!*

"It shocked my sense of fitness . . ." she noted primly afterward, "but then I was not English," and she intended to cling to being a transplanted American.

A day had arrived in Russia when Consuelo caught what seemed to be nothing more serious than a heavy, lingering cold, but infection spread into her ears. She awoke one morning in her hotel room to discover her hearing was fading. The unexpected quietness frightened her, but Sunny made a joke of it when he talked with her.

A new bond grew with Alexandra, who had been deaf for years. So far, Consuelo had done nothing about it, though she was increasingly cut off from the world by her condition, incapable of taking part in the interchange of jokes and gossip that delighted her husband. Hearing of Consuelo's plight moved the queen to act. The duchess must join her for afternoon lessons in lip-reading in a palace sitting room.

Consuelo cherished no great hope for the sessions, but there was no refusing. She went to class gowned and bejeweled in her best, to sit by Alexandra, taking turns in guessing what the overawed instructor was saying with exaggerated movements of his mouth. She did her conscientious utmost to be a good pupil, but the queen's span of attention was limited. Little progress had been made when Alexandra abandoned the effort and canceled the course. Her fellow pupil set her heart on finding a cure, not a palliative, for being deaf.

The year brought an unexpected fragment of news from America. Winty Rutherfurd, aged forty, had finally married, his bride a girl named Alice Morton. Consuelo had not broken her promise to herself. Much less than attempt to see him, she had not been known to mention him. His marriage also passed without comment from her. He belonged to the past that could only be buried.

IX

Worlds Apart

It had become a strain to make sure she understood what English voices, soft and swift, were saying when, toward the close of the year, she sailed with Sunny to India. The king-emperor was enthroned in England; now the coronation must be celebrated at an Indian durbar to impress his eminence over every inhabitant there, from the maharajahs and nabobs to the untouchables who swept the streets.

The viceroy, Curzon, invited the Marlboroughs out with more than four dozen other distinguished friends to see the spectacle he was about to stage in Delhi, old capital of the Mogul empire on a bank of the Jumna River. In his brief meetings with her, he had been drawn toward Consuelo as she was to his wife Mary, the Chicago promoter's daughter. The duchess noted two major variances between herself and Mary: Mary loved Curzon as he loved her, and she willingly submerged her life in her husband's in a fashion impossible for Consuelo.

A Pacific & Orient steamship carried the party to Bombay, where a vice-regal train waited to take them to the site of the gala. If memories of Winty troubled the duchess, she successfully supressed them; her fellow passengers, peers and commoners, were exceptionally agreeable in their holiday mood.

Curzon of Kedleston drove himself like a man chased by demons, forcing himself by sheer willpower into ceaseless work, writing, attention to detail and violent physical exercise in spite of a bowed spine, a relic of his days as an Oxford undergraduate.

In Consuelo's cool assessment, he deliberately chose to undertake more than a strong man's labor as an anodyne for pain.

"It was a weakness," she concluded primly, "he never learned to cure." Eldest son of the rector of Kedleston, Derbyshire, his childhood, as his friend Harold Nicolson described it, had been "disciplined, narrowed, intimidated, uncomforted, and cold." Not unlike her own. But she was liberating herself from the past while he, she felt, was still a prisoner of his upbringing. In his king's name, he governed India like a Caesar in power, pageantry, and disdain for criticism, delving into the minutiae of a dinner menu and projects as grandiose as the setting up of an entire new province, the North-West Frontier, to impose temporary peace on warring tribesmen. Delhi was called Shahjahanabad by its population after an ancient emperor, Shah Jahan, who reconstructed it from ruin. At present it overflowed with Indians of all castes eager to attend the durbar. With a wave of a wand, the viceroy had created a satellite city of sumptuous tents to accommodate his English guests. A servant burst in by accident on Consuelo as she soaked in the wooden tub installed in one section of the Marlboroughs' silk pavilion. She reacted as calmly as any British memsahib accustomed to thinking of dark-skinned menials as pieces of furniture, until she noticed the anguish in his eyes. Had she been a local lady of quality, she was told, he would have been flogged for his mistake.

She was borne away by the fantasies of a military review; columns of swarthy infantry in turbans and scarlet tunics, white-daubed elephants wearing jeweled pendants on their wrinkled foreheads, ambling camels trained in obedience like their uniformed drivers, regimental bands blaring the same tunes their white comrades played and marched to at home, rainbow-robed princes on Arab horses. Caught again between two worlds, one that ruled and the other that was subjugated, she understood what prompted one of the maharajahs on parade to turn Curzon's face pale by declining to pay respect to the conquerors' proconsul.

The most enduring memory left by the great durbar was not of Delhi itself within its miles of Shah Jahan's crumbling walls. His battlemented palace on the waterfront left no deeper mark than the pillared hall of red sandstone which had once contained the fabulous Peacock Throne, inlaid with sapphires,

emeralds, rubies, and pearls, a gewgaw valued at $30,000,000.
What she remembered best was sitting high in a tower of the
Great Mosque, with its domes of white marble and court paved
with granite and marble, one of the largest Mohammedan buildings in the world yet too small to accommodate its congregations
of fifteen thousand, which overflowed into the courtyard to
kneel and pray. The night's fireworks were a salute to Edward.
The first rocket was as eloquent to her as "The Star-Spangled
Banner." In its dazzling light, she could see an ocean of awed
faces beneath her. She felt their hearts were also upturned to
her in search of—what? Hope, perhaps; she could not put it into
words.

On their return, Sunny was offered the opportunity to enter
public life; he was going to accept it, and she was glad. Service in
South Africa had broadened his perspectives. The potentials of
the whole continent, four million square miles of it under British domination, fascinated him. The appointment as under
secretary for the colonies in Balfour's government was nothing
extraordinary, but it was a good place to start, and the work
would lie close to his sympathies.

He and his immediate superior, Alfred Lyttelton, saw eye to
eye. The colonial secretary was another product of Trinity College, Cambridge, a first-class cricketer, a master at most kinds of
ball game—football, fives, rackets—and at tennis a champion.
As an official civilian investigator, he had been in former Boer
territory at the same time as Sunny. In common with other British rich, the duke had hoped that income taxes, escalated to pay
for the war, would soon be reduced to a more tolerable level, but
mine owners of the Rand, with their property won back for them
by British troops, refused to share in the cost.

Victory had supposedly opened up South Africa for immigrants from Britain seeking new lives as farmers in the same way
that the United States cavalry had cleared Western Indians from
the homesteaders' path. But the British plan had gone awry.
Too few blacks could be dragooned into the gold and diamond
fields to get the mines restarted, so Balfour allowed the owners
to import not Britons but Chinese under conditions which critics like Consuelo judged were akin to slavery. The newcomers
were segregated in compounds and forbidden to hold property
or to work except as coolie labor. They had no legal rights, and

the men who shipped them in were required to ship them out as soon as their labor contracts expired.

But a Colonial Office job might lead to bigger things for Sunny, and Consuelo was willing to do her share in all the entertaining it entailed. Everything would be easier if they had their own house in town instead of being constantly compelled to look for rentals. This was the point at which she mentioned the situation to Willie, who promptly provided the funds for a handsome gray stone mansion, large enough to house a bank in later years.

Willie had surprised himself more than his daughter with his newfound ability to understand some of the forces that had made him what he was. "My life," he decided, "was never destined to be quite happy. It was laid out along lines which I could not foresee, almost from earliest childhood. It has left me with nothing to hope for, with nothing definite to seek or strive for. Inherited wealth is a real handicap to happiness. It is as certain death to ambition as cocaine is to morality."

Well into his fifties now, he reflected, "If a man makes money, no matter how much, he finds a certain happiness in its possession, for in the desire to increase his business, he has a constant use for it. But the man who inherits it has none of this. The first satisfaction, and the greatest, that of building the foundation of a fortune, is denied him. He must labor, if he does labor, simply to add to an oversufficiency."

Some of his melancholy was lifting, Consuelo was glad to find. On April 25, 1903, she and Sunny went to St. Mark's on North Audley Street for Willie's marriage to Anne Harriman Rutherfurd Sands, who had four children by two former husbands. One of Willie's brothers-in-law, Henry White, secretary at the American Embassy, gave the bride away. Consuelo had no reservations about her new stepmother, a gentle, lively woman, by nature poles apart from Alva. Her father, she thought, deserved the change.

The Bishop of London thought otherwise. He supplied a foretaste of trouble to come by protesting that the Church of England must stand fast against uniting divorced couples. Willie was not perturbed. Forty-eight hours afterward at the Saint Cloud track, his horse Biltmore added to his master's contentment by winning the Prix Bataille, and on the same program his Marigold carried off the Prix Soleil.

With the latest donation from Willie, the Marlboroughs bought Curzon Chapel and the churchyard extending through the block from Curzon Street to Shepherd's Market, to have the church razed to make space for their new home. Outraged members of the congregation complained that this was desecration, certain to bring bad luck to those responsible. The duchess paid no more heed than to a wizened oracle on the *rive gauche* in Paris who once warned her that dark days lay in store.

"Marlborough House" would be the best identification for the dwelling, but that was in use for the property now owned by the king, who would never surrender it, affable as he usually was to the duke and duchess. Edward, with his needling sense of humor, joshed her over dinner one night about the chastising they were receiving from the uprooted chapel-goers. What did she propose to call her place when it was finished—"Malplaquet"? She knew quite enough English history and French geography to catch the meaning of the barb. Malplaquet was the French village in the department of the Nord where in 1709 the first duke fought what he called a "very murdering battle," the biggest and last of the Thirty Years' War that cost the Allied forces twenty thousand dead. She could only pretend to smile. "Sunderland House" was the name she decided on.

Her opinion of the cross-grained old man who ruled England had deteriorated. A woman who tried to erase every vestige of snobbery within herself found limited pleasure in the company of the greatest snob in the kingdom. The ritual surrounding every step he took irked her. He dressed her down once at a party for himself and Alexandra when Consuelo arrived wearing a crescent of diamonds on her hair in place of a regal tiara. What impelled her, he asked, to dishonor Her Royal Highness in this unseemly manner? He had a fancy for castigating any man or woman who infringed the dress code he imposed on his circle. Consuelo found it all unbearably trivial and unreal.

Dining with him and most members of the displaced Marlborough House set bored her increasingly. The chatter and gossip that amused him meant nothing to her. She could only admire the stamina of Alice Keppel, who knew how to endure tedium gracefully; Alexandra had come to accept Mrs. Keppel's loyal presence everywhere.

Consuelo set herself to withdraw from royal society as fast as

she was able. She had no desire to stir up scandal or bring the
king's displeasure at her impertinence ricocheting onto Sunny's
head to damage his political career. This disengagement must,
therefore be effected discreetly. Sunny was sure to feel affronted, but he would probably bear with almost anything in the in-
terests of maintaining the flow of money essential for the future
of Blenheim. So long as she made it obvious that the decision
was hers alone, he could be spared any blame. She assuredly
would not allow his opinions to influence hers.

What she must do was to establish an obviously distinct personality to avoid receiving royal invitations which, by the rules
of protocol, could not be turned down. If, by exhibiting a life-
style that failed to conform with the standards of her class, she
made herself *persona non grata* with the personages of the court,
she would be quietly struck off the roster of acceptables. She
would change her mode of dressing and look more like a busi-
nesswoman than a duchess, tread paths unexplored by her kind
to date, speak up for herself when the opportunity arose, even if
it meant seeing her name in the newspapers.

Though she hesitated to label herself as anything in particular, she knew what she was not. Self-pity had turned into a well
of compassion for what later generations would identify as the
underprivileged, the have-nots. Yet she was neither a radical
nor a Socialist. Shyness lingered on, preventing her from casting herself headlong into causes, as Alva was doing. The astonishing Mrs. Belmont was marching briskly leftward in her political thinking while she still frivoled money away on supporting
her usual bountiful style.

Even if it did carry a taint of Communism, Alva with a gift of
$2,000 bailed out *The Masses*, which Max Eastman and Floyd
Dell edited in a converted store on New York's Greenwich Avenue, when it ran into one of its recurrent financial crises as "a
revolutionary and not a reform magazine."

Her daughter went no further than to consider herself an
idealist. She had not encountered many of the same species
among aristocrats or had much success in converting any to her
creed. There was more hope, she believed, in cultivating less
self-satisfied members of the human race. She put a few of her
thoughts together in a speech written for delivery in the slums of
East London when she went there to open a flower show.

"The love of flowers," she said, "is emblematic of that striving after ideals which is embedded in every nature. Do not give up your flowers, and do not give up your ideals." She was anxious to avoid the impression that she was preaching Socialism. "Some people go around talking so much that one begins to think of them as heralds of some wonderful millennium when men will no longer be men and when the government will be perfect—in fact, when all that is impossible will suddenly become possible. One gets carried away by them."

An audience like this cared less about what she was saying than about the astonishing presence of a beautiful young duchess in drab streets of broken-down row houses, barefoot children, haggard women, and work-worn men. Even the language spoken at this end of the spectrum was different. She could catch perhaps every other word of their cockney dialect, and they could barely follow her impeccably crystalline tones.

She reached her final paragraph. "I am a great believer in the sound judgment of the working man and do not believe he will be taken in by such wild schemes. The wonderful millennium will only come about by hard work, not by talking. Let us root out the weeds of envy, malice, and distrust. Let us grow flowers of idealism, strength of purpose and goodwill." They cheered her as wildly as if she were promising Utopia would arrive tomorrow.

She wanted a French flavor for Sunderland House, so Achille Duchêne was diverted from his labors for Blenheim to draw plans for a Louis XVI mansion, to be furnished in the same archaic style. The long gallery on the first floor needed a bas-relief at each end, he told her, for decorative effect. She knew Sunny would be disconsolate if the first duke was not put on view above one entrance, but facing him was old Corneel, who she felt deserved equal recognition as the founder of a dynasty. More than that, it was a personal declaration of independence, guaranteed to raise snobbish eyebrows.

There was no shortage of them in the ranks of guests that Sunny's employment brought into the house. So far, her explorations of the English had been confined in the main to the apex and base of the pyramid. Here, she continually ran into middle-class men and women who aped those they looked up to as their betters. These "colonials," as she described them to herself, had nothing to learn about touchiness in protocol. A high commissioner was apt to adopt the airs of a royal highness if no royal highness was in sight.

She could not warm to these thin-skinned citizens who administered the far-off corners of an empire that stretched over 25 percent of the earth. Half the time, she was hard put to make out a word they said to her. She blamed that on their ingrained obsequiousness to the exalted, herself included. "Do you mind speaking up?" had little effect; they went on mumbling. At first, it was demeaning to have to repeat her request, then annoying, and finally nerve-wracking. She was entering a world of deeper silence, losing precious contact with humankind before it was securely established.

Lip-reading was not the answer. She would go to Vienna before Easter to place herself in the care of Dr. Isadore Mueller for six weeks of tormenting treatment that held no certainty of a cure. Bertie and Ivor traveled with her, along with a nurse for each of them and her own maid.

The baroque capital of the Hapsburgs was past its prime, but it retained an aging dowager's beauty, frivolous, discontented, easygoing, blasé. Armed with letters of introduction to aristocratic Viennese, she got caught up in the same kind of social swirl from which she was disengaging herself at home. She was taken for drives on Emperor Franz Josef's new Ringstrasse which encircled the cobbled streets of *alt Wien*. She attended uncounted performances in the Opera House, as ornate inside and out as its Paris counterpart. She conducted her sons around the museums and picture galleries and marveled at the towering Gothic spire of St. Stephen's. Each day, she presented herself at Dr. Mueller's surgery.

The method of treatment was to insert long, flexible wires up through the nostrils to reach and drain the inner ear with medicated wadding. Since anesthesia was impossible, a patient's suffering was acute at every session, while the knowledge that it would be repeated tomorrow and for weeks after that increased the tension. The pain she experienced may have explained her lusterless reactions to the city and its people.

Rich, well-bred Magyars were friendly, she found, but scarcely to be termed intelligent. They were fluent in several languages as a rule; yet she might have echoed Bismark in saying this was an ability most useful in head waiters. The ordeals with the doctor turned her thoughts inward. She looked for some crumb of spiritual significance in what she observed around her and found none.

At the Imperial Palace, she was introduced to the little, disgruntled old man who reigned over the remnants of his domain as the last tetrarch of the Holy Roman Empire. "I have an unlucky hand," Franz Josef had acknowledged once before, and she attributed his coolness toward her to the assassination of his wife seven years earlier, following the suicide of Rudolf, his only son, at a hunting lodge at Mayerling.

Gloom settled over her like a winding sheet when she saw Franz Josef again, the centerpiece in Maundy Thursday's operatic ritual of washing the pre-laundered feet of a dozen of Vienna's beggars in a parody of Jesus' deed as he knelt in humility before his disciples. In Rome, the pope performed the same rite with twelve bishops, but the English custom was more appealing to her. There, the king gave annual Maundy money to as many elderly poor as the total of his years.

Her time was wasted; the treatment was ineffective. She would return to try again with other specialists, but meanwhile she bought a hearing aid to hide in her coiffure or conceal under her hat. When the remedy she longed for still eluded her, she sailed for New York, where Alva and Oliver stood waiting on the pier for her arrival. It was an American doctor's turn to try surgery on her at his sanitarium on East Thirty-third Street. "The duchess," the official announcement explained in a masterful understatement, "has suffered from catarrh for several years." Dr. Buller had no more success than his European *confrères*. She would be deaf all her life and do her best to resist the desire to be left in solitude, addicted to books and walking alone in the countryside, imagining the music of birdsong and the rustle of leaves. She was then twenty-eight years old.

In England and in France, friends of hers were searching for happiness in other ways. Winston had brought a ravishing young American actress, Ethel Barrymore, to Blenheim as a prelude to asking her to marry him. He was rejected as he was by another girl he courted, handsome Muriel Wilson. On the other side of the Channel, Gladys was accumulating a long list of conquests. One patron of hers was the aesthetic art historian, Bernard Berenson; she was on the scene as a proselyte at his villa, I Tatti, in the hills above Florence.

She was also, in the language of the times, an "intimate" of Edgar Degas, white-bearded now and busy making lithographs of Parisian nightlife. A similar relationship developed with Auguste Rodin, honored by the city's building an exhibition hall devoted exclusively to his sculpture. Provided the men were artists, Gladys' tastes were eclectic. She attracted the Austrian poet-playwright Hugo von Hofmannsthal; the patriarchal Anatole France, his country's most celebrated man of letters and aspiring revolutionist; and Rainer Maria Rilke, who was Rodin's secretary before he turned to writing lyric poetry. In 1904, she promised to marry Count Hermann Keyserling, a budding German philosopher, but she broke off the engagement. Gladys was conserving herself for better things.

On trips to Paris, Consuelo sought out Gladys, and so did Sunny. Husband and wife were equally captivated by the sparkle of her personality and her sharp mind. The two women, heiress and protégée, had much in common. Consuelo took Gladys to the opera, where the duchess maintained a box. Gladys drew Consuelo into her circle of admirers in the ateliers of the city, knowing that as a patroness of the arts, the duchess would be welcomed.

Gladys admired and envied her friend simultaneously. Here was an American girl, a Vanderbilt, who had made it to the top rank of the aristocracy. Though there was no family fortune to support her, Gladys was determined to do as well if not better. In some respects, the two women were totally different. Consuelo was altogether lacking in Gladys' ruthlessness, and she was bereft of the vanity that one day took Gladys to a plastic surgeon for the purpose of beautifying her Grecian nose.

The concealment of Consuelo's search to correct her deafness amounted to mild deception compared with the secrecy enshrouding her bankrupt marriage. Discord between the duke and duchess had been obvious to friends and relatives for the last five years. Whenever they could, husband and wife avoided each other. In company, they made little effort to control their bickering. The dinner table sometimes became an arena, to the embarrassment of their guests, with duke and duchess sniping at each other until one or the other flouted all the rules by stalking out of the room. Rumors of estrangement began to circulate as early as 1901, only to be brought down by Sunny as swiftly as he could fire a Purdy shotgun. Now, after more than a decade as man and wife, neither of them chose to continue pretending all was well between them.

The heir was nine and would soon be off to boarding school; the spare was thirteen months younger. They would probably come through the breakup with minimum harm, as their father showed no keen interest in them and nursery rule inevitably made a nanny seem closer than a mother. In any event, both their parents had reached a pitch of nervous stress that made change imperative.

Consuelo weighed the possibility of divorce. The obstacles were mountainous. England was not one of America's western states where incompatability was sufficient. All an Englishman need do was establish his wife's adultery to satisfy a judge. Englishwomen had to prove desertion or actual bodily harm in addition to a husband's infidelity before they could win release. Half a dozen more years elapsed before a royal commission recommended amending the law to place the two sexes on an equal footing. In the interim, it was futile to go outside the kingdom to dissolve a marriage. In the prosecution of Earl Russell on a charge of bigamy before the House of Lords, it had been affirmed that a plaintiff refused a divorce in England would not be relieved from the guilt of remarrying by securing an American decree.

Albertha had committed the unthinkable when she went to court to untie herself from Sunny's father, but he was such a notorious scoundrel that the *beau monde* forgave her. Her daughter-in-law could never follow her example. Apart from being hesitant about stirring up scandal, Consuelo had no grounds for action under the law. Sunny had not assaulted her; he had not abandoned her; and if a Vanderbilt heiress claimed nonsupport, she would be laughed out of court.

The thought entered his mind that they might behave like many another exalted couple in a similar predicament, which meant staying together to preserve appearances while they pursued totally separate lives, accepting each other's right to choose new sexual partners. The king completely approved of such arrangements as a benificiary of them in his liaisons with Lady Brooke and Alice Keppel, to name only two.

His Royal Highness' response to Consuelo's unspoken but

effective declaration of independence from his court had been
to make it clear to the Marlboroughs that he would not tolerate
a breakup of their marriage. Like most of his sycophants, he appeared to take it for granted that she was observing the code he
had established and was engaged in affairs with other men.

Perhaps the most unlikely candidate found by the gossips was
apoplectic Lord Londonderry. One diarist of the day, Tina Whitaker, noted, "When the duchess was in Paris with Lord L., the
duke wired her he would not have her back. But the duchess
took no notice, and it was Lady Londonderry, her best friend,
who saved the situation. The personal intervention of the king
and queen finally put an end to talk of divorce."

Consuelo, objective in her judgment and selective in her
friendships, thought both the Londonderrys were arrogant
snobs. He, she considered icily, "was as ardent a champion of
the prerogatives of birth and postion as his wife."

The tittle-tattle also made mention of a new romance for
Sunny. "Gladys," wrote one of her set of aging males, "has nothing to do with the impending separation of Marlborough and his
wife!!! Who knows, Gladys may be Duchess of M. yet—but on
what?"

Irrespective of the king's views on what was proper and what
was not, Consuelo wanted a legal separation, cut and dried, with
full consideration given to their sons' future as well as the com-
plex financial picture of the Marlboroughs. Willie came from
France to offer consolation and counsel to his daughter. Over
there, his racing stable was chalking up records on the tracks,
and the Rothschilds were hiring Americans to train and ride
their horses in the effort to catch up with him. In May, his
three-year-old Maintenon had won the French Derby, the
Prix du Jockey Club, by half a length, and during this season
Willie collected a total of $123,000. His colors would take the
same race two years hence in 1908 and again in 1909, but he lost
the case he pleaded with Consuelo for reconciliation with Sunny.

The points he could raise when they sat together in Sunderland House were valid enough. Wouldn't she regret giving up
her position as perhaps the most celebrated duchess in the peerage? No, she would miss nothing of the pomp and privilege that
were meaningless to her. What about the investment of years

and money? Were they to be squandered? They must be written off like bad debts while she had enough years left in which to try to find happiness and give love that would be returned. Her father would not argue the sense in that when he, too, knew the difference between a bad and a good marriage.

Her cousin Winston's sympathies were all for her. On October 13, he wrote to his mother: "Sunny has definitely separated from Consuelo, who is in London at Sunderland House. Her father returns to Paris on Monday. I have suggested to her that you would be very willing to go and stay with her for a while, as I cannot bear to think of her being all alone during these dark days." Jennie was in no position to help. Her own marriage was already running into problems over money, which was short, and Cornwallis-West's flirtations with younger women.

When whispers about the discussions under way between the Marlboroughs and their lawyers leaked to the newspapers sixteen days later, *The Times* refrained from printing them. The estimable Tory journal did, however, make space for Sunny's immediate response on October 29:

"We are requested by Sir George Lewis, who is acting as solicitor for the Duke of Marlborough, to deny the statement published yesterday that a deed of separation has been executed between the Duke and Duchess, and that the Duchess will at present have custody of the children. There is no truth in either statement, and the children are in the custody of the Duke, at Blenheim, and are residing with him."

Sunny had to tread carefully to remain in the king's good graces, which was supremely important to him. The duke's job at the Colonial Office was over, lost in last December's election that threw out Balfour's Tories and put Sir Henry Campbell-Bannerman's Liberals back into power after ten years in the cold. If Sunny expected an appointment in a future government, he needed the king's goodwill.

The denial issued on his behalf was a sham. Twenty-four hours afterward, the formal separation was confirmed, and the reverberations rattled porcelain teacups in Mayfair and Manhattan, though divorce was not even contemplated at this stage by either of the Marlboroughs. A head count showed that to date some five hundred wealthy Americans had been taken as brides by European noblemen whose mode of living had been imperiled by soaring taxation. None of the women aroused the attention focused on Consuelo. *The New York Times* waxed indignant over the unhappy Marlboroughs.

> The same melancholy moral is to be drawn from the rupture most lately reported of an international marriage which is described and describable as an "alliance" that is to be drawn from so many preceding ruptures of such marriages. The moral in this case is more glaring and obvious than in most of the others. It is so for the reason that the present husband, when he was a bridegroom in expectation, gave out for publication that his marriage was merely an "alliance" and had nothing to do with the inclination of the parties . . . There was no pretense that the loving and honoring and cherishing which he was presently to promise for the future corresponded at all to his past or then present sentiments. This was strange language in American ears, especially in the ears of American girls.

The *Times* editorialist found only one thing in Sunny's favor:

> It does not appear that the Duke of Marlborough, having completed by the money of one American Duchess the reinstatement of Blenheim, which was begun by another, has taken any particular pains to insult his wife. It appears only that the money having been spent, an "incompatibility" has developed. But the danger of the "incompatibility" was of the essence of the "alliance," and the present state of the household adds another to the innumerable warnings against looking on marriage as a business transaction, especially as an international business transaction.

The newspaper had two of its facts wrong and appeared oblivious of another. The money had not run out, and work on Blenheim was far from complete, in Sunny's eyes. His $100,000 a year was not to be discontinued under the terms of the settlement which, as a quid pro quo, granted Consuelo a rare concession in giving her and Sunny equal custody of their sons. The boys were to divide their time between Blenheim and Sunderland House, where the carved likenesses of John Churchill and Corneel Vanderbilt confronted each other in frozen hostility from the two ends of the gallery.

Any number of people attempted to bring the Marlboroughs together again. Willie tried repeatedly because he knew his daughter in her loneliness sometimes questioned the prudence of the step she had taken. His visits from France to stay with her were one of her great joys, but she abided by her decision to exist without the duke.

Acquaintances among the English nobility argued for peace to be restored between the estranged couple for a different reason. The king kept court circles closed to separated couples as a matter of two-faced principle, and he allowed no exception to be made for his former friends. The exclusion fell harder on Sunny than on his wife, but she listened to what Lady Londonderry had to say on the subject over tea in the Tory stronghold of Londonderry House, whose flower-laden rooms overlooked Hyde Park.

Theresa Londonderry, a formidable figure, exercised more influence in politics than any other hostess of her day. Charles, her apoplectic husband, stuffed with pride like a turkey with chestnuts, might be a Knight of the Garter and a privy councilor, but in common with Sunny he had been deprived of his office of lord president of the council by the Liberals' victory at the polls. The shattered party could well use the services of dependable young men like Sunny. Theresa set about reconstructing the Marlboroughs as a team acceptable to the court and the king.

A dinner party in Londonderry House for Edward and Alexandra, to which Consuelo and Sunny could be invited, was Theresa's crucial move. After the ladies had left the gentlemen to their brandy and cigars, Consuelo was so eager to create an effect with Alexandra that she grabbed the coffee cup about to be served by the butler and, with a curtsey, handed it herself to the queen. In *her* family, she explained, it was the practice to treat royalty with the veneration they deserved. The manoeuvre failed. The doors of the court stayed closed to the Marlboroughs. Edward, the fountain of honor, was a stickler for propriety.

Winston applied his hand to the affair and pleaded his cousin's cause, an act of political altruism on his part, since he had crossed the floor of the House of Commons to take on Sunny's old job as under secretary for the colonies in Campbell-Bannerman's government. He met with less success than Theresa. Peevish with bronchial trouble, the king instructed his private secretary, Sir Francis Knollys, to ask Winston to notify each of the Marlboroughs that they "should not come to any dinner or evening party or private entertainment at which either of their majesties are expected to be present."

The snub put Sunny and Consuelo on a par with two Socialists, Victor Grayson and Keir Hardie, who by the king's command were excluded from a parliamentary garden party at Windsor Castle as the penalty for speaking up and voting against a visit Edward intended making aboard the royal yacht *Victoria and Albert* to meet his niece's husband, Tsar Nicholas, and listen to a firsthand account of conditions in Russia as Nicholas interpreted them.

Sunny's fealty to his king and his respect for tradition caused him to suffer more than his wife. He yearned to be readmitted to the king's circle, which she had long since tired of. The unexpected backing she received consoled her in her isolation. Letters from unknown well-wishers poured into Sunderland House. In a situation where friends and relatives tended to pick sides automatically, she was delighted to have Albertha as her principal Churchillian ally. Alva arrived to stay for a while, eager to stand by her daughter in any emergency arising from clashes with a member of the male species. Willie was on call when Consuelo needed a man beside her to host a reception or a party.

In spite of her family and friends, she felt her life was empty. She had not wrenched herself away from Sunny and Blenheim to resume the rounds in a society for which her respect had vanished. She wanted to make common cause with people like herself, idealists perhaps, but not political radicals in any sense of the word, as she continually emphasized.

She found what she was looking for among the dregs at the bottom of the social swim. The Church Army was a comparatively new religious organization, seven years younger than she. Its founder, the Reverend Wilson Carlile, had patterned it along the lines of the older Salvation Army under "General" William Booth, beginning by banding together a handful of working men and women, designated as "officers" and "soldiers," and training them to work as evangelists in the slums of Westminster, whose absentee landlord was the duke of the same name.

The bespectacled little clergyman knew these rookeries where poverty and crime festered together. It was no wonder to him that their inhabitants were godless outcasts when squalor drove them to sin and blinded them to hope of salvation. His chosen mission was to redeem them for the Church of England by recruiting his troops from the same deprived class of people.

Before William Booth's *In Darkest England* horrified his readers with accounts of men made drunkards and women prostitutes by pressure of the tenements, Carlile established headquarters in Bryanston Street near the Marble Arch where, put into uniform, men were drilled as preachers and women as mission sisters, to be recommitted to the warrens, the prisons and workhouses, carrying the word of God on bare wages paid from funds collected for the work.

Carlile, made an honorary canon, or prebendary, of St. Paul's Cathedral in recognition of his battle for righteousness, sent Church Army vans circulating through country parishes with soldier-drivers equipped to expound the gospel free of charge on a vicar's request. He set up homes in city slums to give destitutes "a fresh start in life," many of them out-of-works who, with their families, went as emigrants to fill jobs found in advance for them in Canada. The army ran lodging houses, employment bureaus, cheap food depots, old clothes departments, and a dispensary supplying free medicines.

Consuelo had opened Sunderland House once before for an "at home" to raise money for the prebendary with a concert and a sale of blouses and needlework. Now he wanted to enlist her in a new undertaking, saving men and women released from their first term in prison from going back to a life of crime.

The spark was lit. In her own fashion, she knew something of what it meant to be a prisoner. In adolescence, she had felt the impulse to dedicate herself to Christ and the Church. She had sensed there were things more vital than material wealth. She had an idea of what salvation might amount to, and she had learned, as she said, "To be punished for the guilt of others is essentially unfair." With her hearing aid tucked under her hat, she set out on an expedition of discovery among the outcasts.

BOOK THREE

X

The Greatest of These

Charity was becoming more fashionable now that the pharisaical Victorian age was over. The king himself made a point of spending three or four days every July surveying the obvious hardships of life in some noisome industrial center while he stayed in a house party with a neighborhood magnate who had grown rich on the profits of his factories. Edward had the necessary personal reasons for his interest in hospitals and medical research. The ulcer that developed under his right eye was first diagnosed as cancerous, but radium treatments cured it. In gratitude he induced his Anglo-German financial adviser, Sir Ernest Cassel, to found a radium institute in London like that of the Curies in Paris.

Over there, Willie's new wife, Anne, was teaching him some principles of philanthropy. He donated $250,000 to Columbia University, more than $1,000,000 to Vanderbilt, and a similar sum for a housing development between Avenues A and B in New York City, earmarked for victims of tuberculosis.

After Oliver Belmont's death in 1908, Alva gave most of her time and a good part of her fortune toward a different kind of purpose: votes for women. Her motives for taking on a fight more challenging than the struggle to make herself queen of American society were as intensely personal as Edward's. "My first experiences in life," she said, "gave birth to my belief in militant woman suffrage." As a seven-year-old in Alabama, she rebelled when little boys taunted her with being "only a girl." The memory still made her gorge rise. "No young would-be masculine bravado ever expressed twice such slurring belittlements of me." The day had come "to take this world muddle that men have created and turn it into a peaceful, happy abiding place for humanity."

She dashed off articles on her favorite theme for any magazine that would print them. The doors of Marble House stood open for fellow suffragists. She financed a national press bureau and leased an office floor on Fifth Avenue as headquarters for the National Woman Suffrage Association and the Political Equality League, its founder and president: Alva Vanderbilt Belmont.

In England, a duchess was expected to contribute no more than her name and a suitable amount of cash as a benefactress, but lip service and a check were not enough for Alva's daughter. Consuelo rented two next-door houses on a London street near Euston Station to fit them out as a commercial laundry and sewing factory with a day-care center attached. Wives of convicted first offenders could earn a wage there to support themselves and their children until their men came home. The duchess was on hand to end most working days with a prayer.

Nobody remotely like her existed anywhere in the land. She was rich, still young, beautiful, and willing to take on any project that promised to add meaning to her life, meaning which she appreciated had been absent until now. What she was doing was hardly philanthropy, she reasoned, but help for herself in establishing an identity. She was the one who benefited most from the effort she put in.

She was drawn to look back on what she had once been, and her words carried an echo of Willie's view. "The responsibilities of great wealth are often puzzling, discouraging and strenuous. There are many hours spent in futile endeavors to make the time pass—in self-culture, sports, frivolities, psychological experiences often dangerous and exhaustive, and much money, time, and energy is spent in rounds of expensive and luxurious entertaining that leave [a woman] empty and disheartened at the end."

The danger of mental decay had passed. Dozens of invitations to enlist in fresh causes gave her the feeling she might drown in the flood, but she accepted them. The Band of Hope, which preached the evils of drink and the virtues of temperance, went on her list. She found herself appointed the only non-professional member of the National Birthrate Commission, set up by the National Council on Public Morals to determine why fewer babies were being born.

The conclusions of her male colleagues enraged her. They were opposed to contraception because, they concluded, the world needed more people to reap the benefits of civilization. "Fertility," said a summary of the final report, "is closely related with social status. The more prosperous the social class, the lower is the fertility." The alarming decline in the birth rate was traceable to the improved education of women. Consuelo ticked off another campaign deserving her attention: birth control for wives and mothers.

She saw less of her boys after Bertie entered Eton and Ivor followed him. Ivor's heath worried her; doctors reported there appeared to be a weakness in his lungs. He had another problem in common with the younger sons of every duke as he grew up in an elder brother's shadow. In nurseries and schoolrooms, Bertie was deferred to as "the marquess" and heir to the title. Ivor inevitably was made to feel second best, the spare. The injustice of this brand of discrimination rankled with Consuelo, sharpening her attachment to her younger son.

With only school vacations to look forward to—and her sons would be with her for only half of those weeks—she wanted more to do to crowd her timetable and keep her occupied. Again she tried to see her problem in perspective:

"Domestic requirements no longer sufficiently employ either the modern woman's time or her intellect," she wrote. "We are speaking now of the woman who has servants to accomplish what in former days used to be her duty. Neither do children fill up her leisure. Public and private schools, governesses and tutors have taken away one of woman's most sacred duties . . . Her time is not filled and, failing more serious interest, a funny attention to small details will monopolize her mind. And this is what many brilliant women are apt to degenerate into from lack of opportunity and purpose."

She thought of herself as an intellectual, though not all her friends accepted that evaluation. They agreed she was well read and intelligent, but no more. Winston approved of her looks and her courage, but not of her passion to reform human living. He had grown to power in the Liberal Party, first as president of the Board of Trade in the government of Herbert Asquith, who succeeded the fatally ailing Campbell-Bannerman, and then as home secretary. Consuelo forecast greater things in store for him, but his wife, Clemmie, whom he had courted at Blenheim, was not so optimistic about his prospects. Until events long afterward proved her wrong, she advised him never to count on being prime minister.

Consuelo's depth of feeling for Ivor was transmuted into empathy for children infinitely more pitiable—the ragged, homeless urchins who begged on city streets. The Waifs and Strays Society sought them out, as did investigators on the staff of the chain of institutions known as "Dr. Barnado's Homes." Both groups had important places on her roster of worthy charities. Destitute youngsters were boarded, clothed, educated, and where possible trained in skills to earn good wages on the labor market. Sunderland House's gallery, large enough to hold three hundred people at a time, was an ideal setting for high-class fund raising.

It was also used as Sunny had originally intended it to be. Consuelo, on a path taking her up and down through society, liked to entertain in style once in a while. The morning might be spent interviewing wary-eyed men fresh out of jail, stigmatized by pallid skins and cropped hair; placing them in jobs was part of her responsibility. The afternoon could take her into the slums, risking infestation by lice and sipping strong tea from a chipped cup in a room reeking of dirt and poverty, as she checked into the needs of a despairing woman temporarily widowed by a judge's sentence. Before the day faded, she would be off to one of her Homes for Prisoners' Wives to look on forty or fifty children in the crèche and utter an evening prayer. She was in a constant hurry. One amusement of her friends was to keep score of her chauffeur's arrests for speeding.

On some gala evenings, she would slip into her house with scant time to bathe and dress. The lights would blaze and the servants scurry on the second floor to ready the reception rooms for guests' arrival. The king kept her written off his books, but the American ambassador, Whitelaw Reid, and his wife made themselves at home in Sunderland House. The Marquês de

Soveral, the squat, gossipy Portuguese minister who was one of Edward's most intimate friends, was another regular visitor. "The Blue Monkey," as he was dubbed, could be counted on to relay to the king the latest tidbits about Consuelo's crusades. She enjoyed his company for another reason: his voice was so loud and clear that understanding him was easy.

Nearly all the cosmopolites in her circle represented a link with the past. Surveying her guests at the dinner table one night, she could recall the roles they had played in the old days. Over there sat Lord Ribblesdale and his American wife, once Ava Astor, whom Consuelo knew as a child. The Marquess and Marchioness of Londonderry? He had ogled her on the sly for years, and Theresa had tried to talk her out of the separation. The Earl and Countess of Derby? They had been shipmates of the Marlboroughs on the voyage to India to attend the Delhi durbar. The other Consuelo from Alva's girlhood, the Duchess of Manchester, was there, devoted to her godchild to the end of her life six months later; a few years afterward her son William, the ninth duke, was declared a bankrupt with assets of only £200, including the clothes he wore.

That night, as on many others, Albertha also came to dine with her daughter-in-law. Sunny as usual was an absentee. Yet any number of people stayed close to each of the Marlboroughs. The same faces that appeared one day at Sunderland House would show up at Blenheim a week later, with the Londonderrys prominent on both guest lists.

Sunny had caught some of Consuelo's enthusiasm for public service. He seemed anxious to keep up with her, as she had once attempted to prove herself to him on the hunting field. He, too, was drumming up contributions for hospitals and presiding over meetings of the Waifs and Strays Society. He ran for election as mayor of Woodstock and, to nobody's surprise, won in a walkover. She noted that his term of office promised to leave the bailiwick untouched. On victory night, he reminded his audience that the first duke had paid for paving the streets, the fourth duke had contributed the town hall, and the chain of office around his own neck had been a gift from Sunny to the town fathers.

Whatever he did, his wife knew she would not allow him to influence her again. He was too hidebound ever to change, too obsessed with his image of what a duke ought to be. Hostile as he was to the Liberal Party, he bore patiently with Winston, but Sunny tackled any political critic who questioned the integrity of the dukes of Marlborough.

The Asquith government planned to introduce the first old-age pensions for ancients like Sara Prattley, whom Consuelo continued to visit when enough hours could be found for the journey from London. Blind Sara complained to her, "You have not been to read to me for a long time, and I have missed you sadly." The duchess accepted the rebuke. "But what a gracious compliment!" she said. It was as sweet as the words of her playwright friend, Sir James Barrie: "I would stand all day on the street to see Consuelo Marlborough get into her carriage." Asquith's budget called for giving 5 shillings a week, little more than a dollar, to men and women at seventy who had an income of £21 a year or less—approximately $100. Tory opinion considered it a dangerous and costly experiment. Consuelo could not credit anyone with such foolishness.

When Sunny voted against the bill in the House of Lords, he drew fire from an irate Liberal member of the lower house. The thirty-eight-year-old duke, he told a public meeting, already received his own pension—an annual £5,000 in perpetuity for every Marlborough dating from the days of Queen Anne. Sunny issued a correction by way of a letter to *The Times*—he liked composing carefully phrased paragraphs for his favorite newspaper.

"It is perfectly true that John, Duke of Marlborough, received a pension of £5,000 a year from this country for services which history has duly recorded. The pension in question was commuted by the British Government in the year 1884 for a certain sum of money." That was his father, George, trading the birthright to settle some of his debts. "You are well aware," the letter concluded, "that I am in favor of the principle of old-age pensions." But not of the terms of what Asquith called the "modest and tentative" measure which Consuelo was happy to note passed into law nonetheless.

From the deficiencies in the plumbing to the interminable meals with Sunny, there was little for Consuelo to miss inside Blenheim Palace, but the hills and woods around it were something else. The land of England was dear to her, if many land-

owners were not. Weekends alone in town or receiving some-
body else's rural hospitality were depressing. She shopped
around for a country retreat of her own and found it in a Tudor
manor house. With its steeply pitched roof and chimneys of
stone, half-timbered walls and thick rectangular windowpanes
sealed in lead, it fitted her dream of attainable perfection.

All this would be hers, the first real home she had made for
herself, tranquil and secluded from the demands of her new universe. She could be content here with no more than the companionship of servants and the owls who nested on one of the
oak beams that reached between the creamy plastered walls of
the hall. It was a joy to set about impressing her mark on the
place with fine oriental rugs spread on the flagstone floors,
French master paintings in the major rooms, crimson velvet
curtains on the windows, and everywhere flowers cut from the
gardens that descended terrace by terrace to water where swans
paddled with a dowager's dignity.

"Crowhurst," hidden in gentle hills, offered tempting solitude. Other people must be asked down to save her from slip-
ping back into the introversion of the past. Politicians, starting
with Prime Minister Asquith and his fiery Welsh chancellor of
the exchequer, David Lloyd George, were eager to stay at a
house where protocol was relaxed and guests were not kept listening for the sound of a butler's gong tolling but mealtimes, or
dragooned into satisfying the whims of a hostess at a bridge table
or on a tennis court.

Herbert Asquith was welcome at Crowhurst. It piqued Consuelo's sense of whimsy to have him there when he was struggling to break the political power of the aristocrats who, sitting
in the House of Lords, could veto any legislation a government
introduced. Sunny, of course, was a stalwart defender of the
peers' constitutional right to the final word on how the nation
should be ruled, which almost automatically placed her on the
opposing side. Asquith, a brilliant talker as he sat at dinner forti-
fying the champagne in his glass with brandy, found an ally in
the duchess, whom he prompted into starting a diary to record
her opinions of people and politics. She needed no prompting to
rattle the nobility with a public speech declaring that everyone,
rich and poor, should be compelled to work during set hours every day.

She was happier to see Asquith alone than with his wife. Margot fell into the category Consuelo privately labeled "clamorous outsiders," as they fished for invitations to spend a weekend with her. Margot's cruel tongue seldom stopped wagging. She bore a vicious dislike for educated American women, pitied their husbands, and did not hesitate to keep on saying so. Her polite hostess saved her response for another speech she delivered in Sunderland House after she took over the post of unpaid treasurer of Bedford College for women, which was collecting funds for new premises in Regent's Park.

"In America," Consuelo declared, "and especially in the western states, girls go in much more for a college course than in England. It is certainly not a fact to be proud of that England, for want of funds, cannot provide the training ground needed in order to prepare its young women to enter useful and successful careers. The old prejudice against women's desire to get away from the cramped and soul-killing position of the unmarried sister at home is still strong."

She made a flying start as a fund-raiser; one contribution alone, Sir Hildred Carlyle's 100,000 guineas, exceeded her target figure. There was no knowing what one could do, she reflected, if one tried hard enough. If she had gone away to college, her entire life would have been different. But regret over yesterdays was futile. Whatever tomorrow held, she was ready for it. She was confident that she had broken out of the shell.

As Consuelo's beliefs swung closer toward the Liberal left, Sunny hewed more firmly to the Tory right. The days when he had politicians of conflicting color to his true-blue as visitors to Blenheim were numbered. He had gone so far as to ask David Lloyd George there once, and now he was rousing the rabble in the impoverished East End of London by defending his latest budget, which replaced an earlier version that the House of Lords had summarily rejected.

"The Lords," Lloyd George thundered, "demand that wealth should be spared, that luxuries should go untaxed and that the burden should be put on the bread and meat of the people. The Lords said, 'Out with the budget,' and now the government asks your help to put *them* out."

The government spends dollars to buy food for Britain, he commented; then came the thrust that enraged Sunny. "Since when has the British aristocracy despised American dollars? They have underpinned many a tottering noble house. The Lords are partly made up of plunderers who came over with William the Conqueror. The aristocracy is like cheese, the older it is—" A voice in the crowd yelled, "The more it stinks."

They roared again when the embattled chancellor contrasted "the plunderers" with a man he had seen in Dartmoor Prison, "sentenced to thirteen years penal servitude for stealing two shillings from a church poor box when he was drunk."

Sunny chose a forum whose respect he could rely on when he made his reply. A meeting was called in Woodstock before the week was out. "Within the last few days," said the duke, with upper-class irony, "Mr. Lloyd George [hisses from the audience] has been down to Whitechapel, where, as he said, no peers reside and where, as he forgot to say, he does not reside himself. When Mr. George did me the honor of staying at Blenheim nearly three years ago, I certainly did not suspect that I should eventually become the target of his insolent and unsavory invective. What do the real poor think, what can they think, of this sham poor man, wallowing himself in every luxury which £5,000 a year can bring, while he stirs up the embers of class hatred?"

In this instance, Consuelo was not too far apart from Sunny in her estimation of Lloyd George. It was all very well for him to claim the government needed money for defense against increasing menace from the kaiser's armies and new navy as well as for the social reforms on which Asquith was so keen. But taxing great incomes, great fortunes, and every kind of luxury to raise £25,000,000 a year could scarcely be done without injuring the country and ushering in Socialism. She could not help feeling uneasy about the demagogue his followers worshipped as "the Welsh Wizard," who expected to be a future prime minister.

To her, Socialism of any variety, including Upton Sinclair's preachments to America, was "rather meretricious," though the unfortunates seduced by its appeal could not be blamed entirely. "The Socialist propaganda," she wrote, "has been called to life in a large measure by the neglect of some of those who occupy prominent positions to recognize the tremendous responsibility that wealth has placed on their shoulders."

The remedy she recommended was simple good fellowship.

"If made in the right way, men do not resent but welcome any effort on the part of the employer animated by a feeling of brotherhood to get into touch with their point of view. The Socialist fallacy dinned into their ears that what is good for the employer is bad for them and vice versa must succumb before such direct appeal."

She wondered whether the irritability increasingly evident in Sunny was his reaction to unrest among the working classes and Asquith's programs, which horrified the diehards. Sunny spoke violently and publicly against "the masters of Europe who inflict upon us all-night sittings and, faithful to the traditions of the Roman model, threaten with extinction those who exercise their right to criticize the performance." Yet it took only a word from Jennie Churchill to transform him, literally, into a knight in gleaming medieval armor, tilting not at windmills but for charity's sake.

She was in the business of fund raising, too; in her case, for building the national theater whose lack incensed men of the stamp of George Bernard Shaw. Her first idea was to hold a Shakespeare Memorial Ball in the Royal Albert Hall two days before the June, 1911, coronation of King George V; Edward, his father, had died thirteen months earlier, within hours of receiving a farewell visit from Alice Keppel and news that his horse, Witch of the Air, had won an afternoon race at Kempton Park. Consuelo did not attend either the funeral or the fancy-dress ball.

Jennie's current project was to turn a section of London at Earl's Court into the likeness of a town in Shakespeare's time, with actors performing every day in a replica of the Globe Theatre, concerts of sixteenth-century music in the Fortune Playhouse, an arena for outdoor country dancing, a Mermaid Tavern, pageants, sideshows, a full-scale model of Sir Francis Drake's ship, *The Revenge*—and from an altogether different era, a genuine tournament between jousting knights, an anachronism that drew the largest crowds in "Shakespeare's England Exhibition."

Consuelo could not resist buying a ticket to the Empress Hall performance to see Sunny under the floodlights, encased in a costume that suited him so well that he might have been born to wear it: dark steel armor etched with gold, a visored helmet over his head, a mighty lance under one arm, a shield bearing his motto, *Fidel Pero Desdichado*, over the other. There was no question about his courage; hunting with the Quorn at Melton Mowbray that spring, he had taken a spill when his horse balked at a fence and broken a shoulder blade. Peering down from her box, she did not feel inclined, however, to toss down a glove for this latter-day champion to tuck into his gauntlet in the tradition of the Middle Ages.

A fanfare of trumpets, hurrahs from the tiers of spectators, and two doughty knights spurred their caparisoned chargers headlong at each other. Only the colors of their trappings—the duke's an appropriate dark blue—distinguished Sunny from his advertised opponent, the valiant Lord Ashby St. Ledgers. Tanbark flew from under the hooves of their steeds as lances were leveled for the collision. The crack of splintering wood sounded like rifle shots as two flowers of chivalry crashed into each other.

When the tourney was over, the herald proclaimed Ashby St. Ledgers the winner, with a cup as his reward. But one blossom of chivalry turned out to be a false bloom. The stout-hearted, visored cavalier who clashed with Sunny was not Ashby St. Ledgers at all. He had sent in an understudy, Captain the Honorable F. E. Guest, MP. The organizers felt compelled to point out that the rules did not allow tilting by proxy. The trophy was duly repossessed and awarded to the truer knight, Sunny.

Consuelo could not waste time lingering around Earl's Court. Preparations had to be made for her next reception at Sunderland House. Delegates would soon be arriving from around the world to confer on the latest subject to capture her attention. Eugenics was defined as "the science of being well born." She believed with her guests in the right of every child to enter life without unnecessary handicaps, this to be achieved by applying the laws of heredity to breed stronger, healthier, brainier human beings.

Eugenists were fond of citing ancient Sparta, land of warriors, as an example, admittedly barbaric, of what could be accomplished when weaklings were disposed of in order to create a race of superior physical specimens. Consuelo respected Sparta's stern training of its citizens from childhood on to serve its goals: "Come home with your shield or upon it." "Let us hasten the day," she wrote on another occasion, "when unity of purpose and nobility of endeavor will inspire the people as in the heyday of Spartan glory to work for the supremacy of the State."

The thought was remote from Mr. Asquith's liberalism, but she was as capable of entertaining contradictory ideas in her head as Alva, who backed striking women garment workers against their sweatshop bosses while she was building a green-tiled Chinese teahouse roofed with copper dragons and curly-tailed dolphins on the water's edge at Newport, with a single-track railway carrying down food from the Marble House kitchens.

There were plenty of men who, Consuelo knew, regarded her as a near perfect specimen without benefit of eugenics. Since she was only nominally married, they viewed her as fair game for their approaches. She could not always stop herself from tempting one or two into making fools of themselves. One already married noble lord who had earned his title in the law assured himself that she was his when she blandly suggested they run away together. He went to London to make blissful preparations for their elopement by getting his professional house in order and resigning from all his clubs. She had to confess she had been teasing him. She could not believe he would take her seriously when work and her sons meant infinitely more to her than any fleeting affair.

A more prodigious suitor was Curzon of Kedleston, a widower since 1906, when his wife died of a heart attack, leaving him with three daughters, no heir. He had resigned as viceroy in a bitter quarrel with Lord Kitchener, commander-in-chief of the armies in India. Curzon served now as both chancellor of Oxford University and chief lieutenant of Lord Lansdowne, Tory leader in the House of Lords. He courted her at Crowhurst and in the brilliant company he invited to his country estate, "Hackwood," where he spent his nights writing in his room, held upright by a steel corset to support his bent spine.

There was no doubt in her mind that George Curzon loved her, as she loved him. The pathetic blend of mental strength and physical infirmity touched her heart. She admired him, but marrying him would entail divorcing Sunny, and she was not ready for that. It would mean giving up the life she had made for herself, which she enjoyed. She and George would be best friends. He would confide in her, weeping, as he searched for an alternative woman to be his wife.

She was overjoyed for him when he found a second Lady Curzon in an American widow, Grace Elvina Duggan, daughter of J. Monroe Hinds, United States minister in Brazil. The first time Consuelo went to Hackwood after the wedding, she found that George, in a gesture of caring, had chosen the books that lay on her bedside table. But she realized that as a wife she would have failed him. Two people as self-willed as they were could never have made a success of it.

Most of the men she came into contact with asked nothing more than companionship. There were few women in public life more beautiful and none with her combined charm and energy. The habit of self-assessment made plain to her the impact she had on her admirers. She would not argue that the best-looking woman in the British aristocracy was Lady Helen Vincent, tall, poised and haughty. This did not diminish the attraction that sparked between her husband, Sir Edgar, and Consuelo, but theirs was a meeting of minds. Edgar, diplomat, one-time Tory MP and lover of the arts, belonged to her father's generation. He did not give her diamonds but a house on his estate at Esher Place, where tennis courts and a private golf course were installed for the purpose of exercise. Consuelo accepted his gift as a vacation home for working women.

She discovered how accurate one commentator had been in delineating the discrepancy between British and American society: "Classes are more sharply marked in England because there is no single test for them, except the final, incontestable result; and there is more snobbery than in any other country, because the gate can be entered by anyone, and yet remains, for those bent on entering it, a mysterious, awe-inspiring gate." Alva had crashed through the barriers in New York; her daughter had slipped in through the gate and, without splashing a fortune around, was on the verge of repeating Alva's conquests.

The duchess would be a prize catch for any organization, the Labor Party in particular. Though she could not envisage herself converted to Socialism, curiosity took her to dine with gnomish Sidney Webb and his commanding wife Beatrice. First a clerk in the civil service and then a lawyer, he was, like Beatrice, an early member of the Fabians, a Socialist group founded with the ambitious object of "reconstructing society in accordance with the highest moral principles." This was the lure that attracted Consuelo to their door.

Agree with them or not, it was a compliment to be invited to join a gathering of cool-headed people who instead of preaching Socialist revolution advocated step-by-step reform of the system, starting at the grass roots of municipal government. Under their prompting, the unions had founded the British Labor Party, which had electrified the country by winning twenty-nine seats in the past election. Working men and women had a secure place in the duchess's affection. She wanted to know more about the Fabians.

The most controversial of them sat beside her at dinner that night. At first she felt as shy in the presence of George Bernard Shaw as though she were still an adolescent. In middle age, the intimidating, bearded Irishman had conquered the London theater with *Man and Superman* and *Major Barbara*. Even *Mrs. Warren's Profession*, banned for its exposé of prostitution, had been performed at last. Consuelo shuddered to think what he would judge her to be. A run-of-the-mill aristocrat stepping down from her pedestal to patronize him and the rest of this company of intellectuals like a meeting of the ladies' aid society in a village hall?

There was nothing to fear. As soon as his wit began to crackle, it was clear he was as susceptible as most other men—"utterly delightful" by her description, "a veritable Zeus." Either then or later, as their friendship solidified, he planted a thought she accepted as gospel: "You should live so that when you die God is in your debt." She picked up another idea from his experience. He had recently completed six years as a member of St. Pancras Borough Council. Perhaps she, too, ought to consider going into local politics.

At present, she could not wait for invitations to see more of this kind of society. After she had earned credentials as a sympathizer at the Webbs', she branched out on her own by holding a dinner party every Friday for the best brains in London. The recipe was simple: stir together brilliant men and beautiful women. The men, competing for attention, would shine even more brightly, and the women would have something worth listening to, for a change.

Feelings that she imagined had withered when her romance with Winty was aborted reasserted themselves; she found herself attracted equally by a man's good looks and by his intelligence. She rated Shaw, a regular guest at her table, one of the most fascinating males she had ever met, though it was a woman's brains, not her sexuality, that attracted him.

"Outrageously handsome" was, she concluded, an apt description for George Wyndham, soldier, courtier and scholar, the handsome, debonair secretary for Ireland whom people called the Admirable Crichton of his day. Besides working to ameliorate British policy toward the Irish, he was active in support of woman's suffrage, another point in his favor. William Butler Yeats, poet, playwright and director of Dublin's new Abbey Theatre, was a third member of her private Parthenon, "an Irish Lord Byron" in her estimation.

She loved to bring these pets of society together in her salon, the most sparkling in the kingdom, and they lionized her in return. She served them some of the best meals and finest wines obtainable anywhere in London, but nothing alcoholic, of course, for Shaw, who was a life-long teetotaller. Protocol was relaxed, but she had to be careful, nonetheless, about some of the seating arrangements. Shaw, for instance, needed to be kept a discreet distance away from another Utopian, dumpy little Herbert George Wells; Consuelo introduced him to the resplendent social scene, impressed by such novels of his as *Love and Mr. Lewisham* and *The Food of the Gods*, at a time when he was overlooked by every other high-flown hostess. But Wells and Shaw would lacerate each other, given the chance, in their duel over Wells' scheme to manoeuvre the Fabians into active radical politics.

Nobody expected to see Sunny at her parties. If she felt a host was called for to preside at the long table set with crystal, a silver service and fresh-cut flowers, she would ask one of the gallants who were always honored to substitute for Marlborough—Lord Rosebery, once prime minister but retired now from party politics, was among those delighted to oblige, asking nothing more than a bottle or two of fine champagne and a brace of attractive women as his neighbors.

Some guests, to her dismay, seemed overawed by her, the house and the company. John Galsworthy, whose best-seller

The Man of Property was introducing its first generation of readers to the saga of the Forsytes, floundered, ill at ease, quite different from another new arrival on the publishing scene, R. S. Hitchens, who had been landed there by the success of his *The Garden of Allah.* He was not shy about sitting down at the grand piano and rattling off duets with his patroness, the other Consuelo, Duchess of Manchester, a widow since 1892.

"Mrs. Marlborough," as some of her followers called Consuelo, felt tempted as some of these evenings drew to a close to hurry upstairs and jot down the scintillating talk she had inspired and joined in. Unhappily, she never did. In old age, she could recapture only impressions, like a painter relying on memory instead of photographs: handsome men in crisp linen and black dinner clothes, charming women in exquisite gowns, the gleam of silver under the chandeliers, serious talk of the troubles in Ireland and what Asquith's Liberal government had in mind for curbing the House of Lords, frothier conversation about the implications of the new books, new plays and new freedoms in a society in which keen ears could detect subterranean rumbling, like auguries within a volcano about to erupt.

She once made a list of the duties expected of her at Blenheim. "Distribution of coal and blankets in winter. Entertainment of school children in summer. Head of all village organizations, the club rooms, nursing associations, bee-keeping society, flower shows, etc. Will have to attend and preside at numberless meetings, visit hospitals and workhouses, care for the poor and destitute, get to know everyone and individual wants."

She updated the inventory with the comment, "In England the time is ripe for women to conquer new territories." Now she was involving herself in "questions of sanitation affecting food supplies, milk, water, drains and ventilation, education of children, child and female labor, administration of relief to poor." These were only a fraction of the things she applied herself to. She corralled donors for the Young Women's Christian Association, and Sunderland House provided a center for a campaign to curb the traffic in women recruited as "white slaves" for brothels overseas.

Under the banner of the National Anti-Sweating League, she

walked in step with Winston in a fight to set minimum wages for women starvelings who worked in chain making, matchbox manufacturing, lace finishing, and garment sewing in the hovels of East London that she knew so well. Her strategy provided a classic illustration of how she used her status at the top of the ladder to combat social evil at its foot.

The Establishment in its splendor was represented for the conference at her house. Gaitered bishops beamed on frock-coated politicos, freshly barbered captains of industry chatted with top-drawer socialites. They all anticipated a congenial afternoon spent over teacups, or champagne goblets for those who preferred them, while they agreed that sweated labor was abhorrent and something would have to be done about it one day.

Consuelo stage-managed a different sort of show. Instead of being called on in turn to express the customary platform platitudes, the conferees were compelled to listen. Twelve veterans of the sweatshops occupied the stage, some of them with half a century of toil behind them. She had them do all the talking. A widowed worker in a candy factory kept herself and her child on eight shillings a week—less than two dollars. A shirtmaker held up a sample of her work for a silent audience to see: "A dozen of these right out before earning ninepence [fifteen cents]." Working with her husband for seventeen hours a day, she could make fourteen dozen shirts a week and earn two dollars.

The act that was passed by an aroused Parliament doubled some women's wages. Consuelo was not satisfied. Another 150,000 women and girls needed the same kind of protection under an extension of the law.

For reasons of personal need, an inhibited girl, transplanted in an alien land, had forced herself to grow into a resourceful professional woman, one of a kind who were striving to improve life for their sex throughout the Western world; in doing so, $2,000,000 of her inheritance was spent. One cause remained to be included on her list: votes for women.

She could not walk anywhere in London without seeing evidence of the suffragists. Their slogan cropped up on every side. They chalked the sidewalks, paraded in sandwich boards, peddled their newspapers, picketed Parliament, marched on the prime minister's home in Downing Street and flooded the city with their leaflets. Asquith was unmoved; he was determined not to yield.

Militancy increased. Soon after Asquith entered office, two of the suffragist leaders, Christabel Pankhurst and Annie Kenney, were ejected from a meeting in Manchester and arrested for obstruction when they held a protest meeting outside. Given the choice between paying fines and going to jail, both chose prison. Now their followers openly courted arrest. In their cells, they went on hunger strikes. The warders' response was forcible feeding, strapping the women down while metal funnels were forced between their jaws.

Asquith, standing fast, announced that he proposed to introduce a new franchise bill "for male persons only." The suffragists stepped up their violence, smashing windows, burning houses, destroying factory property, chaining themselves to railings on Downing Street. The government answered with repression, spearheaded by legislation called the Cat and Mouse Act: a woman released from prison to avoid death from starvation could be rearrested and reincarcerated to complete her sentence when her health had improved. Miss Pankhurst, sent down for three years starting in 1913, was reimprisoned eight times.

That summer Consuelo witnessed a pilgrimage of women who marched on London from all over the country for a gigantic rally in Hyde Park. The processions, miles long, came tramping in behind brass bands, picking up supporters from the towns and villages through which they passed. She was not convinced that militancy was the way to win over Asquith. The forced feeding of women prisoners horrified her, but as a sympathizer of the Fabians, she believed in change by easy doses, not in organized efforts to pull down the government, and Christabel Pankhurst's contempt for the entire breed of men struck Consuelo as inane.

Alva endeavored to raise the level of her daughter's enthusiasm for sterner deeds. The redoubtable Mrs. Belmont staged a demonstration of the strength of the Women's Suffrage Association by marshaling a parade of fifty thousand white-clad members down Fifth Avenue from Fifty-ninth Street to Washington Square. Puffing along in the lead came Alva and the party's principal beauty, blonde Inez Mulholland, astride a white horse.

Inez was a summer guest at Marble House, honored by a fare-well fete arranged by Alva in the fairground at Easton's Beach, where midnight supper was served by white-tied women waiters. "I am in favor of employing waitresses at all large entertainments," Alva explained. "They are just as efficient as men, and they do not have the habit of waiters of drinking much of the wine meant for the guests."

Then it was Consuelo's turn to star in Newport. The call from Alva caught her in a mood of depression. By her own choice, she had taken too much onto her shoulders; she was weary and overworked. In this blazing July, the air carried the scent of danger of war in Europe, in which her sons, growing up without her, would soon be old enough to fight. To all intent and purpose, she had no close family of her own. In spite of the pressures she applied to herself, she was lonely. Yearning in solitude for a husband's love promised at that moment to be her permanent fate. Seeing her mother again might offer temporary comfort.

Women covered every square foot of the back lawn at Marble House when Alva, spectacles on the tip of her nose, stood up on a platform emblazoned with VOTES FOR WOMEN to introduce her solemn-countenanced daughter. The solemnity disguised the impish desire to say a few kind words in favor of men, and risk the jeers, but her mother would never condone such aberration. "Call on God, my dear," Alva once advised. "She will help you."

The duchess controlled herself and delivered the speech expected of her, a veiled criticism of Sunny and an endorsement for her mother. "Many persons wonder why wealthy women want the ballot. There would be little wonder if they knew the story of women whose sons-in-law have squandered the last penny. Legislation is the only protection for the wealthy mothers-in-law of many a young spendthrift. It is the only way in which they can save themselves from ruin."

She was equally critical of the tactics of skirted revolutionaries and "the Englishmen who favor letting militants die in prison." "Militancy will never win the ballot for women in England. If the methods of the Pankhursts and their followers are persisted in, I cannot say what will be the result. In America, the only militants are anti-suffragists, but women sorely need the ballot here, or rather the country needs women voters. Votes for women is a movement for the uplift of the sex, and I am for it, heart and soul."

On the steamy last night of July, her mother gave a ball in Marble House to honor her dearest disciple. Only the faces and costumes of the milling stream of guests seemed to have changed since Consuelo had entered Newport society behind these same walls. Lights in the thousands twinkled on the terraces, in the shrubbery, and around the new Chinese teahouse. Servants kowtowed—they were males tonight; corks popped; and Conrad's orchestra supplied more waltzes than ragtime for the younger ones present to dance to.

Consuelo matched her outfit to Alva's choice of *chinoiserie* as the theme for the evening. The dress was made of black velvet and cloth of gold, the headpiece of black velvet. She wore golden rings in her ears and serpent bracelets on each wrist. If anyone asked, she was Lady Chang, consort of a Ming emperor. Alva won the unspoken contest between the two women in her turquoise dragon headdress, on loan from a London museum, slippers studded with real pearls, skirt and tunic a warranted three hundred years old. She was Tzu Hsi, empress-dowager of the Manchus.

Less than seventy-two hours later, on August 3, 1914, Europe was at war.

XI

Away in a Balloon

After what seemed like a lifetime spent among them, the English continued to surprise her. Europe's war filled the front pages of American newspapers. German armies were steamrollering a road toward Paris, impeded only briefly by the ring of Belgian fortresses at Liège. The puny British expeditionary force—one division of cavalry and four of infantry under the overall command of France's General Joffre—was in imminent danger of being trapped at Amiens.

Consuelo imagined she would find a dour and strained England when a United States liner, steering a course through Allied submarines and German U-boats, brought her safely back to her adopted homeland in the second week of August. On the contrary, the land surged with patriotic enthusiasm. Most people talked of "putting the kibosh on the kaiser" by Christmas at the latest—it was as senseless to her as the forecasts of a quick victory over the Boers. She could not joke about an enemy they usually called "Fritz"; to her, Germans were barbarians, "the Hun," responsible for launching a cruel and drawn-out war which she believed would spell the end of the epoch before it was over. The lightheartedness of the English amazed her; they were equally astonished by her gloom.

Sunny, back in uniform as a brigadier, was one of the few who felt similar foreboding about the problem of defeating Germany. Anticipating that Britain would run short of food sooner or later, he had reluctantly given over a thousand acres of Blenheim Park to the plough for harvests of wheat, oats and barley. Cabbages grew in flower beds, sheep instead of machines kept the grass mown, and every likely man on the payroll was released to enlist. Voluntary recruiting was the order of the day until the draft began in 1916. Billboards plastered everywhere with Lord Kitchener's image proclaimed YOUR KING AND COUNTRY WANT YOU.

Extra income from the farming would go toward fulfilling the duke's insatiable desire to beautify Blenheim. As the bills mounted, he had already sold his porcelain collection and personally served as auctioneer to sell more acreage for new housing. Glorifying the palace itself was the justification for everything. "Blenheim," he wrote, proud of what he had accomplished to date with the help of Willie's contributions, "is the most splendid relic of the age of Anne, except Versailles, which so perfectly preserves its original atmosphere."

He was haunted by the fear that his labors would be in vain. The veto power of the House of Lords was shattered after Asquith and Lloyd George threatened to create enough new Liberal peers to ensure a voting majority. "It may be," Sunny added despondently, "that the time will come when democracy, in the nation's name, will try to recall the nation's gift. Meanwhile, on behalf of the family to whom this trust was committed, I offer my tribute of gratitude to the memory of the Queen by whose hand it was bestowed."

Consuelo conferred with him at intervals about the future of their sons, but the final decisions were his. When Bertie left Eton, he would enter Sandhurst Royal Military College for a limited course of training, cut down to four months in the present emergency, as an army officer, then serve as a subaltern in the First Life Guards. If Ivor proved fit enough he was to follow his brother into the army.

She felt she had always been deprived of their companionship, first by nannies, then by tutors, boarding school and her fractured marriage. Now there were darker prospects to be faced. In the trenches that stretched from the Swiss frontier to the sea, the survival rate among young officers was appallingly low. As the death toll mounted on the Western Front, she lived in terror that both of them would be included in the casualty lists. In the meantime, the sight of silly girls pinning young "slackers" with the white feathers of cowardice overwhelmed her. It was unbelievable that after a few short months, votes for women was a forgotten issue and her sex had stooped to this.

She could not allow herself to mope. The best remedy was the same as ever: hard work. As the structure of England crumbled, there was enough shoring up to be done for the sake of the victims of change to occupy her for a lifetime. Enrolling as she did to help the Red Cross was nothing extraordinary when ladies flocked to wear the uniform. Organizing an employment service to look for jobs for the 400,000 servants displaced when mansions were shut down or handed over to the government for the duration of the war was a typical Consuelo touch.

She was the obvious first choice to chair the American Women's War Relief Fund. In twelve months, her appeals brought in more than $300,000 from her compatriots to open up a four-hundred-bed hospital, and a contingent of New York nurses arrived to join the staff. Like the hospital ship *Maine*, she served under two flags. The Englishwomen who were setting up the Women's Emergency Corps wanted her expertise in coaxing cash from sympathizers to provide mobile canteens at the battlefronts.

The ten thousand who volunteered to help after Her Grace the Honorary Treasurer addressed an inaugural meeting in His Majesty's Theatre sent her imagination racing off on another tangent. Here was a heaven-sent opportunity. "A certain purposelessness and want of union," she had thought once, "have prevented woman achieving an equal place with man in activities of a political or commercial nature Especially in the middle and upper class, where woman's duties are reduced to overseeing, woman is in danger of becoming a more or less useless companion to man."

These women could be inspired to be different. When peace returned, the training they had received should be applied to continue the "long march toward the gates of freedom." She urged the setting up of a permanent register of disciplined volunteers so that they might be drafted for "congenial" work at any time. "The war has proved," she said, "that if woman wants to be useful, she must also be efficient." The spirit of Sparta hovered overhead like the night-raiding zeppelins, silvery in the searchlights, that dropped bombloads on the city. Consuelo opened the basement of her house as a shelter but personally stayed in bed, hearing no thudding of explosives or rattle of shrapnel from the anti-aircraft guns in Hyde Park without her deaf-aid in action.

She kept away from polite society; her private life had virtually vanished; public service was all that counted. She had to be *useful*—a favorite word—and seek for gold in the dross of war. The fighting that drained millions of men from the country was a useful chance for women to improve themselves.

Consuelo stayed out of the ranks of the militants, though Alva invited Christabel Pankhurst to the United States and organized a rousing lecture tour for her. The duchess was not sorry when Miss Pankhurst, staging her last demonstration, conducted a procession of 30,000 suffragists down Whitehall, chanting, "We demand the right to serve." Christabel subsequently got absorbed in religious prophecy, predicting that the Day of Judgment would soon be at hand. Consuelo reflected acidly that, if this were true, then a sword would serve the man-eaters better than a ballot.

The sheer numbers of women going out to work for the first time staggered her. Nearly 200,000 entered departments of the government, and 500,000 took over men's jobs in private offices. Almost 800,000 went into war production factories, learning to bob their hair and shorten their skirts as well as to operate a lathe or a winch. Women were hired to run trams and buses; 100,000 new nurses, 100,000 more employed as "land girls" on the farms—there were no limits to Consuelo's ambition as a recruiting officer for the army of emancipation.

Now and then, glancing back over her shoulder at the disappearing past, she sounded more like the mistress of Blenheim than an enlightened "new woman." While factory work, she told one upper-crust gathering, was certainly developing a love of freedom, it had its disadvantages. "A lack of discipline makes it increasingly difficult to obtain domestic servants. Can we not persuade a more educated type of girl to go in for nursery training? I think it necessary to raise the status of these girls and improve the conditions of their lives, probably giving them more freedom and expecting higher service." Hiring staff for her own household was a worry, when even the girl who chauffeured Consuelo's little French Renault was itching to be off driving a Red Cross car, and the turnover in housemaids reached a phenomenal rate of five a week.

Toward the end of the war, she would finally have to give up
Sunderland House. Shortages of fuel had led to life there dwin-
dling into a chilly, cramped existence in a few little rooms on the
third floor, with the heating shut off and the gallery opened only
for public gatherings when enough people could be crowded in
to counteract the cold. She lent the house to the government
until the time came to sell it and moved into a smaller place near
Regent's Park. Here she was much happier, living with Ivor,
who resembled her in many ways except in the matter of health.
Bertie was in the trenches, but Ivor had failed his medical. Until
he put on uniform as a humble lieutenant in the unglamorous
Royal Army Service Corps, he would be a War Office civilian,
subjected to humiliation on the streets by girls brandishing
white feathers. Ivor became increasingly special to his mother.

By her standards, a particular hardship of the war was her isolation from Willie. Where she was non-committal about America's neutrality, he was incensed by President Wilson's refusal to
commit United States arms and men against the despicable
Hun. Of course, he gave $40,000 to the American Hospital at
Neuilly, where Anne Vanderbilt's work earned her the rank of
Chevalière in the Legion of Honor, and he remembered the
Italian Red Cross with a gift of $200,000. But what aroused his
maximum enthusiasm was the arrival in France of American
daredevils, eager to take to the skies for France.

They needed training and recognition as an elite unit of the
French Air Force. He was eager to pay every volunteer's transatlantic fare and all other expenses, but only a seasoned professional aviator could tackle the job of organizing a squadron. He
knew the very man for it—Jacques Balsan, captain commanding
Cavalry Aviation and former balloonist.

Balsan had been acquainted with the Vanderbilts from the
time of Consuelo's coming-out ball at the Duc de Gramont's,
which he attended as one of the blithest young bachelors in Paris with a keen eye for a pretty face. He had not found a wife or
lost his appreciation of a handsome woman at his present age of
forty-seven, though it amused him to pretend he had gone
through one divorce and fathered a brood of children.

He had to be careful not to joke about such matters in front of
his aunt, Madame Charles, head of the *haut bourgeois* family of
industrialists whose cloth mills in the province of Touraine had
been founded, like the Gobelins' tapestry works, by Jean Bap-

tiste Colbert, right-hand man of the inescapable Louis XIV. Madame Charles and the rest of the Balsans were rigid Catholics who had no truck with divorcées.

Ballooning remained one of Balsan's true passions. The Wright brothers were still tinkering with gliders when he made his ascents in fragile wicker gondolas to rise higher than any Frenchman before him, a record he held for fifteen years. One test of a woman was to take her up with him. "It is impossible to know her," he explained, "until she has been carried away in a balloon." No one so far had passed the examination.

As soon as flying machines made their appearance, he wanted one. His license qualified him as number eighteen among his fellow pilots. In July, 1909, Louis Blériot made history by crossing the English Channel in a contraption incorporating wire struts, stretched silk and bicycle wheels. Jacques had bought his first airplane by then.

He'd had a foretaste of war in 1913, flying craft not much more advanced than Blériot's as part of General Lyautey's army quelling rebellious Moroccans on the plains of North Africa. Two years later, Balsan supplied the experience and Willie the cash to found the Escadrille Lafayette to join battle with Germans in dogfights over France. At the end of 1917, with the United States in the war and the squadron placed under American command, a grizzled but still debonair Lieutenant-Colonel Balsan, Legion of Honor, Croix de Guerre, arrived in London to take over leadership of the French Aeronautic Mission and extend his friendship with Willie's daughter, accustomed to seeing him during visits to her father.

She had invariably enjoyed Jacques' blithe companionship. In her heart now, she was prepared for something more enduring. The times provided a spice of danger as the romance developed against a backdrop of theater going, convivial dinner parties, and quiet evenings when Jacques captivated her with his attentiveness and Gallic chivalry. For nights on end as they sampled the excitements of wartime London together, German zeppelins hovered overhead, undeterred by the barrage of defensive gunfire that lit the skies or the steel "aprons" suspended from balloons that were devised to shield the city.

When Gotha bombers were added to the raiding fleets, the destruction and death below increased. Piccadilly, Eaton Square,

Warrington Crescent—bombs fell closer and closer to Sunderland House, and shrapnel from the anti-aircraft batteries rained on its roof as an accompaniment to Jacques' mannerly courtship of the prim woman who captivated him.

He had found her caught in a political web of her own making, a reluctant contender for one of the 124 places on the London County Council, which ran most public services in the community, from schools to streetcars. The Women's Municipal Party was her creation, assembled when she concluded that neither Liberals nor Tories cared a hoot about getting members of her sex elected, even though women would shortly have the vote at last.

Lloyd George had been giving thought to a postwar election, calculating that the bigger the ballot the better the odds would be on his being kept in power. If men serving their country overseas deserved a new law to include them on the voting lists, why not women also? Opposition in the Commons was feeble. Even Asquith switched to an aye, saying, "Some years ago, I ventured to use the expression, 'Let the women work out their own salvation,' Well, sir, they have worked it out during the war." After six months of hemming and hawing, the Lords fell into line. The turmoil of the suffragist militants ended without further fuss.

The Fabians and Alva planted the seed that grew into Consuelo's pet party. Her group planned to introduce women candidates as a third, independent force in local government, achieving their program by threatening to vote with the opposition against whichever party held a majority in the council chambers.

In America, where the suffragists' marathon remained to be won, Alva was queen of the National Woman's Party, headquartered in a $146,000 mansion she bought near Washington's Capitol. She still liked to bask in limelight. Her name had appeared in headlines again as the librettist of an operetta, *Melinda and Her Sisters*, that was undisguised propaganda for woman suffrage, with music written by Elsa Maxwell, future purveyor of bland society gossip in a syndicated newspaper column. Meanwhile, Consuelo, as her party's president, would gladly have remained in the background if members of her committee had not pushed her forward. The unburied desire to assert herself over

Sunny might have been an unacknowledged factor in her resolve to offer herself as a candidate. He was back in politics, a junior minister in the coalition War Cabinet from which a sulky
Asquith was excluded in favor of Lloyd George as premier with
Curzon second in command. Sunny took his unpaid appointment, joint parliamentary secretary to the Board of Agriculture,
as seriously as his obligations to Blenheim.

Even his sentiments about horses and hunting were put aside.
Cart horses filled his stables now. Since the new government
wanted to prohibit all racing until victory was won, he was willing to cross swords with any other nobleman in defense of the
ban. Sir Edgar Vincent, elevated to become Baron D'Abernon,
complained that the breeding of throughbreds was dependent
on keeping the race tracks open. Viscount Chaplin pleaded the
case of "most respectable people" engaged in the bloodstock
trade who faced "actual ruin." The Earl of Mayo foresaw irre-
trievable damage being done to the entire Irish industry.

Sunny dismissed all arguments. "At no far distant date, the
people of this nation will be asking whether they or the horse are
to be fed." Food supplies were in danger of being cut off by the
U-boat packs that prowled the seas around the British Isles.
"Five hundred horses in training require a thousand tons of
oats. That is the equivalent of 400,000 loaves of bread." There
were mutterings among the diehards about his flirting with
treachery to his class. Consuelo must have wondered whether in
middle age he was a changed man, but the idea had to be dismissed as incredible.

She won her seat as a councillor without a contest, since elections as such were suspended until the war was over. All she was
asked to do was satisfy a meeting of her constituents from
Southwark, a rabbit warren of poor houses and sooty factories
on the far side of London Bridge, that she was capable of serving
them. The strain of competitiveness in her rose to the surface.
Though she had not sought the job in the first place, her pride
would suffer if it was denied her. After an oration that lasted for
an hour, she was asked to wait outside the committee room.
Spirits sagging, she sat trying to guess the verdict, as vulnerable
as ever to rejection; some wounds went too deep for healing. Inside, the debate centered on a key question: how could a
duchess know anything about catering to the needs of working-

men? But her supporters convinced the skeptics one by one. A final show of hands told that she was the unanimous choice.

At the first postwar election five months later, she was voted in at the top of the balloting, and her devotees urged her to take the next step and run for a seat in the House of Commons. She backed away because her whole outlook on the future was in a state of confusion.

She had been a councillor for less than a month when, from a window in Westminster's County Council Hall, she watched troops of the Allied armies march in victory down the Mall. The guns in France were silent; the kaiser had fled to Holland. She gave thanks that both her sons had been spared while she mourned for the friends among the three quarters of a million Britons who had died to restore a peace that left Europe in ruin. The passing ranks of Americans brought an instant of pride; a deeper emotion was stirred in her by the sight of the French. There were not many of them in the contingent led by Marshal Ferdinand Foch, generalissimo of all the British, American, Italian, Portuguese, and his own country's fighting men. Of all the Allied nations, France had lost the most in winning the war to end wars.

Now, the veterans who tramped past the window behind the colors of their regiments sent Consuelo into uncheckable tears. She had a reason, not yet declared, for her emotion about a land she had known only as a visitor. France and one special Frenchman were linked in her mind. She had been afraid that Jacques Balsan might be recalled to his native land to fight more battles, and she believed that with him she could find contentment.

Jacques exuded warmth, wit and Gallic charm, whereas Sunny kept himself detached from humankind, denying the existence of emotion. Consuelo may well have set the pace of the courtship, but Jacques delighted her with his attentions—fetching a book from a shelf, opening a door in advance, surprising her with sentimental keepsakes, instilling the feeling in her that she was important not only for what she tried to achieve but also by the very fact of her being.

Jacques' tastes in the paintings to be hung and the furniture to be placed matched hers, and that was essential for her. He, too, could laugh good-naturedly at absurdity and shrug his shoulders at inconvenience. With his constant kindnesses he was capable of making her believe that the slate could be wiped clean of sorrow and that at heart she was young again. Physically, she towered over him—he stood no taller than Sunny—and in sublety of mind she was also his superior. But he was the antithesis of Marlborough, and it was impossible to contemplate marriage with another Englishman.

Did Jacques put her to the test of a balloon ride? No record exists to indicate yes or no. But in spirit she soared high over France and wrote as if she had seen it from cloudless skies with love in her eyes.

"I loved France, that country of changing lights, of smiling plains, of innumerable rivers. I loved the poplar-lined canals, the discreet villages where life was lived behind walls. I loved the wheat fields where peasants garnered life's sustenance. I never tired of her varied landscapes, from the orchards of Normandy to the dour hills of Auvergne, from the lazy Loire to the rapid Rhône. I loved her acacias and planes and lindens, the tapering cypresses and squat gray olives of Provence." In France, she told herself, she could even hear more clearly.

Balsan could not be suspected of being fascinated only by her money. He would soon be chairman of the family business as well as a director of other companies. Her intimates thought the secret of his appeal lay much deeper. He did not compete with her; of the two, she had the greater strength of will.

Sunny appeared to sense that the ultimate marital break was in the making. He had never wanted it. The war and his public career came to a simultaneous end. Lloyd George reshuffled his Cabinet and set about raising taxes to meet the country's crushing debt, nearly $32 billion of it, part of the price of victory. Great new fortunes had been made in industry, but landowners like Sunny had not gained from wartime profiteering. He realized he belonged to a system that had been destroyed. The society that produced him had passed away. As Winston was to write, "He saw with not unfounded apprehension that the world tides which were flowing would remorselessly wash away all that was left."

Chilled and saddened, Sunny determined to hold on to Blenheim for future generations of Marlboroughs at whatever cost. Whether that could be done without Vanderbilt income he did not know, when death duties were imposed on top of crippling income taxes. The letter he wrote to *The Times* only hinted at his troubles:

There are, I take it, two sections of the community whose activities it is intended to curtain and eventually to destroy. The first category is comprised of men with great sums of more or less fluid capital at their disposal. Money is power. Its transmission from father to son is obnoxious to democratic opinion. Hence it is attached in the name of economic freedom.

The second section consists of persons whose wealth is no longer fluid but is fixed in great homes and their surroundings. These fortresses of territorial influence it is proposed to raze in the name of social equality. But the owners of these houses play a part in the national life. It has been their pride to share the amenities of their homes with their fellow citizens and their happiness to bid their neighbors, as the homely phrase has it, put their legs under their mahogany. The new tax makes it impossible for their heirs to carry on the tradition.

Are these historic houses, the abiding memorials of events that live in the hearts of Englishmen, to be converted into museums, bare relics of a dead past? What of the probable future of the disinherited? I fear that when stripped of their duties and responsibilities they may be tempted to join that pleasure-seeking class in other lands.

Willie, taking his own precautions against the sharpening bite of American taxation on income and legacies, neglected to go to the aid of his embittered son-in-law, but as Consuelo prepared for divorce he made her a gift of $15,000,000 and set aside $1,000,000 for each of her sons.

With Bertie and Ivor provided for regardless of Blenheim's fate, Consuelo had to prevail on Sunny to cooperate in terminating their marriage. If he balked, it would be impossible. The blizzard of attendant publicity might wreck her reputation as the best-hearted of all duchesses, but it was a risk she had to accept. She intended to start a new chapter as the wife of Jacques Balsan. The desire outweighed any other consideration—work, charities, title, the esteem of her friends, almost everything except the well-being of her sons.

The attorney she chose to represent her, Sir Edward Carson, divided his career between politics and the law. At sixty-five, he had been Balfour's solicitor general, Asquith's attorney general, and Lloyd George's first lord of the admiralty before quitting that non-Cabinet appointment to become minister-without-portfolio. He resigned from that job in protest against granting home rule to Ireland; saving Protestant Ulster from domination by the Catholic majorities outside its borders was his life's main political purpose, with time spared to challenge any voting by women. She forgave him that. He was the most celebrated lawyer in the kingdom, a courtroom terror with a scathing tongue.

The scenario outlined for husband and wife to play read like a curdled comedy. A judge must be provided with evidence that Sunny was guilty of both desertion and adultery. Since a separation agreement freed a man from blame on the second count, the duchess would have to start afresh by returning to live with the duke, if only for a matter of days, so that he might go through the prescribed ritual of leaving her and mating with another woman.

Complying with the script, Sunny raised the curtain with a Monday morning note: "Dear Consuelo—May I come and see you for half an hour any day convenient to you? I wish to discuss something about the boys with you which it is preferable to do verbally than by letter. Believe me, Yours ever, Sunny."

Her reply went off the next day: "Dear Sunny—In answer to your letter, I can see you on Friday next at four o'clock if this suits you, or four-thirty if more convenient to you. Faithfully, Consuelo."

The letters were all that was required to revoke the Marlboroughs' separation in favor of a new deed they signed, covering nothing more than provision of allowances—Willie's money for Bertie and Ivor. The duchess declined to move back into Blenheim for act two of the humiliating performance. Sunny brought his sister Lilian, always sympathetic to Consuelo, as chaperone when he came to stay at Crowhurst on a sunless December afternoon. In these dying days of their marriage, husband and wife had decisions to make affecting their elder son.

Bertie, soldiering on as a captain in the Life Guards, was due to be married before the winter was over to Mary Cadogan, daughter of Viscount Chelsea and a lovely girl, in Consuelo's opinion, who would not be twenty until February. Had they wished for it, but neither of them bothered about such things any longer, Consuelo and Sunny could have been readmitted to royal circles; George V was less hypocritical than his father. The king and his queen, Mary, would both attend Bertie's wedding together with widowed Alexandra, stone deaf but still behaving as if age were insignificant. For the sake of their son, the duke and duchess agreed that secrecy about the impending court action was essential.

In the middle of December, Sunny stole away from Crowhurst, leaving the material evidence: "We have tried our best to amend the past and start life afresh, but I fear that in the long period of our separation—now upwards of twelve years—we have grown too far apart to live happily together again. I appreciate all you have tried to do during our reunion, but I am now convinced it is impossible."

On the same day, Consuelo's reply contained more feeling— or was it a sham?—than the law's requirements demanded: "Dear Sunny—I have received your letter. I wish you had spoken to me instead of writing. It seems a pity now that we ever came together again only for everything to end like this. It is useless to say more. I must go away and rest for a while. Yours, Consuelo."

Maintaining the pretense that they had made a serious effort to bridge the gulf was more than her health could stand. Her energy ebbed away. She knew she must go somewhere to recuperate, before they played out the concluding act of the comedy of errors, when she slipped into sleep in the midst of a council committee meeting with a sheaf of documents clasped in her hands. Her doctor prescribed a spell of rest outside of England, where the magnitude of the problems to be handled tormented her.

She went to her mother. There was no better refuge than the villa Alva had bought on the Mediterranean shore at Èze in the French Riviera and then, being Alva, redesigned much of it. No rebuke would be heard from Alva for her daughter's giving up both the man and the title she had contrived to capture for her. Alva was impatient with men of any description nowadays, aristocrats included. Men brought more pain than pleasure to women. "The wife of the multimillionaire and the peasant woman have a common ground," she believed. If the years could have been reversed, she would never have browbeaten her daughter into a loveless marriage. All she could do at present to relieve her remorse was to offer Consuelo her sympathy.

A London lawyer traveled to Èze on Carson's behalf to take

Consuelo's testimony and save her the trouble of making personal appearances in court. Toward the end of January, she felt well enough to go back to Crowhurst and resume the masquerade.

"Dear Sunny—While I have been away I have thought over everything, and you, too, have had the time to reflect, so I am writing to ask you to reconsider your decision and to return to me. If you will do so, I can assure you nothing on my part will be wanting to try and make you happy. Yours, Consuelo."

Unexpectedly, he let ten days pass before he replied. She could only guess why when everything so far had been cut and dried. Obviously, he was hesitant about declaring his refusal to make a last try for happiness with her. The reason had to be ascribed to fears for Blenheim, not love for her. Either way, it was too late to feel a shred of pity for him.

She received the following on February 1, 1926, from Blenheim: "My dear Consuelo—I have received your letter of the 21st, written on your return from the Continent. As I wrote to you in December, when we parted, I am convinced that it is impossible for us to live happily together. Yours, Sunny."

The day his note arrived, she went with her lawyers to petition a judge to order "restitution of conjugal rights." If Sunny disobeyed, half the case she had to prove to regain her freedom would be complete.

There progress rested on the morning they came by separate routes to St. Margaret's, Westminster, the noblest site in the land for a wedding. Bertie, a formidable six feet six inches tall, towered over the pretty bride in his full-dress uniform with sword at his side. The king and two queens appeared, as they had promised, to set the royal seal of approval on the union of the next Duke and Duchess of Marlborough. Balfour and Winston, Lloyd George's secretary of war, signed the register together.

Consuelo's confidence that the succeeding generation would be well cared for by Mary, the new Marchioness of Blandford, was not mistaken. "All those who come to be connected with Blenheim," said Mary on a future occasion, "feel pride they never really lose." Today, Consuelo experienced nothing akin to pride. This was her leavetaking from London society, from England, and her whole mode of living. In not many more days the secret would be out and the breakup of the Marlboroughs would be evident to anyone who understood the intricacies of the law, though here in church only the family knew what was brewing. She would soon be off to live in the house in Paris her father had given her, feeling as though she were ascending from the top of a pyramid in a balloon.

Sunny scrupulously adhered to his side of the arrangements. Reuben Butler, a private detective hired by Consuelo's lawyers, stationed himself on schedule outside Blenheim Palace to trail the duke and a female specialist in such ventures to Paris, accompanied, as the inquiry agent testified, by "lots of baggage, kitbags and large boxes."

At the Hotel Clairidge on the Champs Élysées, Sunny registered as "M. Spencer *et* Mme. Spencer," to be escorted to room 193 while Butler engaged the room next door. A French investigator joined him to corroborate his evidence. On the night of February 28, 1920, they saw Sunny leave at half past eight, the young woman an hour later. The demands of justice had been served. Sunny took a train to Nice to relax, his duty done. Here, the court's order for him to restore Consuelo's "conjugal rights" had been served on him, and the news broke on March 23.

Consuelo had only a few days of satisfaction that plans were proceeding on schedule before she was plunged into fresh despair. Willie, out watching his horses run at Auteuil, was stricken with a near fatal heart attack. He held on until July, still entering his thoroughbreds in every major program until, on the afternoon of the twenty-first, he canceled his entries from all events at Le Tremblay.

Consuelo and her brothers were with him when he died, uncomplaining. "It seemed to me," she said when her grief had softened, "that nothing ignoble would ever touch him." Not even Jacques could replace her father, but she needed him more urgently than before. They took the body back to New York for burial in the monstrous family sepulcher. Alva stayed away; she had never tolerated Willie's second wife, Anne, or those who accepted her hospitality, and she had no intention of doing so now. The reading of the will disclosed the breadth of the discrepancy between Vanderbilt and Marlborough fortunes. Willie's estate totaled $54,530,966.59. The inheritance tax of $1,934,571.73 was the highest yet charged in Suffolk County, Long Island. Consuelo shared equally with her brothers, Willie II and Harold, in an outright $5,000,000.

Once again, she went to Alva when the funeral was over. Her mother's fury to build was incurable. In Manhattan, she owned a new townhouse at 477 Madison Avenue, on Long Island a colonial manor in Hempstead as well as a neo-medieval castle at Sands Point that commanded Long Island Sound. It was there that Consuelo took shelter from the impending legal action.

In August, 1920, one more of Alva's ambitions came to fulfillment: Secretary of State Bainbridge Colby certified the Nineteenth Amendment, granting nationwide suffrage to women. Neither mother nor daughter found reason to celebrate. Consuelo faced more months of agonizing over whether she was to be released from her marriage. Alva's heart was set on moving to France and building one more mansion to prove she deserved the honorary membership she had won in the American Institute of Architects.

The duchess was absent, due to "indisposition," on Carson's word, in November when her case was heard in a London courtroom. The public benches were only sparsely occupied; interest in the Marlboroughs' quarrels had faded fast. Sunny, wrapped in an astrakhan topcoat, had engaged Sir George Lewis to deny the allegations, then instructed him to offer no evidence in his defense. Carson's fee was easily earned. He droned through the transcription of Consuelo's deposition and called on Reuben Butler as a witness; Sunny grinned at the description of the night in Paris with an unnamed *femme fatale*. After twenty minutes, Mr. Justice Horridge granted the duchess costs and a decree nisi. Unless the judgment was to be contested during the following six months, she could be married to Jacques next spring.

She installed herself in the new country she regarded as home, living in a rented villa close by her mother's on the Riviera. She spent only enough time in London to have her possessions packed and crated, hand in a dozen or more resignations, and bid farewell to her downcast associates. The elation of the spring, when she had contemplated Bertie's happiness and her own escape to freedom, was gone. She had probed her motives after her father's death. She was being selfish in running away from all the tasks she had undertaken; there was no denying it. But she had spent twenty-five years in a kind of no man's land, looking forward to nothing except fresh jobs to occupy her and the growing up of her sons. Jacques wanted her as she wanted him. She was forty-four years old and starved of affection, which money could not buy. She might not be given another chance. She justified the course she was taking with an excuse all her own: "Niches give me claustrophobia."

She chose Independence Day, July 4, as the most fitting date for the wedding. Ivor, studying at Magdalen College, Oxford, in a niche of another kind, escorted her to the registry office on Henrietta Street in Covent Garden market at eight-thirty in the morning. At that hour, the cobbled streets were thronged with delivery wagons and cheerful cockney costermongers balancing stacks of fruit and vegetable baskets on their heads. It was a good time to avoid curiosity-seeking crowds. With primroses pinned to the black satin hat which she wore with a sea-green satin dress, she sparkled like a young girl, untrammeled by adversity.

Colonel George Harvey, who had coaxed her into writing for his *North American Review,* was one witness; her cousin, General Cornelius Vanderbilt III, United States ambassador to England, the other in this civil ceremony conducted to conform with French law. Consuelo and Jacques were married twice within the hour. Cousin Cornelius gave her away in the Episcopal rites conducted more formally in the Chapel Royal, with Bertie and his marchioness looking on. "Later," as *The Times* reported, "the bride and bridegroom left by aeroplane for France."

Sunny was in Paris already, residing with his new bride on the Rue Auguste Vacquerie. Consuelo had let almost two months go by after the divorce decree was made absolute under British law on May 14; Sunny announced his engagement on the first day of June. His new American duchess, seasoned in her relations with him and other men of a different caliber, was Consuelo's ambitious protégée, Gladys Deacon, successful at last, after more than twenty years of climbing, in reaching the uppermost branches of the social tree but notably lacking in a dowry.

If he had hoped his choice would wreak vengeance on his first duchess, he was sadly disappointed. A certain ironic amusement was the limit of Consuelo's feeling. Sunny was welcome to Gladys. It was impossible not to share the thought that crossed many another person's mind. Gladys was the new mistress of Blenheim—"but on what?"

The new duchess and the old maintained a distant friendship—meetings were rare except when they revisited the haunts they had known in Paris. Consuelo encountered no problem in forgiving Gladys because she found nothing that needed to be forgiven. Gladys had used her, without any doubt, had schemed to replace her in Sunny's limited affections, had been consumed by ambition, to the exclusion of gentler feelings. But she and Consuelo had something new in common now—the knowledge that the one true love of Sunny's life was Blenheim Palace.

XII

Mercies of the Law

Marriage with Jacques was as agreeable as she had imagined it would be. For the first time she could remember, the tensions released their hold. She had no need to justify her life to herself or to him. Her conscience was calm about what she had left behind. She could live at ease without the nagging compulsion to be lady bountiful and enjoy being rich without feeling guilty.

The marriage deserved a setting to complement it, like a polished diamond on black velvet. The house at 2 Rue du Général Lambert was ideal for the purpose. Windows looked out over the Champ de Mars, whose lawns reached down to the Seine. She watched the children at play in the sandboxes with no remorse over those who had spent their days at her crèches in London. Contact with them was limited to an exchange of *bonjour,* as it was with the workmen who came to the benches under the trees to lunch on crusty bread and cheese and a bottle of *vin ordinaire.* Jacques, she was delighted to find, was good with children, though he would have none of his own.

The house was only an imitation of eighteenth-century style, but the furnishings must be genuine. She was in no rush to have everything completed. Together, they took their time as hobbyists, strolling the back streets of her enchanting city in search of antique shops that had exactly what they were hunting for: mellow paneling for the walls, the finest in period furniture, rare and beautiful vases, Isfahan rugs, paintings—the prize among these was a Renoir, "La Baigneuse." One tapestry, too, was a particular treasure because it had been Willie's.

No other place on earth attracted her in springtime like Paris, but gray winters there were to be avoided if possible. She thought they should have a second home in the Riviera's unfailing sunshine at Èze, near Alva's house, the "Villa Isoletta." Much of the pleasure in this new life was having a husband to share every minute of it. Jacques set about buying up the holdings of fifty-two small holders to assemble an estate of one hundred and fifty acres among the steeply banked fields of flowers and vegetable crops they grew for the market.

She marveled at his skill at haggling, an art she lacked practice in. Some of the peasants were reluctant to sell for any amount of money. Jacques applied a different appeal to them. They surrendered their land, at a price, because he was a colonel-aviator, a veteran of battle against *les Boches,* who so stubbornly declined either to disarm or to pay the reparations dictated by the Treaty of Versailles.

For inspiration for the house itself, she dipped further back into the past than her mother had ever done. Consuelo wanted something with an air more ancient than Blenheim's, a building of weathered stone and cloisters encircling an interior garden. The two of them roved the countryside until they came across a Cistercian abbey, the Romanesque convent of Le Thoronet founded in 1146 AD at Brignoles in Provence. They put up at an auberge to spend weeks studying and sketching the place before they called in an architect, who could only be Achille Duchêne.

The six brothers who built the house—which she named "Lou Sueil," meaning "The Hearth" in local dialect—trudged a dozen miles each Monday morning over the Maritime Alps from their Italian villages, lured by the wages she paid them, then tramped home again on Saturday. She could not wait for more than two rooms to be finished before she and Jacques took possession. The rest of her plan would be fulfilled when imported craftsmen installed the paneling that her connoisseur's taste judged necessary as the only possible backdrop for her furniture from Crowhurst.

She came as close to being a housewife as a millionairess could, plumping up cushions on the enticing sofas, replenishing the stationery on the writing tables, filling the rooms with flowers cut from the terraced gardens where cypress trees broke the mountain skyline. Though she was not of his faith, the *curé* called to sprinkle holy water for keeping Lou Sueil safe from evil spirits. When every room had been furnished to her satisfaction, their contents were worth approximately $3,000,000.

Peasants were their only immediate neighbors, living across the ravine that separated the house from the village and eking out an existence by selling garden produce in the markets of nearby Monaco. The sight of black-clad women plodding along with panniers on their heads induced a twinge of shame as she passed them on the steep road in her chauffeured Rolls-Royce. Once, she asked Jacques to walk with her over the same route, five miles each way. She was not tempted to try it a second time.

In Paris and on the Riviera, she began to establish her salons as meeting places for the same sort of exalted guests she had grown to shun in England. Since the French were slow to ask the Balsans into their homes, she would invite some of them and mix them in with a selection of cosmopolitan visitors similarly endowed with money, power, or reputation. The after-dinner protocol of the English, when the ladies withdrew from the table to leave the gentlemen to their cigars, was dispensed with here. Consuelo held the company together over liqueurs as deftly as she had chaired a fund-raising rally.

French noblemen were as eager to be on the calling list as the English had been. The Duc de Gramont could be relied on to reminisce about her father, whom he admired as "a fine and honorable sportsman"; the Comte de Gautier-Vignal about Alva, whom he had known as Madame Vanderbilt before she became Madame Belmont. The Vicomte de Noailles preferred simply to talk with Consuelo, whose deafness, thanks either to the climate or to new hearing devices, was less acute in France.

The French she had spoken since childhood made conversation simple, but there was another bond with her adopted countrymen. Like them, she detested Germans at a time when, clause by clause, the punitive terms hammered out at Versailles were being mollified by Britain's willingness to compromise. Her regained prestige as a hostess brought constant invitations from the diplomatic corps. Of all the parties, she liked those at the British Embassy best until she clashed with the recently appointed ambassador.

Baron D'Abernon, her old friend of Blenheim days, arrived in Paris after service on the wartime liquor control board so anxious to amend the terms of the peace treaty that she could only consider him pro-German. She had no qualms about telling him so, to taunt him into arguments. Finally, she chose between a long-standing friendship and allegiance to France. "I hear," she snapped, "the Germans so appreciate your policy that they are taking the nails out of Hindenburg's statue to put them in one for you."

The companionship with Curzon was more durable. For one thing, his views on punishing Germany coincided with hers. For another, his personality was so flexible that he was described as "a political jumping jack," and she had something of the same pliancy. He had expected to be prime minister or at least foreign secretary after the Tories took over power in England in 1922. Instead, he was saddled with the inferior post of leader in the House of Lords. Early in 1925 he wrote to Consuelo, complaining only of being extraordinarily tired. Might he spend a little time recuperating at Lou Sueil alone with Consuelo and Jacques?

She knew from past experience that he would need unusual care—a flow of conversation to divert him, heavy curtains to exclude all light when he slept during the day, bedroom snacks to nibble on as he worked through the night editing his manuscripts for publication. When he eased himself out of the car on his cane and straightaway wanted to climb to the top of their private mountain to take in its view of the whole shimmering coastline of the Côte d'Azur, a surge of emotion was aroused in her for the old man who had once spoken of his love.

Perhaps because her feelings about him were too confused in their blend of affection and pity, she concentrated on a chatelaine's duties to make him as comfortable as possible and delegated Jacques to handle the talking over the next two weeks. The house as well as its mistress fascinated Curzon. He loved antiquities, as she did, buying and preserving a castle in Lincolnshire and another in Sussex as gifts to be made to his nation.

The Balsans took him with them to the garish gingerbread palace of Monaco to dine with Prince Louis II, who ruled over all eight square miles of his realm with the pomp of an emperor and had only an illegitimate daughter, Charlotte, to succeed him. Consuelo disliked the place on sight. It reminded her too much of a Victorian anachronism, with bewigged flunkeys ushering the guests into position to stand waiting for Louis to make his entrance dressed up like a hero of opéra bouffe. She resented the delay, when Curzon was suffering obvious pain. It was a pity, she thought, that despite the cash pouring in from casinos that the Monegasques were forbidden to enter, the artless prince hadn't the vision to surround himself with a more distinguished court. It would be the last evening out she arranged for Curzon.

Before he left Lou Sueil, he posed a question to her: had it been worth the sacrifice to achieve what she had become? There was only one answer. Of course; she regretted nothing. She sensed it was unlikely they would meet again. He returned to London, to die there toward the end of March from a lifetime of overwork.

For five years, a glittering set of artists and writers, diplomats and statesmen, society lions and the elite of half a dozen nations descended on the villa and the house on Rue du Général Lambert, enticed by her hospitality. One category of guests stayed away. All of Jacques' family turned their backs on her. In their stern Catholic judgment, he lived in sin with a divorced woman whom he could not marry because her religion was not theirs.

Their intolerance did not bother her, since in her mind she was the bona fide Madame Jacques Balsan. She could live without them in her happy little universe. It was painful for Jacques, though, when the boycott persisted, and embarrassing for him to work with brothers, sisters and cousins who refused to have anything to do with her. Something must be done to restore peace among the Balsans, but what? Her London lawyer, Sir Charles Russell, another Catholic, suggested a solution that had been effective in similar instances before. If her marriage to Sunny were to be annulled, she could be accepted into the church and re-wed to Jacques.

But on what grounds, she asked, when she had borne Marlborough two sons?

It would be sufficient, the lawyer told her, to establish that she had been compelled to become the duke's bride. Three steps in all might be involved. First, she must appear with supporting witnesses before a Roman Catholic court in the diocese she resided in or where the first ceremony had been performed. The court's finding would be confirmed or rejected by the Holy Rota,

a universal tribunal of twelve priests representing all the principal Catholic countries, which had originally been convened in
Rome in 1326. If the Rota decided against her, she could appeal
to the pope himself, who might appoint a commission of cardi-
nals to re-examine the case. Nothing must be regarded as certain. One pope, Clement VII, Russell cautioned her, had refused to annul the union between England's Henry VIII and
Catherine of Aragon.

The prospect of exposing her life to strange priests appalled
her, but there was no alternative. Through all the years, she had
saved the few letters Winty had managed to smuggle through to
her. Ingrained, irrepressible sentiment made it impossible for
her to discard them, though from reading the newspapers she
knew his first wife, Alice, had died, leaving him with six young
children to raise. He had found a second wife in stately Lucy
Mercer of Washington, D.C., once a part-time secretary to
Eleanor Roosevelt when her husband, Franklin, was assistant
secretary of the Navy. The love affair that had developed between Lucy and the aspiring politician whom polio later crippled
was a closely held secret, totally unknown to Consuelo. Lucy
Mercer was no more than a name to her, and she did not contemplate restoring contact with her Rosenkavalier only to have
him testify as a witness on her behalf.

She could possibly trace her old governess, Miss Harper, the
one person who had consoled her on the eve of the 1895 wedding. She could rely on her aunt, Jenny Tiffany, formerly Mrs.
Yznaga, to describe how her sister used to intimidate her daughter. Another aunt, Lucy Jay, who had lived next door, might be
willing to tell about Consuelo's imprisonment in her own bedroom. But it would take Alva's testimony to convince the jurors
of the church beyond any fear of skepticism that Consuelo was
telling nothing but the cruel, scarcely credible truth.

When Consuelo went to talk with her mother, Alva welcomed
the challenge to confess her guilt. It would offer the chance to
· erase the memory of the anguish she had caused her child. If
she emerged as a miscreant, she was too old and too indifferent
to care.

When Sunny was approached, he objected, principally in behalf of their sons. If by some ecclesiastical sleight of hand his
first marriage was declared never to have taken place, would that

cancel out their legitimacy and, therefore, Bertie's inheritance? Would it mean that legally they, too, were to be erased and the dukedom on Sunny's death passed on to Winston, assuming he outlived his ducal cousin?

The answer provided by the Catholic authorities was conclusive: "The decree of nullity from the Vatican has no legal force, and therefore in the eyes of civil law the Marlborough offspring are in no way affected." Sunny asked Sir George Lewis and the Jesuit fathers of St. Aloysius, Oxford, to act for him without contesting the course Consuelo was taking.

She was assured that secrecy for everyone concerned was guaranteed by the ground rules of the procedure. The judges of the diocesan court were bound by oath on pain of excommunication not to reveal the slightest detail of the hearings. It would probably be 1932, six years from now, before the official record of her appeal and its outcome was published by the Vatican in its official periodical, *Acta Apostolica Sedis.*

She appeared with her witnesses before a court held in Southwark, which represented some bending of the regulations in her favor—Sunderland House stood in that diocese. Her testimony was given in wrenchingly simple terms, as she and Alva appreciated it had to be.

"My mother tore me from the influence of my sweetheart. She made me leave the country. She intercepted all the letters my sweetheart wrote and all of mine to him. She caused continual scenes. She said I must obey. She said I knew very well that I had no right to choose a husband, that I must take the man she had chosen, that my refusal was ruining her health, and that I might be the cause of her death.

"There was a terrible scene in which she told me that if I succeeded in escaping, she would shoot my sweetheart, and she would, therefore, be imprisoned and hanged, and I would be responsible.

"Having then destroyed the possibility of my marrying the man I loved, Mother told me that she had chosen a man for me whom she considered suitable in all respects, that he was about to arrive in America as her guest, and that she had already negotiated my marriage with him . . . I insist on declaring that I married the Duke of Marlborough yielding to the tremendous pressure of my mother and following her wish absolutely." She felt compelled to add a few words about Sunny. "The arrogance of the duke's character created in me a sentiment of hostility. He seemed to despise anything that was not British, and therefore my feelings were hurt."

He did not try to deny that when he gave his own evidence to the judges in a move that bewildered her. "She told me," he avowed, "that her mother had insisted on her marrying me, that her mother was strongly opposed to her marrying Rutherfurd, that she had used every form of pressure short of physical violence to reach her end."

Mrs. Tiffany came forward to corroborate her niece's statement: "My sister was continually making scenes. Despite all this, Consuelo did not easily fall in with her mother's wishes. It is on record that she broke down and wept when first told she must marry the duke, and did so again the next day when her engagement to him was announced in the newspapers."

Miss Harper related her version of the events, and Mrs. Jay confirmed it: "This marriage had been imposed by my sister on her daughter."

Then Alva spoke. It took only a paragraph to acknowledge her guilt to these judicial men of the cloth. "I forced my daughter to marry the duke. I have always had absolute power over my daughter, my children having been entrusted to me entirely after my divorce. I alone had charge of their education. When I issued an order, nobody discussed it. I therefore did not beg but ordered her to marry the duke."

The priests who sat in judgment found that, under canonical law, coercion was proven and the marriage was invalid. Their report to the Rota spelled out their reasoning. "Born of a very distinguished American family, baptized but not of Catholic religion, Consuelo Vanderbilt, the appellant party in the case, plighted her troth when she reached the age of seventeen to Rutherfurd, whom she violently loved, and her mother, who strongly opposed the match, brought overwhelming forces into play to wrest the heart of her daughter.

"As Consuelo was endowed with every womanly grace and with great wealth—and this is most important—the mother, who was driven by a desire for a title of nobility, substituted another man for the one whom Consuelo loved passionately. When she met in London Charles, Duke of Marlborough, she invited him as a guest of the family to Newport, where for about fifteen days he lived with the Vanderbilt family. On the day before his departure, he asked Consuelo to be his wife. Consuelo ran to her mother, but the next day the news was unjustly spread in the newspapers of her wonderful engagement to the duke. This was her mother's doing.

"She had nobody to whom she could turn, not even her father, because her father and mother were separated by divorce and because, as all the witnesses unanimously declared, she would have fallen under the influence of the obstinacy and imperiousness of her mother, anyway. That Consuelo was coerced is further shown by the fact that her mother, fearing that she might at the last moment change her mind and retract her consent to wed Marlborough, placed a guard at the door of her room on the day of the wedding so that nobody could speak to or even approach her.

"A most unhappy sequel, indeed, did this wedding have. Shortly after the wedding, in fact, the wife herself revealed to her husband that she had not gone to the altar of her own free will, but was compelled by her mother and that she, therefore, had destroyed the love of another man. Though their souls drew apart, two children were born of the marriage.

"In the year 1905 the couple were legally separated and in the year 1920 obtained a civil divorce by common consent, whereafter each remarried. In 1925 Consuelo appealed to the Diocesan Court at Southwark for an annulment of her marriage with the Duke of Marlborough. The court, having conducted a trial according to approved rites, on February 9 emitted a sentence declaring the marriage annulled for violence and intimidation."

The Rota did not question the rectitude of the court's decision, which it confirmed in July, and Consuelo and Sunny were formally notified. As a not especially devout convert to the faith, she was remarried to Jacques in a quiet Catholic ceremony in France and welcomed as a validated bride to the Balsans' château. Madame Charles, in black satin, presented her in turn to the assembled members of the family, all new faces to Consuelo. The grande dame had been the instigator of the boycott, but her latest niece bore no grudges; she had learned another lesson about the spadework necessary to bury the past.

Sunny delayed his next manoeuvre until November, when he took himself to Rome. The resulting publicity shattered peace for the Balsans. Consuelo could not determine whether it was a desire for revenge that led him to seek an audience with Pope Pius XI, announce that he wished to be received into the Catholic communion so that he might be remarried to Gladys—and appeal for an annulment that had been in effect for four months. Whatever prompted him, the newspapers scented sensation.

Forty-eight hours later, they had dug up most of the story. Consuelo and Alva, under siege from reporters, felt that silence was the most dignified response. On both sides of the Atlantic, Protestant bishops waged war on the Catholic Church for invading what they claimed as their spiritual territory. The accusation that the Rota had been bribed with Vanderbilt dollars distressed Consuelo the most. She had spent nearly thirty years struggling to release herself from Sunny, but the cost to her in money paid to the Vatican in this conclusive final round was certified in Rome to be only $240.

The duke remained out of sight in his palace, leaving his solicitors, Lewis & Lewis, the responsibility for pinpointing where the action had originated: "Many contradictory reports have appeared in the press recently with regard to the ecclesiastical proceedings which resulted in the annulment by the Sacra Romana Rota of the ceremony of marriage which took place on November 6, 1895, and in this connexion numerous false statements have been made about our client. He desires it to be authoritatively stated through us that the application for this annulment was made by Madame Balsan and not by him."

Progress toward his acceptance as a Catholic was stalled. A London spokesman for the faith sounded a firmly democratic note, which could only have infuriated him: "Our church does not do the sort of thing the duke desires unless there is really just cause. Nothing more can be done for a duke than for a tramp."

Consuelo speculated that possibly problems with Gladys underlaid his behavior. His new duchess was turning out to be a virago. While Ivor stayed single, Bertie and Mary had three children by now: five-year-old Sarah Consuelo; Caroline, who was two years younger; and an heir in the baby, John George Vanderbilt Henry. Consuelo was developing into a fond grandmother; their step-grandmother was not. Young Sarah hated being dragged off to Blenheim in her best party dress after her blonde hair had been curled by Nanny with tissue paper and a hot flat-iron. Nanny would give a pinch to the two girls' cheeks to make them glow before she pushed them through a sitting-room door to curtsey to the intimidating Gladys. No lover of youth, she used to respond with a scream, "Get them out of here!"

The battle of the pulpits ran on into December, sparking controversy in columns of letters to editors and diatribes in church magazines on each side of the firing line. *The Pilot* defended the Rota, *The Church Times* attacked it. Canons duelled with monsignors over the finer points of spiritual law until Consuelo felt sick at heart, clinging to her view that questions of faith were definitely a personal affair. Southwark's Catholic Bishop Amogo was summoned to Rome. The Vatican, in self-defense, was about to release the records of the annulment rather than postpone publication for years. Clamor from the newspapers for a statement from Consuelo increased. She still had nothing to say, but Alva, shrugging off the damage done to her name, explained disdainfully, "This is merely one of those adjustments."

Sunny's confirmation as a Catholic was delayed until the following February. By then, the ex-wife to whom he apparently had never been married had tried to obliterate him from her thinking. There was no way in which to forget his impact on the years of her growing up. She had noticeably aged in the process of freeing herself. Her eyes were bright and her body willowy, but her close-cut hair had turned gray, and laughter covered a permanent wistfulness. She had been too deeply hurt to make a complete recovery.

Repeating their vows before a priest did nothing to strengthen affinity between Sunny and Gladys. The size and cost of maintaining Blenheim without injections of Vanderbilt cash weighed him down. She resented the sacrifices he enforced to preserve the monument. Times changed fast in the early thirties, but he did not, apart from peculiarity in his mode of dressing, which had him turn up at least once at a London banquet in a white linen suit like the one he wore the day he arrived at Marble House.

He moved out of the house he had taken on Carlton House Terrace into a suite of rooms in the Ritz, leaving Gladys alone while he ordered the gas, electricity, and telephone cut off, then sent in private detectives to evict her. He knew death was approaching. Cancer took him quickly and painlessly, and Bertie inherited the dukedom.

Consuelo could detect a pretense or two in the obituary of Sunny that Winston wrote for *The Times*. "His first marriage," Churchill noted, "was unhappy and ultimately unsuccessful. To those who knew both him and his wife and their exceptional gifts of personal charm and kindliness, the breach that occurred seemed unaccountable. But no one can penetrate the mysterious springs of human nature." Winston knew better than to make believe there was any mystery, but she forgave him for the partiality he showed "my oldest and dearest friend."

She settled down with Jacques, cushioned by wealth against any demands more taxing than arranging a party or attending a ball, making up for the gaiety she had been deprived of as a teenage duchess. One ball glittered more brightly than the rest, for it confirmed what she hoped was true—that in middle age she was still beautiful. The Duchess de Doudeauville asked all her guests to wear costumes reminiscent of Louis XV's court. The candle-lit ballroom echoed with applause when Consuelo appeared in white taffeta, with roses in her piled up, white-powdered hair, toying with a fan of Alva's, and the liveried musicians paused in the middle of a minuet. Perhaps she was entitled to a touch of vanity and to her insistence on privacy; reporters calling at Lou Sueil were invariably told by a maid that "Madame Balsan is not at home."

She liked to believe that at heart she remained a sturdy American democrat. In her disarming recollection, "It was not only aristocratic parties that pleased us." Though she had no fondness for the Socialists who came to power in France or for the Communists who invented the technique of sit-down strikes and occupied French factories, she retained a sentimental faith in the rugged common sense of the average workingman. She did not volunteer to return to the kind of work she had done in the slums of London, but she was glad to be invited to help raise money for an ambitious new hospital and win President Lebrun's cooperation. Her reward came after he opened the Fondation Foch du Mont Valérian—the gold cross of a member of the Legion of Honor, which Jacques as a fellow chevalier pinned to her dress.

The circle of visitors constantly expanded. Willie II and his wife Rose were favorites among the coterie who arrived at Lou Sueil. Charlie Chaplin stayed for lunch, though he seemed to be a Socialist, and entertained her with his little-tramp version of a day in the saddle, hunting with the Duke of Westminster's hounds. Winston brought his official bodyguard, Clemmie and his painting gear. Serge Voronoff related tales of transplanting glands from the monkeys he kept caged at his château on the Italian frontier into patients who could afford his surgery to ward off old age. Margot Asquith, widowed in 1926, invited herself to Èze, pleading poverty as the excuse for coaxing Consuelo into buying her new clothes.

All in all, it added up to a delightfully frothy, contented existence: picnics among the ruins that studded the mountainsides; drives into Monte Carlo to watch the tennis championships or to Nice for the horse races; excursions aboard millionaires' yachts that anchored in Monaco's harbor. Consuelo was reverting to type, living in the style expected of a Vanderbilt in an era when the name epitomized wealth inexhaustible, surpassing that of the half forgotten Astors or the industrious but dull Rockefellers.

Though she found herself far more comfortable than in the old hair-shirt days, the price she paid was an indefinable restlessness. Even Paris lost some of its charm: she would prefer to pass their summers elsewhere. They found what she wanted on the border of Normandy by the forest of Dreux. The pink brick, moated château had the right degree of seclusion and aura of antiquity. Legend says that Henry of Navarre, king of France, had occupied one room in 1590 the night before he led his Huguenots to victory against the Catholics in the Battle of Ivry.

The urge to restore the place, which had stood empty for the better part of a generation, was surely an inheritance from her mother. Consuelo set about stripping off all twentieth-century additions to return the house to its pristine beauty. She planted gardens, laid out terraces, renovated an old mill by the river and cottages among the trees to accommodate friends for as long as they cared to stay. The cost meant nothing. Surrounding herself with congenial people was a good way to spend money.

Winston, she was sure, would love this château by the village of Saint Georges-Motel—population 350—almost as much as she did. He often came there to set up his easel and paint along-side his mentor, Paul Maze, a Norman artist in oils, pastels and watercolors who spent summers with his Scots wife in the old mill. Maze had met Churchill in the trenches after persuading the Royal Scots Greys to take him on as an unofficial interpret-er. He belittled the rumor that he taught Winston how to apply pigment to canvas. "But maybe," he would say to friends like Consuelo, "some of his paintings have a little touch of me in them, because he gives me his brush."

The accounts Consuelo relayed of the joys on hand at Saint Georges-Motel prompted Alva into buying a fifteenth-century château close by. She was lonely, indomitable, and plumper than ever, driving herself around the grounds behind a Sicilian donkey harnessed to a bath chair which had once been Queen Victoria's. The incurable fury struck her immediately; she moved into her latest home at Augerville-la-Rivier. The parish church, she decided, could do with a life-size statue of one of her heroines, Joan of Arc, which she proceeded to donate. Con-suelo marveled at her incorrigible mother; there was no knowing what she would turn to next. One week when Consuelo called, she found a regiment of laborers cutting back the banks of the river that Alva regarded as hers in order to double its width. On another visit, Consuelo tried in vain to convince her it was rath-er late in the day to install a full-scale American bowling alley. The architect within Alva was repelled by the vast expanse of plain sand covering her forecourt; she considered it much im-proved after she had it paved with ancient stone hauled in from Versailles.

Consuelo's feeling toward her stopped somewhere short of love. She admired the tenacity with which Alva clung to the cause of rights for women. It took her to The Hague when she was nearing eighty to rally with other suffragist leaders in de-manding equality for women everywhere under international law. But Alva was beginning to recognize the frailty of some oth-er kinds of glory. She sold Marble House to a Boston meat pack-er for $100,000, and Consuelo felt no pang of sorrow. Alva had one last commission for the profession she had supported so lav-ishly: she ordered a tomb designed and built ready for her arrival in Woodlawn Cemetery, New York.

Her daughter took her to the house Alva owned at 9 Rue

Monsieur in Paris after a stroke left her paralyzed, her heart and lungs faltering. Consuelo passed hours by her bedside, sometimes alone, more often with a trusted friend. Alva was calm about the approaching end when it lay only two days away. "I think she has not much longer," Consuelo said matter-of-factly to her companion as they left together one winter's evening. He appreciated what that signified. Consuelo's forgiveness did not extend to forgetting how Alva had always intimidated her.

On January 26, 1933, Alva died, eighty-three years and nine days old. Consuelo and Jacques sailed with the casket to New York. Her mother had asked for a suffragist's funeral, but a man and not a woman conducted the service in St. Thomas' Episcopal Church, where she had coerced Consuelo into marriage. A hymn the choir sang was of Alva's composing, and suffragists filed up rank by rank to the altar. Among the faded banners they carried, one seemed to summarize the creed by which Alva had lived: FAILURE IS IMPOSSIBLE.

In a sense, Alva's death represented the final phase in her daughter's liberation. While she lived, she had been the unchallenged leader, while Consuelo followed in her footsteps as a public figure, championing the rights of the downtrodden and expanding life for women. With Alva's influence gone, Consuelo's embrace of her mother's causes was over. The time and the money she had devoted to them had been an essential part of Consuelo's discovery of herself as a personality, but the self-imposed responsibilities were recognizable now as a substitute for loving and being loved. In marriage with Jacques, the impulsion had already withered.

The two of them stayed on in the United States for some weeks to visit with Harold and young Willie. She recalled the devastating feeling of instantly growing old when Alva had first told her she must be Sunny's wife. Now she could erase the past years and feel suddenly young again as she joined her brothers in remembering the childhood they had shared. She had been dragged away from them as a girl and had lived apart from them for so long that they had been something akin to strangers. That would not be allowed to happen again.

Children, everyone's children, claimed her attention now. There was a standing invitation for Bertie's small son and his three sisters—Sarah, Caroline, and little Rosemary—to come on holiday to Dreux. A visit to Grandmother and the jovial man she taught them to call "Jacques" was always a treat, when they had mixed feelings about growing up in Blenheim, a dreary place to rattle around in, according to Sarah, who lacked her parents' infatuation with ancestral halls. Bertie was adopting the style of a nineteenth-century country gentleman, pottering in the gardens and tramping the park with a shotgun. He was hard put to pay expenses; at Grandmother's, money did not matter. She let them do as they pleased—fish for trout, go canoeing, swim in the pool, ride ponies through the woodland trails, or pedal bicycles along the paths winding about the estate.

The supply of playmates was unlimited. Her friends brought their young families, and children from the village were free to come as they pleased, with presents waiting for all when she held a garden party. Every summer, she ran a play school, concerned to find that Provençal boys and girls were brought up so solemnly that they had little idea of how to enjoy themselves. At the farewell concerts they put on when vacation was over, they sang "The Star-Spangled Banner" and the "Marseillaise" for the elegant and genteel Madame Balsan.

The compassion for the young she had experienced in England reasserted itself, making her feel, as she joked, "like the old lady who lived in a shoe." On a hill outside the village she built a sanitarium large enough to accommodate eighty children at a time, ranging in age from twelve months to five years, along with wards, playgrounds, playrooms, and quarters for the nursing staff. Vanderbilt dollars paid for some expensive innovations. Each new arrival was admitted into a separate glass-walled cubicle, with crib, built-in bath, toy supply, and a little outdoor yard, to be kept under observation until the risk of infection spreading had passed. Pad and pencil in hand, Consuelo made a brisk daily tour of the hospital, tempted always to pause and join in a nursery game.

As the reputation of the place grew, the government in Paris asked that she expand the work to care for young tuberculosis patients. She ordered open-ended shelters containing fifty beds to be erected in her pine woods and started a nursing school. "We never," she reported contentedly, "experienced the tedium of country life."

In the back of her mind the thought arose that someday it

might be necessary to return to America, not to a city but somewhere in the sun. Since her brothers liked Florida, she decided
on an oceanfront villa some fifteen miles from Palm Beach, a
sun-soaked, Spanish-looking house of white stucco walls, par-
terres and lavish wrought-iron, to be named "Casa Alva."

For all the satisfaction gained from being occupied and useful
again, she was troubled by the undercurrents she detected
among the French. It was not that they were "decadent" by
comparison with the "trusty" Germans, as her spirited friend
Nancy Astor of England's notorious Cliveden set claimed whenever they met. Consuelo dismissed Nancy's preaching as blind,
pro-Nazi prejudice. But as Hitler bullied Europe, France
seemed to be dangerously divided, its people bereft of faith in
their leaders, and many of those leaders undisguised defeatists.
Ministers of the government spoke to her of their pessimism,
hinting that compromise with Berlin was preferable to inevitable
defeat in another war. She considered herself something of an
expert on the rigid French social structure that set workingmen,
bourgeoisie, aristocrats, the army, and the bureaucrats as far
apart in their loyalties as if they were citizens of different nations.

Caution advised starting preparations against disaster; the old
order could not endure under these strains. She directed Basil
Davidoff, her White Russian majordomo who had once been a
page to Tsar Nicholas, to oversee the packing of some of her
prized possessions for shipping to the United States.

In the Communist zones of the industrial cities there was already talk of deliverance by the Soviets when she crossed to
England during the sweltering summer of 1939. Sarah, eighteen
in December, was being given her debutante ball, and Blenheim
came alive again with lights, orchestra, bevy of guests including
one royal, the Duke of Kent, and magnums of champagne.
Consuelo's outward cheerfulness hid a presentiment of doom.
She remembered having the same eerie sensation as a scared
young duchess seated beside the tsar in the Winter Palace at St.
Petersburg, which was Leningrad nowadays. Talking with Winston was in no way encouraging; Prime Minister Neville Chamberlain would not tolerate a war-horse like Churchill in his Cabinet stable at any price.

Neither did her next meeting with Winston do anything to lift her gloom. She had returned to Paris when he arrived for a Bastille Day parade that filled the Champs Élysées with a display of regiments on the march, accompanied by every tank in the French army. If these rumbling machines were all that the generals could command, she failed to see how the country could be defended, though she fancied the men of the Foreign Legion made a more soldierly appearance even than Britain's Brigade of Guards, in which Bertie had served.

On August 23, 1939, Nazi Germany and the Soviet Union came to terms in Moscow; if Hitler went to war, the USSR promised to stay neutral. Eleven days afterward, Consuelo read the unbelievable black letters spread across her morning newspaper, repeating a phrase used as casually in commonplace French conversation as "C'est la vie." Today, the headlines said C'EST LA GUERRE.

XIII

The Years of the Locusts

Consuelo learned from the Red Cross that she was listed for capture as a hostage by the enemy she still referred to as "the Hun." If they caught her, she would be held for ransom. There seemed little likelihood of this happening when they were held back by the impenetrable concrete fortresses of the Maginot Line, but nevertheless it was something extra to worry about. Baron Louis de Rothschild had suffered that indignity in Vienna. She was not a member of his tortured race, but neither was she an American, protected by United States neutrality. Marriage to Jacques effectively made her a citizen of France.

At the age of seventy-one, he was back in uniform, eager to help in the fighting that had yet to begin in earnest as the icy winter of 1939 turned into a snow-shrouded new year. When Jacques was away on duty, she stayed on at Saint Georges-Motel with Paul Maze and Basil Davidoff, the three of them bundled in fur coats beside logs crackling in a marble fireplace. The black market offered fuel to keep them warmer, but it went against the grain to patronize profiteers. Talk about a "phoney war" repelled her. She had heard similar nonsense twice before in her sixty-three years and seen how long the killing lasted once it started.

No amount of money could spare her anxiety for Jacques and herself. The way to ease the strain was to go on working as if nothing were unusual, doing the rounds of the sanitarium and the tuberculosis center, then adding to that the task of inspecting the lodgings provided in surrounding communities for refugee families who were being evacuated from potential battle zones in the north. Vanderbilt money went to pay for certified milk and immunization shots for the displaced children. The extra *bidons* of scarce gasoline that went with her official job were useful when her scruples kept her away from every kind of under-the-counter trading.

She would have been more comfortable, she knew, in Paris, seventy kilometers away to the east, but living there would involve a certain sense of shame. *Le Journal* and *Le Matin* persisted in denouncing Stalin and barely mentioning Hitler, trying to convince their readers that the real enemy was the Soviet Union. The couturiers on the Rue de la Paix continued to parade their mannequins in exotic fashion shows, and Maurice Chevalier packed the Casino, singing *"Paris sera toujours Paris."*

The spring days grew longer, warmer, tenser. Consuelo was still asleep in her canopied bed on the morning of May 10 when her maid scampered in. The radio had just broadcast the calamitous bulletins. German paratroops were descending like locust plagues on Belgium, Luxembourg and the Netherlands. German tanks were rolling southward unopposed. German planes controlled the skies, and bombs were falling on Lyon. Consuelo reached for her hearing aid and ordered the girl to pack a bag. Jacques was confident that France's defenses would hold. His wife was equally certain that they would not, but she kept the opinion to herself and, as soon as she had dressed, went off to reassure the sanitarium staff that she had no intention of evacuating the place. If the sirens wailed, they would somehow have to get the children out to hide in the forest.

The rich, riding in limousines, made up the first freshet of refugees. Consuelo stationed herself at the bank in Dreux, the closest town of any size on the highway, to help those who had left in such haste that they were short of ready cash, the essential ingredient for continuing a smooth escape. When the rivulet expanded into a wave of farmers and peasants arriving in her own village on foot, in oxcarts, on hay wagons and bicycles, she opened the doors of the château to them, set up a canteen on the street to feed them, and organized temporary sleeping quarters wherever there was space for a mattress.

The outlook darkened day by day. The radio consistently reported the impossible, interrupted by only a single note of hope.

The Hun had broken through, and France was the battlefield, but Winston was England's new prime minister, promising "victory at all costs, victory in spite of all the terror." She had scarcely a moment to remember her forecast that this was bound to come to him in the end, or her thought about his wife Clemmie's want of faith in his future which Consuelo once expressed to Paul Maze: "You know, she's really a stupid woman."

The odds against her being taken prisoner had shortened immeasurably. The fact that she resided at Saint Georges-Motel was known to the German High Command, as to everybody with an interest in her. Her money was the lure that made her vulnerable, like a lamb tethered to a tree to attract tigers. The question was no longer whether but when the sanitarium and the refugee children should be evacuated. At first, Health Ministry bureaucrats at the other end of the telephone line opposed the move; then they left it for her to decide, recommending that she take her patients and charges to some sanctuary farther south, with the stipulation that the transfer must be carried out under conditions of secrecy to avoid alarming the villagers.

She admitted to herself that the courage she showed was a sham. The project, she knew, was futile, a hopeless cause. But getting the children away became an obsession. If they went, she could leave, too, and with an easier conscience. She marshaled every truck, ambulance and automobile she could lay hold of for a dress rehearsal, loading them with mattresses, boxes of food and canned milk, and clothing stowed in laundry bags.

The preparations were interrupted by a summons to Evreux, the district capital, twenty kilometers away. Madame Balsan must consider the prefect's request an order. Trains bearing forty-five thousand homeless and wounded would shortly be arriving at the station. She was to take charge of arrangements to feed and shelter them overnight until they could be sent on their way again southward, always southward.

The job was achieved, the beds made up with clean linen, a first-aid station opened, an evening meal cooked. Along with the sanitarium's matron and some nurses ferried in from Saint Georges-Motel, she spent the night waiting. Their guests did not appear until the next day. The Luftwaffe had knocked out the railroad tracks. Automobiles brought some of the contingent into Evreux; the rest had no choice but to walk, strafed by dive bombers that forced them off the road into ditches and woods. Consuelo had never witnessed such a spectacle of agonized humanity, so much suffering of body and mind that it was beyond her power to accept it as reality. A woman who had seen her two children machine-gunned. Another mother of seven who had been walking for the past week and was now about to give birth to her eighth baby. Men in rags, men with wounds, men with gangrene.

After she and Jacques bought clothes for those in direst straits, she went to make herself useful in the hospital wards, where the count of the wounded had leaped over the past twenty-four hours. Nothing more than the habit of working kept her going. She had no thought that France might escape defeat in this disaster. The country she loved best was doomed to be destroyed. German planes had already circled the town. It was only a matter of time before the bombs began to fall. The idea of issuing some sort of appeal for help to friends in the United States crossed her mind. Infinitely more money than she had access to was needed in this catastrophe. It was inconceivable that nothing had been heard from the country she must flee to, if that proved possible. But there was no time left to organize anything more than the evacuation of those in her immediate charge. The next imperative duty was to drive back to the château.

The detachment of French troops that had turned up in the village had to be taken care of as a priority. She ordered a sheep killed for cooking in their mobile kitchen to give them dinner. As for sleeping accommodations, protocol could not be ignored. The three officers would sleep in the house, the one hundred and fifty bedraggled soldiers on straw spread on the stone floor of the glass-enclosed orangery.

In the first week of June, permission was granted by the Ministry of Health for her to set off with Jacques for Pau in southwestern France, a drive of almost seven hundred kilometers that would take them close to the Spanish border. There, she hoped to find the refuge she desperately wanted for her children and nursing staff. Jacques would chauffeur the little Citroën. One suitcase each, they fancied, would serve for the trip, since they would soon be back at the château.

Pick-and-shovel brigades were throwing up feeble barricades along the road against the imminent arrival of the Panzer divisions. Here and there, a French seventy-five cannon had been hauled into place. Everywhere rumors spread like a blight. Soviet and German troops were advancing side by side; America had declared war; Paris was burning; Paris was secure. At every stop, the townspeople muttered about treachery and blamed the Fifth Column of Nazi agents for the Germans' invincibility. Every last man of the British Expeditionary Force had either been captured or evacuated at Dunkirk. Hitler had won the war in the west at one blow. Winston, shuttling between London and Paris, found Marshal Pétain, who had joined Paul Reynaud's disarrayed government, already talking about an armistice. Everything she saw sharpened the acid taste of disillusionment.

Time was running out for her. They reached Pau on the second day and found the streets swarming with refugees while gendarmes combed the crowds for Nazi sympathizers. Money spoke its universal language, cutting short her frantic search and producing an empty villa that could serve her purpose. They left the querulous resort city before dawn the following day, the highway north empty of traffic before the car's headlights.

They traveled fast enough to reach almost the halfway mark on the road home before they stopped for a meal at Périgueux in the Dordogne, town of truffles and brandy. In a café there they encountered friends who passed on the news: the Germans had reached Saint Georges-Motel, and Reynaud's government had abandoned Paris for Bordeaux. Jacques dismissed this as more tittle-tattle; they started heading north again.

She had to face the question of her own life or death. She expected at any minute to see German soldiers blocking their path. She must make up her mind whether she would submit to being taken captive or break and run for it, risking their bullets. It took only a moment. She would prefer dying to captivity, but Jacques must be allowed to do what he thought best.

Instead of enemy troops ahead, she recognized another car of hers in the stream of traffic fleeing south. Her butler, Albert, sat next to the driver. It was unfortunately true, he told her gravely when they had stopped; the Germans had moved into Saint Georges-Motel. The village had been bombed as expected, but the house and sanitarium remained intact. Paul Maze, who had

scouted a getaway route across the fields in advance, had led a
convoy of automobiles carrying the children out onto backroads
on a course for Pau. In the confusion of this hour, she felt a
mysterious resentment of Maze. She wished, perhaps against all
logic, that she had been the one to make this decision.

Albert also was on his way to Pau, with the most essential of
the Balsans' portable possessions. Davidoff, her majordomo,
chose to stay on at the château to guard its treasures against
German plundering. He spoke their language; he was a White
Russian; he would take his chances along with Jacques' valet,
Louis Hoffman, born in Luxembourg and accordingly a neutral.
Jacques turned the Citroën around to squeeze it into the stam-
pede bound for Pau.

The city was as divided in its loyalties as by the ravine of the
Hedas River that rippled through its heart. There were those like
Jacques who thought that France must fight on and, if the worst
happened, die with honor. Others, a probable majority,
watched for Reynaud to resign in favor of ancient Pétain, who
would assuredly seek an armistice even at the cost of surrender-
ing northern France and all her coastline down to the Pyrenees
to German occupation, providing a gigantic springboard for invading England.

When the Hun ruled France—and she had no doubt it would
come to that—Consuelo's United States income would be froz-
en at the source. She had not been compelled before to contemplate living bereft of money. Incalculable amounts of it had always been available for spending at her will. She could not con-
ceive being deprived of what she accepted as something akin to
the air she breathed. Did the rich possess their money or did
their money possess them? She was too tense to ponder the rid-
dle when the very reason for her being here, the sanitarium,
could not survive unless she paid the bills.

The breakout led by Maze brought the children safely to Pau.
Their stay, she concluded, must be limited. The healthy could
be restored to their parents wherever they were to be found, the
sickly passed on to other hospitals. The only way to put the arrangements in hand was to eke out the gasoline and make the
round trip of four hundred kilometers to the new seat of government in Bordeaux.

A momentary rush of disjointed pleasure came as she drove

through the antique city's narrow streets lined with beautiful, low white houses. It vanished as soon as, with Jacques, she edged into the throng that filled the United States Consulate. Pétain was in negotiation with the conquerors. "You should cross into Spain immediately," she was told, "while the border is still open."

Jacques took her with him to find an old comrade who might be willing to grant them instant permission to leave France, the air minister. It was accomplished within minutes of coming across him in the chaos that surrounded the installation of the shattered government in unprepared new quarters. With the precious papers in their pockets, they drove through pelting rain and paused for cups of coffee. The "Marseillaise" crackling from the restaurant radio pulled them up from the table to their feet. Standing together at rigid attention, they heard the decrepit marshal of France address his countrymen with funereal dignity. He had made them "the gift of my person," he bragged. *"Il faut cesser la guerre."* When he had finished, lightning exploded in the sky, and thunder rattled the streaming windowpanes.

It seemed to her that seconds counted. The barriers might already be up across the frontier. Finding the car and returning to the consulate had the quality of helplessness that marks a nightmare. They handed over their French passports to a harrassed State Department aide. The documents were inadequate, he said. They could be allowed into the United States only as immigrants. To obtain the vital visas, they must produce their certificates of birth, marriage, and divorce. But all of these were stored in Paris . . . Return in the morning, she was told.

She was reduced for the first time in her life to the common level of frustrated humanity. The title she had once held and the fortune she commanded were meaningless in this situation. If the escape hatch into Spain were closed, she could not see how to avoid the choice: accept captivity or elect to be killed in a bid to flee.

The best advice came from a fellow fugitive: go to Bayonne and at the Spanish and Portuguese consulates there, obtain visas permitting them to cross Spain into Portugal. In Lisbon, departure point for flights to New York, they could try their luck again with the Americans, and meanwhile she would be freed from fear of capture.

Nightfall overtook them on the road to Bayonne. They were unable to find a room to rent anywhere until a retired sea captain, equally impressed by Jacques' uniform and Consuelo's weary beauty, gave them shelter. They would spend the next night on sofas in a stranger's house in Bayonne while more checkmated hours slipped away.

She could not sleep after four AM. They would have to start counting pennies the moment they left France, assuming that ever happened. They still had a good supply of francs, but nobody outside the country wanted them now. The few dollars and British pounds Jacques was carrying might not be enough to pay their way to Lisbon. Some of their francs had gone to buy waterproofs and umbrellas to protect them from the atrocious weather. They needed them when they arrived at the Portuguese Consulate soon after dawn, to stand on line for four hours in rain that never ceased.

The mob jammed into the courtyard outside the building that housed the consul had to be tackled before they reached the foot of the wooden stairs leading up to the entrance three flights above. Jacques, in his telltale colonel's cap, was too conscious of the discipline expected of an officer to bring himself to wrestle a way through. Alva's daughter, half a head taller than most of the crowd, had no qualms at this moment. She thrust ahead to elbow a path for herself, figuring that her husband would follow close behind to protect her from a mauling.

With their passports stamped, she again led the struggle through the crush, and they hastened to the consulate of Spain. Only a handful of hopefuls waited on the steps there. According to the sign on the door, the issuing of visas was finished for the day. She tugged and kept tugging on the bell pull until the door opened, then forced herself inside. Monsieur and Madame Balsan soon had clearance to cross the frontier; there was no denying her. She primly told herself that "prerogative" and not aggression had won the day, but "I almost felt a transgressor."

They reached the Spanish border by way of the coast road south from Biarritz. The beaches they passed along the Bay of Biscay, dull as tarnished brass under the sullen sky, were bare of people, unlike the shoreline farther north where the sands were black with the thousands of those who had failed where she had succeeded, mostly Poles and Czechs and Austrians who could flee no farther from Nazi terror, only wait for their pursuers.

The barriers at the frontier had been lowered. She spent one more uncertain night on the French side in the home of a friend of Jacques before they made another start at dawn. The way ahead was open again when they returned at six o'clock on a July morning. They cleared customs and immigration, and the Citroën started for San Sebastian. In London, Charles de Gaulle was organizing the Free French. On a future day, Jacques would leave her in America and take up a role alongside him.

In San Sebastian, they ran short of cash to pay the train fares to Lisbon. The expendable Citroën should have a considerable resale value, but she discovered that the law prohibited Spaniards from buying such cars from refugees. The travel agent steered them to a dealer on the black market. She found the experience degrading and the pesetas they received outrageously few, but their visas were good for only a few more days in Spain. If they overstayed the date, she and Jacques would be pushed back into France.

In Lisbon, the Vanderbilt name and valid passports were enough for the United States consul to issue them immigrant visas after her brothers cabled word that they had bought them plane tickets. Her aura as a former duchess sufficed to bring an invitation from Prince George, Duke of Kent, to dine with him in the Portuguese palace that was his temporary home during his official visit from England. She had been drilled too long in the niceties of society for her not to hesitate about accepting. How could she and Jacques sit at table with royalty when neither of them had any proper evening clothes to wear? The prince was insistent. At his side in a simple dark dress, she noticed the reproving glances cast on her by other guests and marveled at their bland ignorance of the crumbling universe.

She had to calm herself as the clipper flying-boat taxied through the pale brown water of the Tagus, ready for takeoff; flying the Atlantic was another new challenge. But she was going home, adversity over, to be insulated by money against further hardship. She landed at New York with a pixy smile under a perky hat, disclosing no sign of stress or of having lived out of a suitcase for longer than she cared to recall. All she had to tell reporters inquiring about the war she had left behind was, "I saw it coming for a long time."

She went to earth like an exhausted fox after a hard run eluding hounds and huntsmen, burrowing herself out of sight of all but Jacques and her most trusted friends, keeping her name out of newspapers for more than a dozen years. The personal peace she sought was not to be interrupted by any more endeavors on the scale of the abandoned sanitarium. Her charities had to be much less conspicuous, more guarded, and her money more carefully spent, as property and income taxes rose every year.

Casa Alva continued to be her favorite winter home—she would also buy and sell equally distinguished houses on Long Island. With American citizenship restored, she settled down to wait out the war, her age denied by an unlined face, slim ankles, and a back as straight as a guardsman's.

Letters seemed abysmally slow in delivery from England, as she yearned for news of her family there, but when they did arrive there was little in them to worry her. Bertie served as a liaison officer with the United States forces after America joined the fighting. Ivor, physically frail as he was, worked with the Free French and earned the Legion of Honor. Blenheim had been stripped of its finery and put to use as headquarters for MI5, Britain's military intelligence corps. Though Ivor still had to find a wife, Bertie's Mary bore him a "spare," Charles George William Colin, in 1940.

Consuelo confessed to having selfish reasons for praying for Germany to be defeated: she wanted children around her again, her own grandchildren sharing her contentment in the Florida villa. All of them would be familiar faces there after 1945 along with Bertie and Mary, but never Ivor, who refused to fly.

The trickle of information obtainable from France was almost too good to be credible. Louis Hoffman, arrested as a spy, was threatened with a firing squad but then released unharmed. Basil Davidoff, taking up quarters in an old mill, was succeeding in defending the château and its treasures, which the German occupiers were treating with respect even when it was employed as Luftwaffe headquarters and visited by Hermann Goering, who had a greedy eye for other people's valuables. Basil, she decided, deserved a pension.

In America, she saw society as her mother had dominated it wither away to nothing. The great houses on Newport's Bellevue Avenue were locked and shuttered for the duration, the town identifiable only as a base for the United States Navy. Alva's mansion on New York's Fifth Avenue, where she had brought Caroline Astor to heel, had vanished; an office building stood on the site. The fifty-eight-room house at No. 640, on which care-worn Cornelius III paid annual tax bills of $67,000, had been sold to the estate of William Waldorf Astor on condition that after Cornelius' death his family might live there for twelve more months before it fell to the inexorably swinging steel ball of the demolition gangs; Cousin Cornelius was found to have left less than $4,000,000 when his end came in 1942 aboard his yacht in the waters of Florida.

Consuelo stayed away from what remained of Manhattan's social swirl, as secluded as she had been in the first delectable days at Saint Georges-Motel. *The* Mrs. Vanderbilt in the whole tribe of them was Grace, Cousin Cornelius' widow, who allowed neither death nor taxes to curb her style. Madame Balsan, a healthy distance away, noted with gentle amusement how the former Miss Wilson, belle of Newport, behaved more haughtily than Alva in her heyday, decking herself in bursts of jewelry and a Paris wardrobe, hunting for celebrities to attend her ostentatious entertainments, checking on pedigrees to make sure that her guests were worthy of her attention. Madame Balsan's taste in ornaments restrained her from wearing anything flashier than a rope of fine pearls except on extra-special occasions, and she preferred books to banquets. Gertrude, the matriarch, was aptly labeled "queen of the golden Age"; Consuelo, who counted herself fortunate in having survived it, was not inclined to challenge her claim to the title.

Most of her relatives had been more prolific in child-bearing than Consuelo. There was such a swarm of Vanderbilts, and over successive generations the fortune built up by her grandfather, William Henry, had been split into so many fractions, that none of the family ranked any longer among the monumentally rich. In Consuelo's concluding years as a duchess, each of her brothers had annual incomes in excess of $1,000,000. When Willie II died in January, 1944, $30,000,000 of his $36,000,000 estate went in taxes, effectively erasing his heirs as a major force in high-powered commerce or on the grand social scene.

With the same detachment that she applied to herself these days, Consuelo could trace the rise and fall of American dynasties from the time of her great-grandfather. The Commodore, hell-bent on making his way, had been cold-shouldered by the Astors, who continued to epitomize unimaginable wealth until Alva forced open the gates of society for the Vanderbilts. Now their day was almost over. They were out of date as archetypes of style and status.

The glory, if it could be called that, had transferred itself into the hands of comparative upstarts whose names had been unheard of by old Corneel. Men like the Rockefellers and the Fords, after amassing their millions from oil and automobiles instead of from obsolescent railroads, kept their money and their influence intact, not subdivided into ever diminishing fragments. As entrepreneurs, John D. Rockefeller and Henry Ford were no more impressive than William Henry Vanderbilt, but they had a more profound dynastic sense. They had seen to it that their holdings were consolidated, and they did not let their heirs behave like Willie and Uncle Corneel, who set greater importance on frittering money away than on multiplying it by a lifetime's devotion to hard labor.

Consuelo may have reflected—there was time to spare for it—that the law had been harsh on the family as far back as the 1920s, when the Interstate Commerce Commission, in a sudden flurry of trust-busting, ruled that no man could hold directorships of competing railroads. Three generations of Vanderbilts, starting with the Commodore, had taken it for granted that a place on any number of boards was the natural method of exercising the leverage that was the key to propagating a fortune. Her brother Harold felt the impact of that ruling, but he continued his association with what had once been the Vanderbilts' own railroad, the New York Central.

As long as the war lasted, American railroads prospered, hauling materials and men in record numbers. When its end brought Jacques back to her for good, the picture began to fade. A group of Texans captained by Robert R. Young of the Chesapeake & Ohio, with two pugnacious henchmen in the millionaire oilmen, Clint Murchison and Sid Richardson, hungered to control the Central. Brother Harold hurried to defend the status quo by buying more shares to add to the Vanderbilt portfolio. Seven years of skirmishing saw charges of mismanagement fired by the Texans and accusations of brigandage shot back by the Central's board.

The climax came in a fusillade of advertising placed by each side, aimed at convincing shareholders to vote for the appropriate slate of directors at a forthcoming board meeting. When the ballots had been tallied and retallied, Consuelo could be excused a few minutes of rare regret. The Texans had won by more than a million votes. Vanderbilt ties with the Commodore's own creation were severed.

Consuelo was not well acquainted with the new species of rich, nor did she wish to be. These hustlers who drilled for oil or speculated in real estate and mergers were not her kind. These were the lucky ones, because tax laws favored the oil industry, and profits made as a capital gain in buying and selling were subjected to a gentler bite from the Internal Revenue Service than inherited income. The be all and end all of many of the newcomers was crude wealth, not the joy of owning the finer things of life which she, as a third-generation Vanderbilt, had been brought up to value far more highly. The newcomers built commercial skyscapers instead of seaside palaces and Manhattan mansions, and they probably imagined K'ang Hsi porcelain had something to do with Peking duck.

She had not met any member of the unquestionably superior Rockefeller clan until Paul Maze, his renown as an artist soaring, came to New York in the 1950s for an exhibition of his works at the Wildenstein galleries. He brought a Vanderbilt and a Rockefeller together for the first time during the six months he occupied a suite in the Hotel Carlyle, paid for by Consuelo.

She grew more arbitrary in some of her evaluations. After the Renoir canvas "La Baigneuse" came back to her from France, thanks to Davidoff's watch over it, she gave it up for sale by a charity organization, the proceeds going to buy food for French children. The new owner paid $115,000 for the painting; Davidoff himself fared nowhere near as well. The aging majordomo was reluctant to leave when she sold the château in keeping with her determination to obliterate her former days. The chore of coaxing him was left to a granddaughter, Rosemary, who realized that his pension from Consuelo was too small to support him after he and his few belongings were moved to Monte Carlo. Rosemary and her husband brought Davidoff's allowance up to subsistence level out of their own pockets.

As in any household surrounding an elderly couple with large sums of money at their disposal, the choice of dependable servants became a matter of permanent concern to Consuelo's grandchildren. Affection may have been one reason for their anxiety, nervousness over pilferage of the inheritance another. Most members on the English side of Consuelo's family felt more at ease when one suave and persuasive butler left her service and Louis Hoffman, imported from France, took his place. They were even more relieved when Louis married her equally reliable maid, Annie; they suspected that Grandmother made an easy mark for unscrupulous retainers.

Turnover among Consuelo's servants was low. They responded as her guests did to her charm and a kind of feyness inherent in her manner, while *the* Mrs. Vanderbilt alienated battalions of hired help—butlers, footmen, gardeners, chauffeurs, cooks and maids—in the course of spending $250,000 a year, half of which came from dipping into her capital.

Consuelo maintained herself in quiet splendor. Guests earned invitations to her home on New York's Sutton Place by reason of their gaiety and wit more than for social standing, and not in wholesale lots, which was the practice of Grace, who in one vainglorious year entertained thirty-five thousand people.

The Balsans' house and gardens at Oyster Bay, on Long Island's sequestered north shore, were showpieces. Only close friends saw the manicured flower beds, the rooms furnished with the acquisitions of half a century's browsing through the Western world's galleries and antique shops. The most precious of her paintings, furniture, rugs, and bibelots were packed and shipped to and from Casa Alva every year—summer or winter, she counted them essential to her environment.

The agonizing she had done over the annulment of her marriage and her conversion to Catholicism was secreted in her mind like discarded clothing stored away in an attic trunk. When she attended church, which was not every Sunday, it was an Episcopal service, and Jacques went with her. His faraway relatives bewailed the backsliding; she and her husband were indifferent to the complaints.

She felt that finally she had come to terms with herself, but one element was missing for complete peace of mind: Ivor. He stuck by his refusal to fly over to visit her, and she missed him sadly. She realized she had underestimated the loss it would cause him when she left his father. Bertie, always fawned over by nannies in their heir-worship, had taken it much better. He was a mumbling, muttering giant, a formidable figure stamping about with his Malacca cane, but his heart was kind; his children and grandchildren loved him, and he had caught up with the times by opening Blenheim to tourists at half a crown a head while he stood at the gates selling illustrated guidebooks.

Ivor was different, a pale, delicate aesthete who bought canvases of Corot, Pissarro, Matisse, and donated a Cézanne to the Museum of Aix-en-Provence, "an aristocrat of the spirit," as one French painter described him; he had never held a public job. He had been scarred, as she knew, by the absence of a mother to teach him the meaning of maternal love. Though he had a wife now, Elizabeth, he and Consuelo were virtually strangers to each other. Yet she sensed that in character he was closer to her than anyone else, incomplete in some ways, wounded beyond healing, his true nature remaining to be determined.

The serenity Consuelo asked for could not last; money had not the power to fend off sorrow. It struck a double blow within a span of less than two months in 1956. On September 17, she had to accept that she would not see Ivor again after sixteen years of separation; cancer of the brain killed him. She was unable to be there when he was buried in Bladon churchyard, outside the rear gates of Blenheim Park, because Jacques was close to his end, bedridden in the Sutton Place apartment. On November 6, he went the way of Ivor, and she accompanied his body back to France for interment in the Balsan family tomb.

From France she went to pay her last visit to Blenheim and lay flowers on her son's grave. As evening approached, she climbed the stone staircase hidden away behind a wall of the Great Hall of the palace, restored after wartime wear and tear with the help of a government grant of £55,000. In the melancholy bedroom where she had borne two sons out of duty, she wept for the past that could not be kept from intruding itself. Then discipline reclaimed her. Alone, she changed for dinner. At the table with Bertie and his family, she sparkled as brightly as the woman she strove to be.

She needed someone dear to her to save her from solitude.

The role was filled by her eldest grandchild, lively, free-spirited Sarah, a wife and mother now, who stayed close to Consuelo wherever she made her home in the United States. The number of houses Consuelo owned was falling. Casa Alva was the first to go onto the market. Then the house at Oyster Bay was sold for $315,000 to be converted into a country club, but another Long Island retreat remained at Southampton. Taxes continued to gnaw at the fortune. One by one, a selection of the art treasures passed discreetly into new ownership, sold to some, given away to others.

At intervals she crossed to France, to keep in touch with Jacques' relatives and with old friends. A long-term admirer, the Vicomte de Noailles, recalled one re-encounter in Paris: "She asked me to go and see her at the Ritz Hotel, and it was arranged that I should go at five o'clock. After about five minutes, she came in from her room. I had not seen her for almost ten years and was overwhelmed to find her less deaf than she had been thirty years earlier and just as exquisitely beautiful.

"When we had had tea, I was about to take my leave so as not to tire her, but then she said to me, 'Couldn't you remain a little longer? It is so seldom that I can talk about everything with old friends.' So then I stayed, and we talked about whatever she liked, and she talked at length about her granddaughters." (Sarah had four blonde girls—Serena, Alexandra, Jacqueline and another Consuelo.)

"At the end of about one hour, the door of the bedroom opened a little, and I saw a nurse or a chambermaid who signaled to me that I should not remain longer. I said good-bye to her. To my knowledge, she never came to France after that occasion, and I, alas, never saw her again."

There was another terminal meeting, this time with Winston. Cherubic as he looked, he was embittered at heart by the British voters' rejection of the Tory Party when he came to the United States in the spring of 1959, to be met by Dwight Eisenhower, who hosted a stag dinner for him at the White House. He was the weekend guest of Bernard Baruch, self-announced adviser to a string of presidents, who on Monday morning told reporters this was "your last call," because the most celebrated of all Churchills was on his way to Idlewild Airport. Winston foxed him. He ordered his chauffeur to hurry him to Southampton to see Consuelo. Those who knew them guessed that the ex-prime minister, aged eighty-four, and the former duchess, aged eighty-two, talked of the disappointments they had lived through together. They were both creatures of sentiment, but the old man was the one most likely to shed a tear.

One more echo of long ago sounded on another day in Southampton. Consuelo was sitting down with friends to a country club luncheon when one of them introduced a tall, handsome man who came by the table. There were too many people around to allow more than an exchange of pleasantries. Age and a heart attack had overcome his father before the war ended. Her eyes showed only their usual attentiveness when she was introduced to this son of Winty Rutherfurd.

She did not shrink from contemplating her own leavetaking. The rites she wanted were much like those she had arranged for Bertie's wife Mary in 1961. "Fight the Good Fight" and "Jesus Lives" were to be the hymns, and Brahms' "How Lovely Is Thy Dwelling Place!" the anthem sung by the choir. She did not wish to be embalmed, she wrote, but there was a conflict in her desires. The Vanderbilt mausoleum on Staten Island was too grandiose for her democratic inclinations, the Balsans' too cheerless, and Alva's must be hers alone. Consuelo's choice fell on England, in Bladon churchyard next to Ivor, as though she might be able to make amends for their separation in life by being near him in death.

The seventeen pages of her will bequeathed the bulk of her estate, the house at Southampton, personal papers, paintings and jewelry to Sarah, the income from family trusts to Bertie, with provision also made for Ivor's young son, Robert. To Louis Hoffman, her butler, she left $40,000. Of all the millions handed on to her by Willie, less than $2,000,000 remained.

She was eighty-eight years old when she suffered a stroke at her Southampton home. Sarah, with no illusions about the outcome, kept urging her father to take the next flight from London. He postponed leaving until it was too late.

There were fewer flowers in St. Thomas' Church than on the November morning when Consuelo Vanderbilt was joined in wedlock to Charles Spencer Churchill, ninth Duke of Marlborough, but while the jubilation had been false then, the grief among this congregation was unquestionably real. A blanket of

white roses covered the plain mahogany coffin. The mourners—
Vanderbilts and DuPonts, Astors and three generations of
Spencer Churchills among them—sat on burgundy-colored
cushions in polished wooden pews which until three years earlier had been rented and reserved at Sunday services for the vanished elite of old Manhattan. In accordance with custom she
had not cared to break, no eulogy was spoken.

Taking matters upon herself, as she had to if Grandmother's
grave was to be in Bladon, Sarah ignored the instructions con-
cerning embalming. She flew back to England with her father,
her brothers, and the coffin.

The cortege made its way up the steep, winding climb toward
the plain wooden gate of the cemetery at Bladon. The head-
stone, to be set beside Ivor's, would read: "In loving memory of
Consuelo Vanderbilt Balsan—mother of the tenth Duke of
Marlborough—born 2nd March 1877—died 6th December
1964."

Some of those who lined the route were weeping. These English, especially those who remembered from childhood the
kindnesses of a young American duchess, were more openly
sentimental than Consuelo had ever permitted herself to be.

"She's come back to go to her rest along with poor buggers like
us who was murdered by hard work," one stubble-bearded pen-
sioner said, nodding to his neighbor.

"Ah," replied the other, "but she's the best woman ever to be
buried here."

Acknowledgments

Of those who contributed personal reminiscences of Consuelo, particular gratitude is acknowledged to the Duke of Marlborough, Lady Sarah Roubanis, Lady Rosemary Muir, Edwin F. Russell, Paul Maze, Valentine Lawford, Stuart Preston, the Vicomte de Noailles, and Louis Gautier-Vignal. Foremost among those who helped with equal generosity is Hugo Vickers, biographer of Gladys Deacon. Thanks are paid, too, to the staffs of the Bodleian Library, Oxford; of Worcester Public Library, Worcester, Massachusetts; and of the Preservation Society of Newport County. Of research sources consulted, greatest reliance was placed on *The Glitter and The Gold* by Consuelo Vanderbilt Balsan (1952, Harper & Brothers, New York), *The Vanderbilts and Their Fortunes* by Edwin P. Hoyt (1962, Doubleday & Company, Inc., New York), a variety of articles written by Alva (for *North American Review, Harper's Bazaar, Forum, World Today, Good Housekeeping*, etc.), and the files of *The Times* of London and *The New York Times*. Once again, Margaret Davies provided sterling aid with research and interviewing in England, and Kathryn Brough typed the manuscript *con brio*.

INDEX

Index

Abbey Theatre, 187
Abercorn, James Hamilton, 1st
    Duke of, 52, 60
Abercorn, James Hamilton, 2nd
    Duke of, 92–93, 129
Academy of Music, 39, 123
Albert, Prince Consort, 120
Alexander I, King of Bulgaria, 63
Alexander III, Tsar, 62
Alexandra, Queen Consort of Ed-
    ward VII (earlier, Princess
    of Wales), 107, 109, 132,
    146
  at Bertie's wedding, 205, 206
  Consuelo and, 108, 110, 113,
    115, 117, 121–23, 152, 167
  coronation of, 150–51
  deafness, 113, 152, 205
  and Alice Keppel, 157
  at Sandringham, 113–15
Alexandra (Alix), Tsarina, 111,
    150
Alfonso III, King of Spain, 88
Allen, Daniel, 13, 16

Allen, Ethelinda Vanderbilt, 13,
    16, 21, 22
Almanach de Gotha, 36, 118, 150
Alva (yacht), 46–47, 53–54
American Institute of Architects,
    208
American Railway Union, 77
American Women's War Relief
    Fund, 195
Amogo, Bishop, 221
Anne, Queen, 99–105, 178
Annual Register, 110
Anthony, Susan B., 80
Armour, Allison, 138
Ashby St. Ledgers, Lord, 183
Asquith, Herbert, 176, 184, 200,
    203
  and Consuelo, 146, 179–80
  and House of Lords, 179, 188,
    194
  social programs of, 178, 181,
    182
  and woman suffrage, 190, 199
Asquith, Margot, 146, 180, 223

Astor, Caroline Schermerhorn, 29, 43, 78
  Alva's rivalry with, 22, 32–35, 37
  at Consuelo's wedding, 83, 85
Astor, Carrie, 34, 35, 36
Astor, Henry, 22
Astor, John Jacob, 21–22, 32
Astor, John Jacob IV, 78
Astor, Nancy Langhorne, Lady, 227
Astor, Waldorf, 48
Astor, William, 32–33, 46, 53
Astor, William Backhouse, 9, 10
Atchison, Topeka & Santa Fe Railroad, 77
Atlanta (yacht), 46
Augerville-la-Rivier, 224
Augusta Victoria, Empress of Germany, 132, 147, 148
Aylesford, Lady, 97–98, 107, 117, Aylesford, Lord, 97

Baker, Bernard, 137
Balfour, Arthur, 154, 165, 203, 206
  on Churchill's speeches, 140
  Consuelo and, 118–19, 146
Balmoral, 66, 111
Balsan, Consuelo, *see* Vanderbilt, Consuelo
Balsan, Jacques
  Consuelo and, 61–62, 144–45
    courtship, 198–99, 201–2, 203
    marriage, 208–9, 211ff., 219, 222ff.
  death, 243
  family of, 197–98, 215, 219
  flight from Nazis, 232–37
  in French forces, 229, 237
  in U.S., 238, 240, 242
Baltimore & Ohio Railroad, 44

Band of Hope, 174–76
Barrett, Justice, 67
Barrie, Sir James, 178
Barrymore, Ethel, 161
Baruch, Bernard, 244
Battenberg, Prince Alexander of, 62–63
Battenberg, Prince Francis Joseph of, 62–63
Battenberg, Prince Henry of, 62
Battenberg, Prince Louis of, 62
Bayonne, France, 235–36
Beatrice, Princess, 62
Bedford College, 180
Beers, George, 12
Belcourt, 89
Belmont, Alva Smith Vanderbilt
  ambitions of, 7–22 *passim*, 27–28
  and Mrs. Astor, 22, 29, 32, 34–35, 37, 240
  and Oliver Belmont, 59, 68, 85, 89, 119–20, 161
  birth of children of, 22, 27, 43
  builds Marble House, 49–57, 184
  builds "Petit Château," 28, 30–31
  Consuelo brought up by, 27–29, 39–42, 53, 126
  Consuelo forced into marriage by, 73–74, 78–85, 216–18
  Consuelo's relations with after marriage, 126, 131, 161, 168, 191–92, 205, 208, 212, 216–18, 221, 224–25
  Consuelo's romance broken up by, 66–74, 216–18
  cruise to France, 47–48
  cruise to India, 58–60
  death, 225

discord with Willie, 49, 53–54, 55, 60
divorces Willie, 63–64, 66–68
early life, 23–25, 48, 173–74
fancy-dress ball of, 34–37
hunts titled husband for Consuelo, 61–67
political leanings of, 119–20, 158
and suffrage struggle, 173–74, 190–92, 196, 199, 208, 224–25
and Willie's death, 207
and women strikers, 184
Belmont, August, 58
Belmont, Oliver Hazard Perry, 58, 83
Alva and, 59, 68, 78, 85, 89, 161
death, 173
finances magazine, 119–20
Belmont, Perry, 83
Belmont, Sarah Whitney, 68
Berenson, Bernard, 162
Bernini, Giovanni, 144
Bitter, Karl, 52
Bladon, 124–25, 131, 243, 245, 246
Blandford, Albertha, Marchioness of, 92
befriends Consuelo, 107–8, 129, 168, 177
divorces George, 52, 91, 98, 163
pranks of, 117
Blandford, Bertie, Marquess of, see Marlborough, John Albert, 10th Duke of
Blandford, George, Marquess of, see Marlborough, 8th Duke of
Blandford, John Churchill, 1st Marquess of, 103, 130
Blandford, Mary, Marchioness

of, see Marlborough, Mary, Duchess of
Blenheim, Battle of, see Blindheim
Blenheim Palace
Bertie and, 226, 243
Consuelo mistress of, 93–95, 112, 115, 117–23, 130–32, 147
Consuelo's first visit to, 69–70
Consuelo's last visit, 243
descriptions and history of, 101–6, 123–25, 128–29
8th Duke (George) and, 52, 69–70, 90, 122
German Crown Prince's visit, 147
Kaiser's visit, 131–32
Sunny's dedication to, 128–29, 142, 143–44, 166, 194, 202–3, 210
the Waleses' visit, 115, 117–23
in World War I, 193–94
in World War II, 238
Blériot, Louis, 198
Blindheim (Blenheim), Battle of, 101, 102, 128, 132
Boer War, 130, 133, 135–39, 155
Boldini, Giovanni, 145–46
Bombay, 59
Bonner, Robert, 8
Booth, William, 168, 169
Bordeaux, 234–35
Boris III, King of Bulgaria, 63
Botha, Louis, 139
Boya (nurse), 43
Breakers, The, 57, 74
British Labor Party, 185–86
British South Africa Co., 93
Brooke, Frances, Lady, 114, 143, 163

Brooke, Lord, 114
Brown, "Capability," 106, 143
Bryan, William Jennings, 119–20
Buller, Dr., 161
Buller, Sir Redvers, 131
Burdett-Coutts, William Lehman, 137
Burnett, Rev. Waldo, 83
Butler, Reuben, 207, 208

Cabanel, Alexandre, 35
Calcutta, 59–60
Campbell, Lady Colin, 98
Campbell–Bannerman, Sir Henry, 165, 167, 176
Carlile, Rev. Wilson, 168–69
Carlyle, Sir Hildred, 180
Carnot, Sadi, 127
Carson, Sir Edward, 203–4, 205, 208
Casa Alva, 227, 238, 242, 244
Cassel, Ernest, 173
Castlereagh, Viscount, see Londonderry, Marquess of
Cat and Mouse Act, 190
Catherine the Great, 85
Chamberlain, Neville, 227
Chambers, Sir William, 106
Chaplin, Charlie, 223
Chaplin, Henry, 117
Chaplin, Viscount, 200
Charles, Madame, 197–98, 219
Charles I, King, 24, 99
Charles II, King, 99
Charles of Denmark, Prince, 117
Charlotte, daughter of Louis II of Monaco, 214
Chelsea, Viscount, 204
Chesapeake & Ohio Railroad, 240
Chevalier, Maurice, 230

Chicago Limited, 45
Church Army, 168–69
Churchill, Lady Caroline, 220–21, 225–26
Churchill, Charles, son of 1st Duke of Marlborough, 130
Churchill, Charles George William Colin Spencer, 238, 246
Churchill, Clementine Hozier, 106, 176, 223
Churchill, Lady Elizabeth, 243
Churchill, Lord Ivor Charles Spencer, 131, 220, 245, 246
  birth, 129
  death, 243
  early years, 160, 163, 175
  and parents' breakup, 166, 203, 216–17, 242–43
  in wartime, 194, 197, 238
  at wedding of Balsans, 209
Churchill, Jennie Jerome, 23
  and Blenheim, 69, 92, 98, 117
  in Boer War, 136–38
  and Cornwallis-West, 137, 140, 165
  and Prince of Wales, 65, 113, 114, 136–37
  Shakespeare pageant of, 182
  and Winston, 92, 140
Churchill, John George Vanderbilt Henry Spencer, 220, 225–26, 246
Churchill, John Strange Spencer (Jack), 92
Churchill, Lord Randolph, 23, 41, 69, 92, 98, 99
Churchill, Robert Spencer, 245
Churchill, Lady Rosemary, 225–26, 241
Churchill, Lady Sarah Consuelo,

220–21, 225–26, 227, 244, 245, 246
Churchill, Winston Spencer
  and Consuelo, 92, 139–41, 223–24, 244–45
  and the dukedom, 136, 140
  early loves, 161
  in India, 117, 140
  on Marlborough (Sunny), 202, 222
  and the Marlboroughs' separation, 165, 167–68
  political rise, 139–40, 167, 175–76, 206
  prime minister, 231, 233
  proposes to Clemmie, 106
  in South Africa, 133, 136, 137
  "war horse," 227–28
  and women's wage, 189
Church of the Strangers, 9, 19
Church Times, The, 221
Claflin, Tennessee C., 17–19, 21
Clark, Horace, 15, 17
Clark, Marie Louise Vanderbilt, 15, 17, 21
Clarke, Charles E., 50
Cleopatra's Needle, 44
Cleveland, Grover, 77, 91, 110, 119
Clews, Henry, 37
Coaching Club, 41, 58
Coeur, Jacques, 31
Colbert, Jean-Baptiste, 197–98
Colby, Bainbridge, 208
Columbia University, 44, 173
Connaught, Prince Arthur, Duke of, 132
Cornelius Vanderbilt, S.S., 12
Cornwallis-West, George, 137, 140, 165
Corsair (yacht), 46

Cowes, 66
Cristina, Queen-Regent of Spain, 87
Cromwell, Oliver, 94
Cross, James, 13
Cross, Phoebe Jane Vanderbilt, 13, 21
Crowhurst, 179, 184, 204–5, 206
Curie, Marie and Paul, 173
Curzon, George, 1st Marquess Curzon of Kedleston, 118, 146, 153–54, 184–85, 200, 214–15
Curzon, George, Viscount, 118
Curzon, Grace Elvina Hinds Duggan, Marchioness Curzon of Kedleston, 185
Curzon, Mary Leiter, Marchioness Curzon of Kedleston, 118, 153, 184

D'Abernon, Sir Edward Vincent, Baron, 185, 200, 213–14
Damrosch, Walter, 83, 84
Dancer, Matthew, 12
Davidoff, Basil, 227, 229, 234, 238, 241
Davis, Jefferson, 15
Deacon, Edward Parker, 127–28
Deacon, Mrs. Edward Parker, 127
Deacon, Gladys Marie, 127–28, 145, 161–62, 164
  as duchess of Marlborough, 209–10, 220–22
  and Prince Wilhelm, 147–48
Debs, Eugene V., 77
Deems, Rev. Charles, 9, 19
Degas, Edgar, 29, 162
de Gaulle, Charles, 237
De La Rey, Jacobus, 139
Delhi, 153–55

Dell, Floyd, 158
Delmonico's, 34
Depew, Chauncey, 67
Derby, Earl and Countess of, 177
Desha, Joseph, 24
De Wet, Christiaan Rudolph, 139
Disraeli, Benjamin, 107
Dr. Barnado's Homes, 176
Doudeauville, Duchesse de, 222
Dresser, Clarence, 45–46
Dreux, 223, 226, 230
Drew, Daniel, 14
Duchêne, Achille, 144, 159, 212
Dudley, Lady, 110
Duran, Carolus, 29

Eastman, Max, 158
École des Beaux Arts, 35
Edward VII, King (earlier, Prince
    of Wales), 24, 41, 66, 87,
    107, 126
  accession of, 146–47
  Blenheim, visit to, 115, 117–23
  and Lady Brooke, 114, 163
  Consuelo is presented to, 108
  coronation of, 146, 150–51
  death, 182
  and Lady Dudley, 109–10
  and Kaiser, 132, 147, 148
  and Mrs. Keppel, 114–15, 157,
    163, 182
  Marlborough (George) de-
    nounced by, 97
  Marlborough (Sunny) honored
    by, 142
  the Marlboroughs are guests of,
    110–15
  and the Marlboroughs' separa-
    tion, 163–64, 167–68
  in New York, 65, 123
  philanthropies of, 173

snobbishness of, 157
Eisenhower, Dwight D., 244
Epstein, Jacob, 142
Erie Railway Co., 14
Escadrille Lafayette, 198
Eugénie, Empress, 85
Evreux, 231–32
Èze, 205, 212

Fabians, 199, 185–87
Fair, Graham, 144
Ferdinand I, King of Bulgaria, 63
Ferncliff, 33
Fisk, Jim, 14, 18, 20
Fleschmann, Julius and Max, 144
Foch, Ferdinand, 201
Fondation Foch du Mont Valéri-
    an, 222
Food of the Gods, The (Wells),
    187
Ford, Henry, 240
Fortnightly, The, 98
France, Anatole, 162
Franz Josef, Emperor, 160, 161
Free French, 237, 238
French Aeronautic Mission, 198

Galsworthy, John, 187–88
Garden of Allah, The (Hitchens),
    188
Garrett, Robert, 44
Gautier-Vignal, Comte de, 213
Gentlewoman, The, 80
George I, King, 104
George III, King, 19, 106
George V, King, 182, 204–5, 206
Gladstone, William Ewart, 81, 87
Godolphin, Sidney, Lord, 103
Göering, Hermann, 238
Gould, Jay, 14, 46
Gramont, Duc de, 61, 197, 213

Grand Central Terminal, 10, 89
Grant, Nellie, 28
Grant, Ulysses S., 11, 28, 36
Grayson, Victor, 168
Guest, F. E., 183
Guest, Ivor Churchill, 73, 79, 84

Hackwood, 184, 185
Halleck, Henry, 13
Hamilton, Lady Ian, 143
Hammersley, Lilian, *see* Marlborough, Lilian, Duchess of
Hammersley, Louis, 52
Hampden House, 129
Hardie, Keir, 168
Harlan & Hillingsworth, 46
Harley, Robert, 104
Harper, Miss, 72, 78–79, 216, 218
Harris, Frank, 98
Harvey, George, 209
Haucke, Countess Julia Teresa von, 62
Hayes, Rutherford Birchard, 11, 22, 25, 27
Helleu, Paul, 145
Henry I, King, 102
Henry of Navarre, 223
Herter Brothers, 30
Hesse, Alexander of, 62
Hinds, J. Monroe, 185
Hitchens, R. S., 188
Hitler, Adolf, 227, 228, 230
Hoffman, Louis, 234, 238, 242, 245
Hofmannsthal, Hugo von, 162
Homes for Prisoners' Wives, 176
Horridge, Justice, 208
Hunt, Richard Morris, 30–31, 40, 44, 51, 57, 89

Idle Hour, 40–41, 43, 57, 144

Illustrated London News, 95
In Darkest England (Booth), 169
India, 58–60, 117, 153–55
Interstate Commerce Commission, 240

James, Henry, 145
James I, King, 32
James II, King, 99–100
Jay, Julia, 84
Jay, Lucy Smith, 66, 72–73, 74, 79, 82, 216, 218
Jay, William, 41, 79, 82, 84
Jennings, Sarah, *see* Marlborough, 1st Duchess of
Jerome, Jennie, *see* Churchill, Jennie Jerome
Jerome, Leonard, 41
Joffre, General, 193
John, Augustus, 146
Journal, Le, 230

Kenney, Annie, 190
Kent, Prince George, Duke of, 227, 237
Keppel, Alice, 114–15, 157, 163, 182
Keyserling, Count Hermann, 162
Kitchener, Lord, 184, 194
Klunder, Monsieur, 34
Knollys, Sir Francis, 167
Kruger, "Oom Paul," 136

LaBau, Mary Alicia Vanderbilt, 15, 21, 22
Lafitte, Catherine Vanderbilt, 15, 21
Lafitte, Gustave, 15
Lake Shore & Michigan Railroad, 15, 21

Lamsdorf, Count Vladimir Nikolaevich, 149
Lansdowne, Henry Charles Keith Petty-Fitzmaurice, 5th Marquess of, 60, 184
Lansdowne, Marchioness of, 60, 93, 109
Lebrun, Albert, 222
Ledger, The, 8
Lenin, 149
Lewis, Sir George, 81, 165, 208, 217
Lewis & Lewis, 220
Life, 139
Lincoln, Abraham, 22
Linsly, Dr. Jared, 15
Lisbon, 237
Littlejohn, Bishop Abram Newkirk, 83
Lloyd George, David, 179
  defends budget, 180–81
  and House of Lords, 194
  prime minister, 199, 200, 202, 204, 206
  and woman suffrage, 199
Lodge, Henry Cabot, 58
London County Council, 199–201
Londonderry, Charles, Marquess of, 118, 164, 167, 177
Londonderry, Theresa, Marchioness of, 164, 167, 177
Louis XIV, King of France, 100, 101, 198
Louis II of Monaco, Prince, 214–15
Lou Sueil, 212ff., 222–23
Love and Mrs. Lewisham (Wells), 187
Lucknow, 59

Lyautey, Louis-Hubert-Gonzalve, 198
Lyttelton, Alfred, 155

Mafeking, siege of, 131, 138
Maine (hospital ship), 137–38
Major Barbara (Shaw), 186
Malplaquet, Battle of, 102, 157
Man and Superman (Shaw), 186
Manchester, Consuelo, Duchess of, 23–24, 34, 36, 52, 65, 136, 177, 188
Manchester, George, 8th Duke of, 23, 52
Manchester, Louise, Duchess of, 24
Manchester, William, 9th Duke of, 24, 177
Mandeville, Viscountess, *see* Manchester, Consuelo, Duchess of
Manhattan Club, 19
Mann, William D'Alton, 49
Man of Property, The (Galsworthy), 188
Marble House (Newport estate), 49–57, 67, 70ff., 174, 184, 191–92, 224
Marlborough, Bertie, Duke of, *see* Marlborough, John Albert, 10th Duke of
Marlborough, Caroline, Duchess of, 125
Marlborough, Charles Richard John Spencer Churchill (Sunny), 9th Duke of
  Blenheim, dedication to, 143–44, 166, 194, 202–3, 210

in Boer War, 131, 133, 135–38
children of, *see* Churchill, Lord
    Ivor; Marlborough, John
    Albert (Bertie), 10th Duke
    of
and Churchill (Winston), 133,
    136, 139–40, 167–68, 178
and Consuelo
    first meeting, 65
    invites her to Blenheim,
        69–70
    at Marble House, 73–74,
        78–79
    engagement, 79–81
    marriage contract, 81–82
    wedding, 82–85
    honeymoon, 85–91
    welcomed to Blenheim,
        93–95
    in royal circle, 109–10
    at Sandringham, 112–14
    the Waleses' visit, 119,
        120–23
    at Melton Mowbray, 125–26,
        128, 129–30
    accuses her of "Socialism,"
        130
    Kaiser's visit, 131–32
    commissions portraits,
        142–43
    at Victoria's funeral, 146
    Prince Wilhelm's visit,
        147–48
    in Russia, 148–50, 152
    at coronation of Edward,
        150–51
    in India, 153–55
    Sunderland House built, 107,
        156–57
    marriage bankrupt, 162ff.

separation, 164–68
divorce, 203–8
annulment, 215–21
death of, 222
on death duties, 203
early life, 97–98
family of, 91–93, 99ff.
Garter conferred on, 142
and Gladys, 127–28, 162, 164,
    209–10, 220–22
inherits dukedom, 98–99
Liberals attacked by, 180–82
and Lords' veto power, 179, 194
mayor of Woodstock, 177
and his mother, 108–9
and pension bill, 178
public career, 55–56, 107, 158,
    159–60, 165, 177–78, 202
in "Shakespeare" tourney,
    182–83
in World War I, 193–94
Marlborough, Charles Spencer,
    3rd Duke of, 105–6
Marlborough, Consuelo, Duch-
    ess of, *see* Vanderbilt,
    Consuelo
Marlborough, Frances, Duchess
    of, 92, 107
Marlborough, George Spencer,
    4th Duke of, 106, 143
Marlborough, George Spencer
    Churchill, 5th Duke of,
    106, 126
Marlborough, George Spencer
    Churchill, 6th Duke of,
    106
Marlborough, George Spencer
    Churchill, 8th Duke of, 41
affair with Lady Aylesford,
    97–98, 107, 117

and Blenheim, 52, 69–70, 90, 122

death, 98–99

and family pension, 178

marriages and divorce, 52, 90, 98, 163

Marlborough, Gladys, Duchess of, *see* Deacon, Gladys Marie

Marlborough, Henrietta, Duchess of, 103, 105

Marlborough, John Albert (Bertie) Spencer Churchill, 10th Duke of (earlier, Marquess of Blandford)

birth, 126–27

childhood and education, 128, 160, 163, 175

children of, 220, 225, 238

and Churchill (Winston), 136, 140

and Consuelo's death, 245, 246

at Consuelo's second wedding, 209

as duke, 222, 226, 243

marriage, 204–5, 206

and parents' breakup, 166, 203, 216–17, 243

wartime service, 194, 197, 238

Marlborough, John Churchill, 1st Duke of, 100–5, 126, 130–31, 178

Marlborough, John Winston Spencer Churchill, 7th Duke of, 23, 98, 107

Marlborough, Lilian, Duchess of (nee Price), 52, 69–70, 90, 98, 143

Marlborough, Mary, Duchess of (nee Cadogan), 204–5, 206, 209, 220, 238, 245

Marlborough, Sarah Jennings Churchill, 1st Duchess of, 99–105, 107, 130–31

Marlborough, Sunny, Duke of, *see* Marlborough, Charles Richard, 9th Duke of

Marlborough House, 107, 109–10

Marlow, Buckinghamshire, 64, 66

Marx, Karl, 77

Mary, Queen Consort of George V, 205, 206

Mary II, Queen, 100

Masham, Abigail Hill, 101, 103–4

Masses, The, 158

Matin, Le, 148, 230

Maud, Princess, 117

Maxwell, Elsa, 199

Maynard, Lord, 114

Mayo, Earl of, 200

Maze, Paul, 224, 229, 231, 233–34, 241

McAllister, Ward, 33–34, 50

McClellan, George Brinton, 22, 25

McDonald, Dr., 17

McEvoy, Ambrose, 146

McKinley, William, 120, 138

Meissonier, Jean, 29

Melinda and Her Sisters (Belmont and Maxwell), 199

Melton Mowbray, Leicestershire, 125–26, 128, 129

Mercer, Lucy, 216

Metropolitan Club, 67, 81

Metropolitan Opera House, 39–40

Metternich, Count Paul, 147–48

Michael, Grand Duke, 149

Monaco, 140, 214–15, 223

Monet, Claude, 29

Monmouth, James Scott, Duke of, 100

Morgan, John Pierpont, 30, 44, 46, 49, 77

Morning Post, 133

Morton, Edith, 84

Morton, Levi, 83–84, 85

Morton, Mrs. Levi, 83–84

Moscow, 150

Mrs. Warren's Profession (Shaw), 186

Mr. Vanderbilt's House and Gallery, 30

Mueller, Dr. Isadore, 160

Mulholland, Inez, 190–91

Murchison, Clint, 240

Napoleon III, 35, 48

National Anti-Sweating League, 188–89

National Birthrate Commission, 175

National Council on Public Morals, 175

National Woman Suffrage Association, 174

National Women's Party, 199

Nelson, Horatio, Lord, 106

Neustretter, Nellie, 64

New Dorp, Staten Island, 44

Newport, Rhode Island, 50ff., 238–39

New York Central Railroad, 14, 15, 25, 45, 67, 240–41
strike, 26–27

New York Times, The, 28, 35, 64, 110, 166

Nice, 47

Nicholas II, Tsar, 62, 111, 147, 149–50, 168, 227

Nicolson, Harold, 154

Nietzsche, Friedrich, 126

Nineteenth Amendment, 208

Noailles, Vicomte de, 213, 244

North American Review, 209

North Star (yacht), 13, 46

Nourmahal (yacht), 46

Oldham, 139–40

Osgood, Eliza Vanderbilt, 13, 21, 36

Osgood, George, 13–14

Oyster Bay, Long Island, 58, 242, 244

Paget, Lord, 65

Paget, Minnie Stevens, Lady, 64–65, 69

Pankhurst, Christabel, 190, 191, 196

Patriarchs' Balls, 34

Pau, 232, 233, 234

Pauncefote, Sir Julian Pauncefote, 84, 85

Pennsylvania Railroad strike, 26

Périgueux, 233

Pétain, Henri-Philippe, 233, 234, 235

"Petit Château de Blois," 31, 34–37, 40, 43, 66, 67, 239

·*Pilot, The,* 221

Pius XI, Pope, 220

Pless, Daisy, Princess of, 137

Plowden, Pamela, 140

Political Equality League, 174

Polk, James Knox, 12

Potter, Bishop Codman, 83, 85

Poujy, Liane de, 64

Pourtalès, Mélanie de, 62
Prattley, Sara, 125, 131, 178
Price, Cicero, 52
Pulitzer, Joseph, 110
Pullman Palace Car Co., 77

Reid, Whitelaw, 176
Renoir, Pierre August, 29
Reynaud, Paul, 233, 234
Reynolds, Sir Joshua, 125, 143
Ribblesdale, Ava, Lady, 177
Richardson, Sid, 240
Rilke, Rainer Maria, 162
Roberts, Field Marshal Lord, 133, 138
Robinson, Lucius, 27
Rockefeller, John D., 240
Rodin, Auguste, 162
Roosevelt, Eleanor, 58, 216
Roosevelt, Elliott, 58
Roosevelt, Franklin D., 41, 216
Roosevelt, James Roosevelt, 41
Roosevelt, Theodore, 58
Rosebery, Hannah, Lady (nee Rothschild), 87
Rosebery, Lord, 87
Rothschild, Baron Louis de, 229
Roubanis, Lady Sarah, see Churchill, Lady Sarah Consuelo
Roxburgh, May, Duchess of, 48
Royal Army Service Corps, 197
Rudolf, Archduke, 161
Russell, Earl, 163
Russell, Sir Charles, 215–16
Russia, 148–50, 152
Rutherfurd, Alice Morton, 152, 216
Rutherfurd, Lewis Morris, 57
Rutherfurd, Lucy Mercer, 216
Rutherfurd, Margaret, 57–58, 65

Rutherfurd, Winthrop, 57–59, 60, 63, 66–74
    death, 245
    marriages, 152, 216
Rysbrack, Thomas, 105

Saint Georges-Motel, 223–24, 238
    sanitarium, 226, 229, 231–34
St. Mark's-in-the-Bowery, 42
St. Petersburg, 149
Salisbury, Robert Gascoyne-Cecil, 3rd Marquess of, 111, 139, 146
Salvation Army, 168
Sandringham House, 111–15
San Sebastian, Spain, 237
Saratoga Springs, 17, 26
Sargent, John Singer, 143
Schopenhauer, Arthur, 126
Shakespeare Memorial Ball, 182
Shakespeare's England Exhibition, 182
Shaw, George Bernard, 182, 186–87
Shepard, Margaret Louise Vanderbilt, 30, 36
Sherman, John, 45
Sinclair, Upton, 181
Sloane, Emily Vanderbilt, 30, 32, 36
Smith, Armide, 85
Smith, Murray Forbes, 24, 32
Smith, Phoebe Desha, 24–25, 74
Smuts, Jan, 139
Southampton, Long Island, 244, 245
Soveral, Marquês de, 176–77
Stalin, Joseph, 230
Stevens, Mrs. Paran, 65
Stevens, Paran, 65
Stewart, Alexander T., 9–10

Stirling, Lord (William Alexander), 32
Stone, Lucy, 80
Storey, Waldo, 142, 144
Strong, William L., 89
Stuyvesant, Peter, 57
Sullivan, Louis, 31
Sunderland, Charles Spencer, 3rd Earl of, 103, 106
Sunderland, Lady Anne Churchill Spencer, Countess of, 103, 105
Sunderland House, 107, 156–57, 159, 166, 197
Sutherland, Duchess of, 69, 143
Sutherland, Duke of, 69

Theory of the Leisure Class, The (Veblen), 145
Thorn, Emily Vanderbilt, 13, 16, 21, 23
Thorn, Louisa, 13
Thorn, William, 13
Tiffany, Jenny Smith Yznaga, 23, 46, 216, 217
Tilden, Samuel Jones, 11, 22
Times, The (London), 165
    Marlborough's letters to, 178, 203
    Marlborough's obituary in, 222
Torrance, Daniel, 14–15
Torrance, Sophia Vanderbilt, 14, 21
Town Topics, 49, 74

Union Club, 19

Valiant (yacht), 53–54, 58–60, 72, 78
Vanbrugh, John, 102–3, 104, 143–44

Vanderbilt, Alice, 27, 36, 50, 57, 74
Vanderbilt, Alva Smith, see Belmont, Alva Smith Vanderbilt
Vanderbilt, Anne Harriman Rutherfurd Sands, 156, 173, 197, 207
Vanderbilt, Consuelo
    adolescence, 52–53, 56, 57, 58
    Alexandra, friendship with, 113, 115, 122, 155
    and Balsan, 61–62, 144–45, 197
        courtship, 198–99, 201–2, 203
        marriage, 208–9, 211ff., 219, 222–43 passim
    birth of, 22
    and Boer War, 136–38
    childhood, 23–36 passim, 43, 46–48, 50–51
    children of, see Churchill, Lord Ivor; Marlborough, John Albert (Bertie), 10th Duke of
    and Churchill (Winston), 92, 139–41, 223–24, 244–45
    at Crowhurst, 179, 184, 204–5, 206
    and Curzon, 184–85, 214–15
    deafness, 152, 160–61, 194, 213
    death, 245–46
    debut and suitors, 61–63, 65
    education, 39–41, 53
    and eugenics, 183–84
    and the Fabians, 185–87, 190
    and father's death, 207–8
    father's help to, 28, 107, 156, 157, 168, 203
    and father's second marriage, 156
    final years in America, 238ff.

first public speech, 141–42
on France, 202
and Gladys, 127–28, 145, 147–48, 162, 210
in London County Council, 199–201
and Marlborough
    first meeting, 65
    invited to Blenheim, 69–70
    at Marble House, 73–74, 78–79
    engagement, 79–81
    marriage contract, 81–82
    wedding, 82–85
    honeymoon, 85–91
    meets his family, 91–93
    at Blenheim as duchess, 93–95, 97ff., 112, 117, 119ff.
    presented at court, 107–8
    admitted to royal circle, 109–10
    at Sandringham, 112–15
    the Waleses' visit, 117, 119, 120–23
    at Melton Mowbray, 125–26, 128, 129–30
    accused by him of "Socialism," 130
    Kaiser's visit, 131–32
    electioneering, 139–40
    family portraits, 142–43
    at Victoria's funeral, 146
    Prince Wilhelm's visit, 147–48
    in Russia, 148–50, 152
    at coronation of Edward, 150–51
    in India, 153–55
Sunderland House built, 107, 156–57

and his career, 159–60
    marriage bankrupt, 162ff.
    separation, 164–68
    divorce, 203–8
    annulment, 215–21
and mother's death, 224–25
and mother's matchmaking, 60–65, 69ff.
philanthropies, 168–69, 174–76
political leanings, 180–82
portraits painted, 29, 142–43, 145–46
her reading, 53, 126, 145
her religious feelings, 130–31
and Winty Rutherfurd, 57–59, 60, 63, 66–74, 152, 216, 245
sanitarium of, 226, 229, 231–34
and Socialism, 181–82, 185, 222
visit with Victoria, 110–11
withdraws from royal circle, 157–59
and women's causes, 180, 185, 188–92, 196, 199
in World War I, 193–97
in World War II: flight from Nazis, 230–37
Vanderbilt, Cornelius, "Commodore" (Corneel), 7–22, 26, 44, 46, 123
    and the Astors, 21, 240
    and the Claflins, 17–19, 25
    death and burial, 19–21, 45
    his will, 21–22, 25, 29
Vanderbilt, Cornelius II, 11, 27, 36, 63, 80
    and father's death, 44–45
    and mother's death, 120
    Newport "cottage" of, 50, 57, 74
    wealth of, 21, 45, 240
Vanderbilt, Cornelius III, 209, 239

Vanderbilt, Cornelius Jeremiah, 12, 21, 22, 25, 29
Vanderbilt, Florence Adele, 27–28
Vanderbilt, Frank Crawford, 8, 9, 10, 19, 21, 27
Vanderbilt, Frederick William, 27, 32, 78
Vanderbilt, George Washington, 12–13, 20
Vanderbilt, Gertrude, 74
Vanderbilt, Grace Wilson, 239, 242
Vanderbilt, Harold, 43, 225, 237
  in childhood, 47, 66, 67, 79, 82, 84, 89
  inheritance, 208
  and N.Y. Central, 240–41
Vanderbilt, Louise, 27
Vanderbilt, Maria Louisa Kissam (Grandmother Vanderbilt), 21, 27, 29–30, 32, 81, 120, 127
Vanderbilt, Rosamund (Rose), 223
Vanderbilt, Sophia, 10, 15, 16–17
Vanderbilt, Virginia Fair (Birdie), 144
Vanderbilt, William Henry (Billy), 10, 36, 239, 240
  art collection of, 29–30
  and Commodore, 11–12, 17
  and Commodore's will, 21, 25, 28–29
  death and burial, 44–45
  mansion of, 30
  and N. Y. Central strike, 25–27
  philanthropies of, 44, 45
  "The public be damned!," 45–46
  Willie helped by, 37, 41
Vanderbilt, William Kissam (Willie), 7, 19, 29, 34, 42, 211
  Alva, marriage to, 10, 23
  Alva, rift with, 49, 53–54, 55, 60, 63–64, 66–68
  and Alva's ball, 36, 37
  and Alva's remarriage, 89
  Anne, marriage to, 156
  and birth of grandson, 126–27
  Consuelo helped by, 28, 107, 156, 157, 168, 203
  at Consuelo's wedding, 81–85
  death, 207–8
  education, 10, 11, 42
  and father's death, 44–45
  financial help from father, 41
  and Idle Hour, 40–41, 144
  inheritance, 11, 21, 45, 240
  Marble House built by, 49, 51
  and the Marlboroughs' break-up, 164–65, 166–67, 168, 203
  and mother's death, 120
  and "Petit Château," 30, 31
  philanthropies of, 173
  and racing, 127, 144, 145, 156, 164, 207
  railroad executive, 10, 25, 26, 37
  womanizer, 49, 63–64
  in World War I, 197, 198
  yachts of, see Alva; Valiant
Vanderbilt, William Kissam II
  and the Balsans, 223, 225, 237
  birth, 27
  death, 239
  early years, 40, 41, 42–43, 66, 67, 84, 89
  inheritance, 208
  marriage, 144
Vanderbilt University, 44, 173

Van Rensselaer, May King, 25
Van Rosenvelt, Claes, 32
Veblen, Thorstein, 145
Venezuela crisis, 110
Verdict, 119–20, 139
Versailles Treaty, 212, 213–14
Victoria, Princess, 87, 117
Victoria, Queen, 33, 62, 66, 120
  Consuelo has dinner with, 110–11
  death, 146
  and the Marlboroughs, 86, 107
  Tsar's visit to, 111
Victoria and Albert (yacht), 168
Vienna, 160–61
Villa Isoletta, 212
Vincent, Sir Edward, *see* D'Abernon, Baron
Vincent, Lady Helen, 185
Vogue, 80
Voronoff, Serge, 223

Waifs and Strays Society, 176, 177
Wales, Prince of, *see* Edward VII
Wales, Princess of, *see* Alexandra, Queen Consort
Webb, Beatrice and Sidney, 145, 185–86
Wedekind, Fräulein, 39, 42, 43
Wells, H.G., 145, 187
Wharton, Edith, 58, 145
Whitaker, Tina, 164
White, Henry, 156
Wilhelm, Crown Prince of Germany, 147
Wilhelm II, Kaiser, 131–32, 147–48, 149, 201
William III (William of Orange), King of England, 100

Wilson, May, 48
Wilson, Muriel, 161
Wilson, Richard T., 73, 74
Wilson, Lady Sarah, 91
Wilson, Woodrow, 197
Wimborne, Lord, *see* Guest, Ivor Churchill
Women's Emergency Corps, 195–96
Women's Municipal Party, 199
Women's Suffrage Association, 190
Woodhull, Dr. Canning, 18
Woodhull, Victoria Claflin, 18–19, 21
Woodhull and Claflin's Weekly, 18–19
Woodstock, Oxfordshire, 101, 106, 124, 142, 181
  Consuelo welcomed to, 93–94
  Sunny elected mayor of, 177
  and the Waleses' visit, 120–21
World War I, 192–201
World War II, 228–40
Worth, Jean, 61, 89
Wyndham, George, 187

Yeats, William Butler, 187
York, Archbishop of, 151
Young, Robert R., 240–41
Young Women's Christian Association, 188
Yznaga, Don Antonio, 23
Yznaga, Consuelo, *see* Manchester, Consuelo, Duchess of
Yznaga, Fernando, 23
Yznaga, Jenny Smith, *see* Tiffany, Jenny Smith Yznaga